In the late 19th century, an estimated 11 million Americans believed in something called Spiritualism. They believed in it so ardently that it came to be thought of as a religion, and it became the seventh most popular religion in the United States. It's fundamental tenet—virtually its only tenet—was that it was possible for the living to communicate with the dead. America's philosopher king William James believed in it. Thomas Edison believed. Mark Twain believed. Countless number of scholars and scientists—although always a minority—also believed. Or, at the least, they believed that the belief should be tested, not scoffed at; that it might deserve to be part of university curricula, not the raw material of derisive humor. The same was true across the Atlantic, where Spiritualism attracted Marie Curie, Queen Victoria, two British Prime Ministers, Pope Pius IX and Russia's Czar Alexander II, among numerous others. Hundreds of the smartest minds in the world—geniuses all—formed societies in New York and London to investigate the notion of conversation with the deceased. They conducted scores of experiments under the most rigid, secure and sometimes even punishing of conditions, and some of what they discovered startled them. As *When the Dead Talked . . . and the Smartest Minds in the World Listened*, attests, it is still startling today.

WHEN THE DEAD TALKED . . .

and the

SMARTEST MINDS IN THE WORLD LISTENED

by

Eric Burns

author of

1920: The Year That Made the Decade Roar

&

*Infamous Scribblers: The Founding Fathers
and the Rowdy Beginnings of American Journalism*

When the Dead Talked…and the Smartest Minds in the World Listened

Copyright © 2023 by Eric Burns

ISBN: 978-1-970157-38-3

Story Merchant Books 400 S. Burnside Avenue #11B Los Angeles, CA 90036
www.storymerchantbooks.com

Book Interior, Cover and E-book Design by Amit Dey | amitdey2528@gmail.com

ALSO BY ERIC BURNS

Broadcast Blues:
Dispatches from the Twenty-Year War
Between a Television Report and His Medium
(1993)

The Joy of Books: Confessions of a Life-Long Reader
(1995)

The Autograph
A Modern Fable of a Father and Daughter
(1997)

The Spirits of America: A Social History of Alcohol
(2004)

Infamous Scribblers:
The Founding Fathers and the Rowdy Beginnings
of American Journalism
(2006)

The Smoke of the Gods: A Social History of Tobacco
(2007)

Virtue, Valor and Vanity:
The Founding Fathers and the Pursuit of Fame
(2007)

All the News Unfit to Print:
How Things Were . . . and How They Were Reported
(2009)

Invasion of the Mind Snatchers:
Television's Conquest of America in the Fifties
(2010)

1920: The Year That Made the Decade Roar
(2015)

The Golden Lad:
The Haunting Story of Quentin and Theodore Roosevelt
(2016)

Someone to Watch Over Me:
A Portrait of Eleanor Roosevelt
and the Tortured Father Who Shaped Her Life
(2017)

The Politics of Fame
(2018)

1957: The Year That Launched the Future
(2020)

To

Ken Atchity
And
Devon Blaine

For services rendered
and profoundly appreciated

CONTENTS

A NOTE TO READERS

I never thought I would write a book like *When the Dead Talked . . . and the Smartest Minds in the World Listened.* Never thought the topic would engage me for more than a paragraph or two. Yes, the book is, like my previous volumes, a work of history, a subject of research and deliberation. of countless hours spent in public libraries, a couple of musty private libraries, museums specializing in arcana, and in front of the screens of websites no less arcane. It is, thus, non-fiction. Factual.

And yes, the "facts" I have chosen to relate are supported by at least one source, more often two or three. Further, the incidents that the "facts" describe all took place before eyewitnesses, some of them the most prestigious people in their societies: members of royalty, respected political figures, academics. Many of them can, without exaggeration, be called the smartest minds in the world of their time. And what they saw, what they conducted themselves, were experiments subject to the most rigorous of scientific controls, the most unerring supervision. What they saw was free from illusion, trickery, or loopholes in logic. What they saw, in other words, was *real*. If it weren't, why would so many non-believers, literally thousands of them, have switched affiliations? Formerly skeptics, they had made sudden U-turns, now becoming believers.

And yet I have twice enclosed the word "facts" in quotation marks in the preceding paragraph, giving a twist to the meaning of the word and thereby admitting my doubts. For the same reason, I have italicized the word "real." I am, after all, a sensible man who is about to analyze the possibility of communicating with the after--the possibility, in other words, of impossibilities. How do I find myself in such a position? More than once, I have thought of reality as being like a railroad track, its stations proceeding sequentially from A to B to C and so on. And more than once I have asked myself whether it is possible that sidings exist which have been previously undiscovered, or unacknowledged, sidings that exist largely in the shadows.

Actually, I do not think of myself as a spokesman for impossibilities. Rather, I am an author, a lifelong student of the liberal arts, who is about to tell the story of what he has learned in the past few years, a period of diligent research, and if the scales sometimes tip toward the irrational, there is nothing I can do about it. My role is merely that of messenger.

Don't shoot.

Eric Burns
Norwalk, Connecticut
March 7, 2023

A séance, late nineteenth century

PHOTO
GALLERY

BELIEVERS

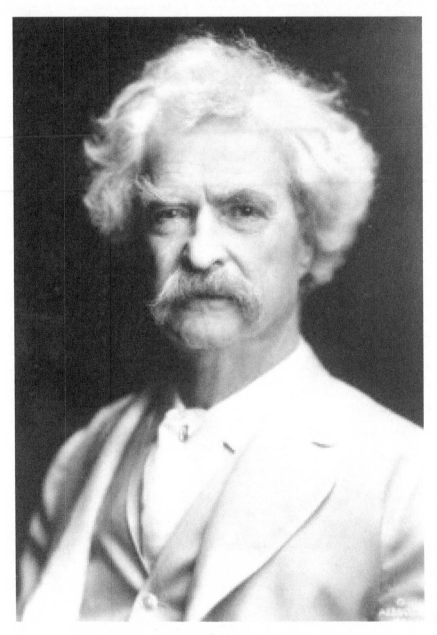

Samuel Clemens

Sir Arthur Conan Doyle

James Fenimore Cooper

Elizabeth Barrett Browning

INVESTIGATORS

William James

Sir Oliver Lodge

Sir William Crookes

Richard Hodgson

PSYCHICS

Maggie and Kate Fox

Eusapia Palladino

Daniel Dunglas Home

Mrs. Leonora Piper

GLOSSARY

Aetheric The adjectival form of "ether," with the "a" at the beginning to give the word a more scientific cast.

Apparition The supernatural appearance of a person or object, often a ghost, which, although seen, or thought to be seen, cannot be explained rationally.

Automatic writing A technique frequently used by mediums. Instead of reciting messages that they have received from the afterlife, they write the messages on paper, transcribing the words of a mystical colleague, called a control. It is the control, serving as intermediary, who communicates directly with the deceased and then whispers their words into the medium's ear.

Clairvoyant A synonym for medium, although Peter Aykroyd, a scholar of matters otherworldly, says that a clairvoyant is "a medium with special powers to see and describe departed spirits." In other words, Aykroyd believes that a clairvoyant is a medium with super-supernatural abilities. To avoid value judgments, I have used the word "medium" almost exclusively in the following pages, saving "clairvoyant" for Mrs. Leonora Piper, the reasons to be stated later.

Cross-correspondences Rather a fuzzy term, referring to automatic writings and trance utterings.

Elongation The ability of a medium to stretch his body, adding several inches to his or her height. A basketball player's dream, it is one of the least common, and certainly the least believable, of a medium's abilities. Few, in fact, have ever claimed such a feat.

Ether The upper regions of the atmosphere, the heavens, or, more esoterically, a magic substance, ingredients unknown, believed by the ancients to fill that space. Also, a term used for the so-called energy field, or aura, that surrounds a human being. In other words, "ether" is a word that can be used to describe just about anything that cannot be seen.

Ghost The soul of a dead person, a spirit that often takes the form of the person when alive. Or so goes the most commonly-held belief. But, says Frederic Myers, who spent much of a lifetime studying one ghostly presence or another, "let us define [ghost] as a manifestation of persistent energy."

Levitation The rising into the air of a human being, usually a medium, without any visible means of support. No easier to believe, is levitation, than elongation. Yet Frank Podmore, an esteemed, often skeptical, psychic researcher of more than a century ago, wrote, "The phenomenon is, in fact, one of the most fully attested of all spiritualist marvels."

Medium A person who claims to be able to bring about a "conversation" between the living (those attending a séance) and the dead.

Mesmerism Similar to hypnosis, the ability of a person to focus so completely on a person, a topic or an object that all else is excluded from his ken.

Paranormal The description of an event or occurrence that cannot be explained by known scientific methods. It is, essentially, a synonym for "supernatural."

Psychic In some cases a noun, in some an adjective, and used as both in this volume. As the latter, it modifies terms that that science cannot decipher and often refuses to acknowledge. As the former, a psychic is another name for a medium.

Psychometry The ability, or alleged ability, to divine facts about the life of a deceased person by examining an object that once belonged to that person.

Séance A gathering of people, as few as one and perhaps as many as thirty (and on rare occasions a full auditorium), usually held in a dimly-lit venue, at which a medium attempts to make contact with persons no longer among the living. Or a gathering at which a medium simply performs tricks, stupefying his audience.

Sitter A man or woman attending a séance. For some reason, sitters are usually arrayed in alternating male-female fashion around a table, and often required to hold hands.

Telekinesis Also known as psychokinesis, it is the alleged ability of a person to move an object although he makes no physical contact with it, causing the movement with mental prowess only.

Telepathy The ability of two people to exchange information silently and motionlessly--no words necessary, no visual signals employed, just mental abilities similar to those required for telekinesis.

Thought transference Best regarded as a synonym for telepathy, i.e., the exchange of thoughts through extra-sensory means, known short-handedly as mind-reading.

Trance A semi-conscious state, residing somewhere between wakeful-ness and sleep, in which a medium functions involuntarily, and usually does not remember what he or she has done upon fully awakening.

Introduction

BEFORE HE WAS
MARK TWAIN

The year was 1858, and a life on the river was the dream of many a young man who had grown up near the Mississippi. One of them was twenty-three-year-old Samuel Clemens. He and his brother Henry, three years younger, both hoped to be riverboat captains one day, and were learning their vocation aboard the *Pennsylvania*, "a big, steam-powered paddle-wheeler." It was just the kind of vessel Sam and Henry yearned to command in the years ahead. The Mississippi was the great American highway of the time; Sam and Henry wanted to master its currents from northern Minnesota to the Gulf of Mexico. It seemed the most adventurous of callings.

One night that summer, the *Pennsylvania* docked in St. Louis. It was not only the busiest port and largest city the Clemens boys had ever seen, but home to one of their sisters. They dropped in for a visit long overdue, and the three siblings spent the evening eating and drinking, reliving old times and old friends, sharing future aspirations. Finally the night grew late, and the men parted--Sam spending the night with his sister and Henry deciding to bunk where he had done every other night of late, aboard the *Pennsylvania*. Such a cheerful evening it had been. Sam was at peace as he nestled under the covers.

Yet at some point during the night, he had the most horrifying dream of his life. Henry, it seems, had died. Sam didn't know how or when, but there his brother lay, stretched out before him, his body displayed in a coffin that had been balanced across the seat cushions of two chairs. The nightmare was a remarkably detailed one; Sam saw it as if his eyelids had suddenly snapped open: White roses covered his brother's torso from chin to waist, with a single red bloom in the middle of the bouquet.

Sam bolted awake. His heart was thumping so hard that he might have been able to see his nightshirt fluttering on his chest; his breaths did not come easily. After a few minutes of collecting himself, he made his way downstairs slowly, ever so slowly, holding onto the railing for equilibrium. He was afraid that Henry's corpse would await him in his sister's parlor, arrayed just as he had seen it moments earlier.

But it wasn't. Sam didn't see anything out of the ordinary on the first floor. The parlor was just as it should have been: dark, quiet and empty. No coffin lying across seat cushions, neither one holding his brother nor anyone else. Sam walked around the room, peering into every corner. Only then could he assure himself that his brother's death had been a figment of his dozing imagination. His breathing gradually returned to normal. He climbed back up the stairs and slid under the covers again, easing himself into a sleep that remained uninterrupted the rest of the night.

In the morning, when Sam found Henry waiting for him aboard the *Pennsylvania*, his smile was an unusually broad one, full of relief. Henry might have found it odd, but it is not known whether Sam offered an explanation. Later, however, he did tell some members of his family about his vision, but according to his niece, they "were not impressed; indeed they were amused that he took it so seriously." This despite the fact that Sam's midnight vision had long since been proven true.

At any rate, the two brothers, began as usual to talk about the future, looking forward to resuming their maritime education side-by-side. But it was not to be.

For reasons unknown, the ship's captain ordered the brothers to be separated. Henry was to remain on the *Pennsylvania*, Sam to report to a smaller craft, the *Alfred T. Lacey*, which would follow the larger one down the Mississippi, trailing it by about two days. The men were not happy with the new arrangement, but had no choice. Sam gathered his clothes and the brothers exchanged reluctant goodbyes. The sun, set to slow bake, beat down on him as he traipsed along the pier, back to the *Lacey* to begin his new assignment.

Three days later it happened. This time it was not a dream. A few hours beyond Memphis, as the *Pennsylvania* continued to head south, its boiler exploded. The sky blackened overhead, a frightening midday nightfall, and the noise reached back not only to Memphis but even farther. The first reports would indicate that a hundred and fifty people had been killed or injured. But who had they been? Was Henry Clemens one of them?

When news of the tragedy reached Sam's ship, the captain ordered it to put ashore. After borrowing twenty dollars, Sam disembarked, hired a horse, and whipped it back to the remains of the *Pennsylvania*, where plans were already being made to bury the deceased. As for the wounded, they were being treated in two hospitals, one of the makeshift variety. Henry had been taken to in the latter.

For the next five nights, Sam sat at his brother's bedside, barely sleeping, perhaps even praying, not an activity in which he normally engaged. He had enough energy to send a telegram to St. Louis, telling his sister what had happened and to expect the worst; beyond that, he could exert himself no more than to shed tears. He was shocked beyond words. This was not what life on the Mississippi was supposed to be like. This was tragedy, not adventure.

On the morning of the sixth day, Henry died.

It was only after looking at his brother for several seconds, perhaps a minute or more, that Sam realized the casket in which Henry lay was balanced across two chairs. He began to tense. A few minutes later a nurse approached, a cascade of flowers drooping from her arms. She covered Henry's chest with roses. White roses. Then she picked out a single red rose and gently located it in the center of the others. Sam watched, benumbed, as his previously senseless dream came true.

Her work done here, the nurse departed, shuffling down the aisles and placing other bouquets atop other victims. Henry's brother did not move, except perhaps for a quivering hand. He simply stared at the display that had just been arranged atop his brother. It is said that someone who saw Sam in that moment thought he was "almost crazed with grief."

That is the story. Clemens swore it happened, swore he neither exaggerated nor contrived so much as a single detail. But could he be believed? As a journalist in Nevada some years earlier, he had shown little regard for the truth, often deferring to the entertainment value of the hoax. Even grisly entertainment. In one of his reports, he wrote that a man on horseback was spotted with "with his throat cut from ear to ear, and bearing in his hand a reeking scalp from which the warm, smoking blood was still dripping." The man died upon reaching an old log house. The scalp belonged to the woman who lived there. Her body was found nearby, with her hair missing and "her right hand almost severed from her wrist." Back in the house, six of her children were found with their brains bashed into mush.

Or so Clemens wrote.

None of it took place. The entire story was pure, frightful fancy. Yet it was printed precisely as the reporter had hatched it in the *Virginia City Territorial Enterprise*. Other examples of Clemens's fiction, masquerading as fact, are numerous, albeit not so grim. And, of course, Clemens he would go on, under a different name, to become one of the greatest of American novelists, which is to say, one of our greatest creators of events did not actually occur.

The incident with his brother, though--did *it* occur? Yes, he vowed, time and again, yes. And as he related to the tale to others, he almost always concluded by saying that he didn't expect anyone to believe him.

But what exactly *was* the tale? If it had not been a dream, had it been a ghastly, nigh-onto-impossible coincidence? Even more unlikely, could it be that Clemens was possessed of psychic powers, which he had never displayed before and in which he often said he did not believe?

In fact, eight years after his brother's death, he was still saying he did not believe. Most of the time. There was at least one occasion, however, when he claimed to have sat in on a séance in which he received a ghostly visitation from an old friend named Smith. The psychic, he said, had a hard time reaching the fellow, struggling to get his attention in the afterlife. Finally, she succeeded. "I got hold of the right Smith at last--" wrote the man now known as Mark Twain--"the particular Smith I was after--my dear, lost, lamented friend--and learned that he died a violent death. I feared as much. He said that his wife talked him to death."

It sounds very much tongue-in-cheek.

According to Mallory Howard, who curated an exhibit at the Mark Twain House & Museum in Hartford, Connecticut, the author "was flippy-floppy about spiritualism and the afterlife. One minute he allows his wife to attend a séance to communicate with Susy [Twain's daughter, who had died at the age of twenty-four] and the next he said it was poppycock."

The exhibit, in 2014, called "Spiritualism, séances and Sam," did nothing to dispel the notion that Twain was, at the least (or the most) a part-time believer. But it was an unsatisfactory state for him. He wanted either to flip or flop one final time and stay put. But how? To whom could he turn to explain how one day's nightmare at his sister's house had become another day's reality? It had to be someone familiar with such occurrences, perhaps even someone who had had a similar, otherworldly experience himself. But it couldn't be just anyone. It had to be a man who was believable, trustworthy, intelligent and respectable, perceptive and unbiased. Did such a person exist? And if so, what were the odds that he was a scholar in the realm of overnight horrors?

As it turned out, he would eventually discover that many such people actually existed, hundreds of them, in fact, and that they had joined together to investigate just such events as Twain had described. It was more than he could have hoped for--two groups of psychic researchers, one on each side of the Atlantic, and they were comprised, virtually without exception, of men whose scientific credentials were unchallenged, whose minds were not predisposed toward the supernatural. Not, at least, at the beginning.

But two and a half decades would pass before these scholars formed their alliances and Twain learned about them. Keeping up with their inquiries as best he could, reading their publications "from cover to cover," he began to work toward a solution to the most baffling mystery of his life. He was diligent about it, though unable to solve the puzzle. He was uneasy about it, though only part-time, it seems, and never for publication. And he was serious about it, though, as befit the mocking creator of Tom and Huck, the father of American drollery, he took an occasional break to scoff at himself.

Part One

THE FOX GIRLS

Chapter 1

APPLES IN THE NIGHT

A t one time, there were probably six Fox children, five of them daughters, although one was believed to have died in infancy. Leah was the oldest by twenty-three years, a full generation, and she will soon appear in these pages in an important supporting role. But the stars of the family were the two youngest girls. Kate was born in 1837 and baptized Catherine, while Maggie had entered the world four years earlier. Her real name, seldom used, was Margaretta, although she was sometimes called Margaret, which was also the name of her mother. The girls' father was a blacksmith and part-time reformed alcoholic, John David. Thus the Fox family tree as it pertains to the beginning of this volume.

Little is known of Maggie and Kate's earliest years, except that they were spent in Canada and were, for the most part, untroubled. By militarism: Neither the Mexican War nor the Civil War had yet begun to the south, and the native Americans who once lived near them in Canada and, later, the United States. had either been murdered, dispersed or tamed. They were untroubled by noise: There were neither factories nor train lines near their homes in either country, and it was donkeys, not yet machines, that assisted farmers with their plows. And they were untroubled by technology: Samuel Morse would not send his first telegraph message from Washington D.C. to Baltimore until 1844. The telephone had not been invented, and although Thomas Alva Edison might have begun to think about the phonograph, he was still decades away from creating it.

There seem to have been few witnesses to Maggie and Kate's first steps on the paths to adulthood. One schoolmate remembers the girls as "adept mimics," and a general impression exists that the girls were friendly, cheerful. But no other memories seem to have been recorded. Except for the headaches. Both sisters suffered from them, and at times they were sharp, perhaps migraines, sapping the girls of strength as well as their usual sunny dispositions. It is not certain how often they occurred, though, or how long they lasted, or whether they tormented the sisters all their lives. Their parents never felt compelled, or were never financially able, to seek medical help for them.

But maybe that was all for the best. Or, at the least, was inevitable. Maybe the headaches were some kind of perverse necessity for the sisters, given their eventual life's work.

Maggie and Kate were still thought of as little girls when the family departed from Canada, crossing the border at Ontario and taking possession of a farmhouse in what was once described as the "infected district" of New York. It later became known as "the Burned-over District," a reference, it is believed, that suited "the prevailing western analogy between the fires of the forest and those of the spirit."

Still the term, like the place, was an odd one. It was coined by a man named Charles G. Finney, a minister known to some as the Father of American Revivalism. It refers to the western corner of New York, where centers of population were neither central nor well-populated, and the woods that surrounded them sometimes appeared to run on into ever darkening depths. The majority of residents were evangelized Christians, and that led Finney to believe--via a complicated metaphor--that there was no more "fuel" in the area, by which he meant no remaining heathens, to "burn," by which he meant "to become converted" to the true faith. The Burned-over District, then, was closer to paradise than perdition. Of course, there had to have been a few heathens scattered about the Foxes' new residence, but it is not certain into which category--Christian or heathen--the family fell.

Imagine a newcomer standing at the edge of the Burned-over District in the mid-nineteenth century. He knows nothing about it; he just comes across the territory and stares before him, finding nature at its shabbiest and civilization at its least civilized. Little of the land was cultivated, and the residences barely qualified as shacks. Today we would think the word "godforsaken" might come to mind. But since religious fervor was the district's principal raw material, no term could have been less appropriate.

Yet the newcomer might have wondered. He might have wondered whether those who resided in western New York prayed out of fervor, or because there were so few human beings to talk to. He might have wondered whether the settlers read the Bible out of piety or because there were few other books to be found. He might have wondered whether they went to church out of desire to share their faith or because there was no other organization to join. And perhaps they attended church social events with the same people not for enrichment but because there was no other form of culture or social activity and no desire for it anyhow. He might have been right. It was a strange place for the Foxes to have encamped in their new country--barren in some ways, zealous in others. But inexpensive in all ways, and but a short journey from Ontario; these are likely to have been the most compelling reasons for the Foxes' destination.

Hydesville, the village in which the family now lived, was about twenty miles from Rochester, the largest community in the Burned-over District and the closest thing to urbanity that its dwellers knew. But today, neither the family's home nor the surrounding community exists any longer. The name "Hydesville" continues to appear in small print on a few local maps but, for the most part, the land has been reclaimed by wilderness, and its history is little known. At its peak, the population of the village is believed to have reached about forty.

John David Fox and his wife probably got an especially good deal on their new home. It was, after all, haunted, and everyone knew it. In fact, it was referred to by their neighbors as the "spook house," with people believing that a benign ghost roamed the hallways in the most fearful hours of night. At least, he was *thought* to be benign; so far, there was no evidence of his ever having harmed anyone. Actually, there was no evidence of him at all; he had never been seen or heard or, as far as anyone knew, had never provided a sign of his presence. No matter. The belief in his existence was unquestioned by all who knew the house and its lore, and it was too good a story to doubt.

The ghost, so the story went, had been a man who once visited the place, perhaps five years before the Foxes moved in. And he never left, for he had been murdered there. No one knew who he was, no one knew how he met his maker, no one knew who the perpetrator was. No one was ever tried for the crime and, for a while, there was reason to believe that the offense might never have occurred; a search of the dwelling at one time or another revealed no signs of foul play. But, as would later be discovered, the search had been nothing more than cursory.

Nonetheless, Maggie and Kate were titillated by the tale, even though they thought it could use a little work. Gradually, they enlivened it, fashioning "a gruesome portrait of the spirit in the house. He was a peddler, killed for his money by previous occupants. His throat had been cut with a kitchen knife, and his body had been dragged, smearing blood, through the buttery, down the stairs, down to where he now lay buried in the earth-floored cellar."

It would have made a perfect story for a future edition of the *Virginia City Territorial Enterprise*.

Before long, many people would swear by this account of the spook-house murder. But how had the girls concocted the tale? Why? Even those who dismissed it as legend wondered how it was that such sweet, young lasses had suddenly displayed such horrid imaginations? They had never given so much as a hint of grotesque fantasizing before.

And even more baffling, what if their description of the murder turned out *not* to be fantasy? What if it were later proven to be authentic, as if the siblings had somehow, through some kind of mystical process, witnessed the long-past event. What would *that* say about Maggie and Kate Fox?

They were different from others girls their age, these two girls, and as they grew into adolescence, more and more people in the Burned-over District seemed to know it. Just *how* different had yet to be revealed.

By 1847, shortly before Christmas, several of the Foxes had gone their separate ways, leaving Hydesville behind. The older children, most of them married, scattered to places of their own. Son David stayed close to home, farming a small, barely arable plot of land less than two miles down the road from his mother and father. Only Maggie and Kate continued to live with their parents, and it was there, within the walls of the spook house, that it all started.

Once the holiday season was over, the winter grew more wintery. It was 1848 now, the most violent year of the century. Uprisings against the established order broke out all across Europe, one seeming to ignite the other. It might also have been in that year when the French intellectual Pierre Proudhon coined the term "anarchy"; many of those subscribing to this new form of non-government were responsible for the overthrow of King Louis-Philippe in France, and turbulence in Germany, Venice, Vienna, Rome, Czechoslovakia, Bohemia, Denmark, Hungary and elsewhere. The number of dead and injured was incalculable, the political confusion almost impossible to sort out in the aftermath.

In South Africa, the British took up arms again Dutch settlers known as the Voortrekkers, presaging the later Boer Wars; and in North America, the Mexican War, an exercise in self-aggrandizement for the United States no less than violence, came to a close after less than two brutal years. It allowed Americans to claim--some would say steal--more than 800,000 squares miles of the southwest that had once belonged to their foe.

Meanwhile, the unlikeliest of people with the unlikeliest of motives were igniting a different kind of revolution, nonviolent and, according to many, nonsensical. It was a revolution that would start in the outback of New York and before long thrill and mystify much of the world, even going so far as the czarist court of Russia.

Maggie Fox was now a "[s]light but sturdy, a country girl," and biographer Barbara Weisberg continues her description by portraying her as "an ebullient fourteen-year-old with glossy dark hair, a broad-boned face, and frank brown eyes. Black-haired Kate was slim and soulful, at ten years old still very much a child, with compelling eyes that struck some people as deep purple and others as black or gray." They were attractive youngsters, and ordinary enough, unless one looked more closely. It was then that something not so ordinary became apparent, an intensity in the eyes, a quality that suggested they were concentrating on something far away, something no one else could see.

Or perhaps they were just feeling the pain of their headaches.

"The first way in which the Fox sisters made themselves a nuisance was innocent enough," writes Gilbert Seldes in his classic work, *The Stammering Century*. "They used to tie strings to the stems of apples and, after they had gone to bed, bounce them on the floor in the dark to frighten a little niece who slept with them."*

Innocent enough? Yes.

Foreboding enough? Also yes.

But it was not just the little niece who heard the after-hours apple-thumping; Mrs. Fox also heard it and was no less disturbed. She thought of the ghost who was reported to dwell in her abode and immediately believed that he was the source of the sound, swearing that "sometimes it seemed as if the furniture was moved; but on examination we found everything in order. The children had become so alarmed that I thought it best to have them sleep in the room with us. . . . On the night of the first disturbance," she continued, "we all got up and lighted a candle and searched the house, the noises continuing during the time, and being heard near the same place."

Mrs. Fox speaks carelessly. When she says that "we all got up," she refers only to herself and her husband. Maggie and Kate, who by now constituted the rest of the household, remained in bed with their fruits of Edenic temptation, dropping them and then yanking them up by the strings, dropping and yanking; they might have been playing with yo-yos. One imagines them feigning sleep and stifling giggles as they listened to the commotion they created beneath them.

---

* Virtually nothing is known of the niece. It is not certain where she lived, nor how often she spent the nights with the Foxes.

That is one version of the story. Another makes no reference to a niece. Instead, it is said that the sisters heard sounds in the night similar to that of apples clunking against wood; deciding that the ghost was trying to get in touch with them, they started to clunk back.

Regardless of the truth, and the former version certainly seems more likely, one realizes in retrospect that the girls were planting the seeds of the idea that would later make them famous. And infamous. But at the time it was regarded as nothing more than a harmless diversion. Such a tender ruse, the youngest Foxes might have thought, yet so much of a fuss.

Soon there would be even more of one. After Maggie and Kate had given their first surreptitious performance, they decided on an encore. Actually, there were several encores, although accounts vary on how many. During one of them, Mrs. Fox, having become less fearful of her deceased boarder with increased exposure to him--he was, after all, harmless--decided to respond more boldly than before. Rather than waiting for the ghost to take the lead, it was she who would give the orders, starting by telling him to count to ten.

Ten apple-thuds followed.

Then Mrs. Fox told the ghost to give the ages of her two young daughters.

The ghost complied again. Fourteen thuds, pause, then ten.

Next, she asked whether the sounds she heard were being made by a human being. Give one thud for yes, two for no, she said.

The response was no.

Were they being made by a spirit?

Yes.

A spirit who had once been a human being?

Another affirmative.

Whereupon Margaret Fox said, "I then asked if it was injured in this house, and it manifested it by the noise. If the person was living that injured it? and got the same answer. I then ascertained by the same method that its remains were buried under the dwelling and how old it was."

Margaret Fox was ecstatic with her performance, especially its duration; she had spoken to the apparition for the longest period of time yet and elicited information never confirmed before. She was ready for another interrogation. Was the ghost ready as well? she asked, not knowing what to expect.

After a brief pause, he thumped his approval. The show would go on, with an unknown number of encore performances that winter and early spring. After the first few, Margaret began to tell friends and neighbors about the strange goings-on that she moderated. She invited them to sit in, to hear for themselves. The first non-Fox to hear from the ghost seems to have been a neighbor named Mary Redfield, and the occasion was April Fool's Eve, 1848. As usual, Maggie and Kate had secreted themselves upstairs, under the covers, and nervously awaited their introduction. Mrs. Redfield, nervous herself, sat downstairs with Margaret and John David.

Margaret requested quiet. It descended like a night gone suddenly starless. Then she began.

> "Now count five," she ordered, and the room shook with the sound of five heavy thuds.
>
> "Count fifteen," she commanded, and the mysterious presence obeyed. Next, she asked it to tell the neighbor's age; thirty-three distinct raps followed.
>
> "If you are an injured spirit," she continued, "manifest it by three raps."
>
> And it did.

Mrs. Redfield was astonished, especially by the fact that the spirit knew her age. How to account for that? In the days that followed, she told everyone she met about the miraculous occurrences in the Foxes' lair. As a result, more and more local denizens began stopping by--no formalities, like invitations, required. Shopkeepers and farmwives, itinerants and small town idlers--some knocked at the Foxes' door; others just tramped right in when the sun went down and made themselves comfortable in the family's living room. Among them were men who usually spent their nights fishing on a nearby river; there might have been as many as half a dozen of them. Supposedly, on another occasion, more than 300 people wedged themselves into the Fox house for the descent of the apples, although the number seems surely an exaggeration.

Soon, it is said, the ghost and Mrs. Fox collaborated on an alphabet of sorts; it was based on the number of times the apparition rapped, but involved more complexity than just "yes" and "no" replies. It might even have involved some creativity on the part of Mrs. Fox. One night, with her living room full of neighbors with mouths agape, she led the spirit to disclose "that it was murdered in the bed room, about five years ago, and that the murder was committed . . . on a Tuesday night, at 12 o'clock; that it was murdered by having its throat cut with a butcher knife; that the body . . . was taken down cellar, and that it was not buried until the next night . . ."

Rap, rap, rap, rap, rap.

As the size of the audiences increased, a problem grew along with it. Maggie and Kate had decided they could no longer rely on apples to transport their messages from the afterlife. It would have been too hard to keep replenishing the family's supply, and just as problematic, the use of a foodstuff would soon become obvious. Surely someone would discover pieces of dented apples in the girls' room, or in the garbage, and the game would be up. In addition, the family's shrinking spools of string would soon be noted.

A more subtle approach was called for, and it did not take the girls long to concoct one.

In time it was learned that the victim of the spook-house murder was a man named Bell, and it was discovered that the details of the crime were just as his ghost had related them. Hydesville and its environs were stunned. And it is reasonable to assume that, in their own way, Maggie and Kate were no less taken aback, for with confirmation of the crime, they had apparently completed an astonishing transition. Having started out as practical jokers, they were now, somehow, revealing themselves to be possessors of the dark arts. "William Duesler [who lived close to the Foxes] summed up the positions of neighbors by saying, 'I never believed in haunted houses, or heard or saw anything but what I could account for before but this I cannot account for.'"

Could Maggie and Kate account for their suddenly acquired knowledge? We do not know. They never spoke about a sudden onset of otherworldly gifts. And, in fact, of all the mysterious events associated with the Fox sisters, this seems to me the most mysterious. How *did* tricksters suddenly evolve into oracles? As far as I have been able to determine, it is a question unanswered by anyone who has ever written about the girls, or the phenomenon they brought into being. It is, in fact, a question that has never been asked, as one book after another, one essay after another, leaps over the trickster-to oracle chasm without even trying to build a bridge.

Unless, that is, there is such a thing as psychic DNA, and the sisters' gift was a genetic inheritance that suddenly manifested itself. Biographer Barbara Weisberg writes that

> Margaret Fox's sister, Elizabeth Smith, also reportedly evidenced the gift called second sight or clairvoyance, the ability to see what the eye can't at a distance in time or space, even foreseeing her own death. At age nineteen--or so it was later said--Elizabeth told her parents, "I dreamed I was in a new country, walking alone, when suddenly I came to a small cemetery, and, walking up to one of the most prominent head-stones, read the inscription. . . ."

> Elizabeth confided that she had seen her own name on the headstone, the first initial of her husband's last name, *H*, and the information that she had died at twenty-seven years old.

But at this point, Weisberg makes her own contribution to the chasm, by neglecting to tell her readers whether Elizabeth Smith did in fact yield her mortality at twenty-seven. And surely there *is* no such thing as psychic DNA. Is there?

However it happened, the transformation of the Fox sisters from practical jokers into soothsayers had repercussions that far exceeded the boundaries of the Burned-over District. Writing in *The Smithsonian* magazine more than a century and a half later, author Karen Abbott insisted that the people who sat in on the performances at the Foxes' dwelling were not seekers of eerie thrills so much as pilgrims who took the first steps toward "[o]ne of the greatest religious movements of the 19th century."

It is not as laughable as it sounds. It is, in fact, prescient.

At the time, the United States was nearing the end of an era of profound trust in forces that the eye could not see. The Second Great Awakening,** a commitment to the Almighty among Protestants prone to excitable expression, a commitment that attracted preachers who declared that they were "God's chosen people in the redemption of the world," had begun around 1790. By 1848, it seemed to be trickling out of relevance. But if the faithful were no longer as overheated in their means of worship as they had once been, no longer as apt to shout out hosannas, weep in joyfulness, faint in contemplation of heavenly glories--if they no longer behaved so manically, they were still as committed to their religion's underlying tenets.

And more than a few of them were thinking that it might be nice--if not even essential--for something to come along that gave the Second

---

** The First Great Awakening, which was the model for the Second, swept through the United States before it officially existed, reaching its peak in the 1730s and 1740s.

Great Awakening a boost, a few more years in which the fires of heavenly fervor continued to burn. In fact, one historian would write that, by 1850, the awakening had fallen asleep, for all practical purposes no longer existing. But this was an exaggeration; something continued to stir in the embers. And because it did, the oldest of the Fox sisters, waiting in the wings, was only a few tumultuous months from entering our story.

Unlike the other members of her family, Leah knew something about the Burned-over District's past, that it had already established itself as ground for a new movement in American religious history. It was here that Jesus reputedly spoke to Joseph Smith in a vision, and also here that the ultimate results of Smith's vision, *The Book of Mormon*, was published in 1830. If, after almost another two decades had passed, the Fox sisters had not yet gone so far as to hint at the development so bold as a new religion, they seemed to be getting closer. And Leah would not have been surprised at Karen Abbott's later conclusion.

The pilgrims who squeezed into the Fox abode to hear ethereal taps from the afterlife were a diverse group who came from locales increasingly distant from Hydesville. Among others, they were "[s]enators, judges, and professors said they believed that communication was possible with the dead," it was reported, and the so-called "Rochester rappings,"--although they had not yet been heard as far away as Rochester--seemed proof of the contention. After all, when spoken to, the ghost could always be counted on to chat back in that distinct way of his.

Maggie and Kate not only continued to ride the wave they had created; they took a giant step to give it even more momentum. True, they did so warily, having begun to fear the monster they had created, that it might overwhelm them, taking on a life of its own; they were, after all, just two young ladies, one of them not even in her teens yet. They also did so with a certain degree of fatalism, believing that they had no choice but to cast aside their doubts and accept the reality that their ghost, who had already become a status symbol in their indigent hometown, would be even more of an attraction if he had a name. How they came up with one nobody knows, but they eventually decided on Mr. Splitfoot, a sinister term because it was thought by some to be associated, even synonymous, with the devil.*** It was a risky choice for the girls to make, but something about the sound appealed. Besides, in for a penny, in for a pound.

Soon the sisters and their playmate *were* heard as far away as Rochester, then even beyond. More and more people now "regarded them with awe," according to *American History Magazine*, "as divinely inspired individuals chosen to interpret messages from the dead--an attitude that may have contributed to Maggie and Katy's continued reluctance to confess to the prank."

Of course, the prank was more than just a prank by this time. Otherwise, how would the sisters have known Mrs. Redfield's age? How would they have known the details of the crime that took place in their house? So many questions about what the girls had wrought, questions to which no one yet had an answer, and perhaps never would.

And then another question arose, one that should have arisen before, and suddenly mystery enshrouded Maggie and Kate again, this time more deeply than ever. Although they were widely acknowledged to be the spirit's allies, they were never seen with him, never part of the audience that listened to his echoes from the afterlife. Why not? Where were they at the time? What did their absence signify? That the three of them had formed some perverse kind of bond with one another, and that Mr. Splitfoot required the sisters' company for reassurance as he waited for his cues in his otherworldly realm? Or was it that, since Maggie and Kate, being only children and the ghost a murder victim,

---

*** Pan, the Greek god of nature, was half man, half goat and all carnal appetite, the very antithesis of Christian restraint and virtue. Because of him, the cloven hoof possessed not only by goats, but by sheep, cattle, and other ruminants had long been regarded as a satanic symbol. "Cloven hoof" is, of course, another term for "split foot."

he felt safer with them than he would have felt with adults? Even Mrs.
Fox, apparently too wrapped up in her newfound fame as ringmas-
ter, had never asked herself about the girls' constant absence from the
Splitfoot showcases. Perhaps she thought that, because of her daughters' youth and innocence, they were simply afraid of the extra-sensory
proceedings.

Neither she, nor anyone else, seems to have wondered whether the
sisters *were* Mr. Splitfoot.

Eventually, someone had a suggestion: remove Maggie and Kate
from the Fox abode when Mr. Splitfoot was meeting his listeners. Stash
them away somewhere, perhaps with neighbors who were appointed
to stand guard over the girls. They would ensure that the young Foxes
had no communication with the ghost, not of any manner whatsoever,
when he was answering his audience's questions. Would he respond
to them nonetheless? Or would the strange visitor from the afterlife
be silenced?

The girls did not like the idea, afraid it would reveal their secret. But
they had no choice. So one night they were taken to a friend's house,
remaining under watchful eyes until morning. Or maybe they stayed
for longer than that; what actually happened is not certain. What *is*
certain is that, for the first time since Mr. Splitfoot's debut, the elder
Foxes and a houseful of friends and the psychically curious, found
themselves immersed in stillness. Margaret asked her usual questions,
but those who hoped to hear from the ghost were instead subjected
to such mundane sounds as the breathing of others, the scurrying of
nocturnal creatures in the surrounding woods, and the occasional
whistle of wind through the trees. But from supernatural precincts all
was hushed.

So the question was answered. Or seemed to be. The ghost *had*
accompanied the girls into temporary exile; there was, apparently, no
breaking up the act. But rather than the brief separation having blown
Maggie and Kate's cover, the perception was that it revealed more
clearly than ever the strength of their bond. Mr. Splitfoot *did* feel more

comfortable with Maggie and Kate--and why not? Even spectral entities needed unthreatening companions, and the sisters obviously had a
special affinity for the ghost. And vice versa.

Which, as it turned out, brought a different and more troubling
issue to the forefront: the closeness of the relationship between two
young human beings and a phantom, a wraith from another world.
And the phantom's name was Mr. Splitfoot; suddenly the sinister
implications could not have been more obvious. Innocence on the one
hand, deviltry on the other. People became appalled by the connection,
even frightened. The girl's association with the Hydesville ghost, it was
now believed by some, proved that the girls were witches at the least, or
at worst, the very handmaidens of Satan, angels of darkness.

The members of Hydesville's Methodist Episcopalian Church led
the protest. They demanded that the entire Fox family be exiled from
the village and never show their faces again. Prayers were said for them
at Sunday services; in public they were shunned. In addition, good,
churchgoing folks of other faiths were now changing their minds, now
aware of, and of course opposed to the devil's presence in their midst,
regardless of how entertaining a show he put on. No longer a novelty in
the Burned-over District, Maggie, Kate, and company were now being
seen as a threat.

For a time, the elder Foxes tried to ignore the commotion. But
opposition to them only grew more insistent. Reluctantly, John David
and Margaret yielded to it. Having lived in Hydesville less than a year
and a half, they were now forced to depart. Possessed of few material
goods, they were able to load them all into the family's ramshackle
wagon. For reasons unknown, however, the family set out in different destinations, with the parents taking the wagon and heading off in
one direction and the girls being dropped off at the railroad station to
journey elsewhere.

At first, Maggie and Kate did not know what to make of the plan.
On the one hand, they did not want to be separated from their parents;
on the other, they were relieved that they would no longer be exposed

to their mother and father's failing marriage and the arguments that accompanied it almost daily. John David was drinking as much as ever, probably even more since Mr. Splitfoot had joined the family. As for Margaret, it may be that her newfound celebrity had gone to her head and that it turned to notoriety was more than she could bear.

What awaited the adults as they left the spook house behind, other than the end of their union, is a puzzle; they went their own ways and disappeared from history. What awaited their offspring, however, was not ignominy, as people of Hydesville expected, but stardom to a degree that no one could have foreseen.

First stop: Rochester. The bright lights, the big city. If there is such a thing as destiny, this is a prime example of it, for Rochester, the capital of the Burned-over District, was where the Foxes' big sister had situated herself. A single mother of one girl, she had kept her husband's name after divorcing him. Unfortunately, that name was Fish. She was leading a lonely life when her siblings arrived, and thus was only too happy to welcome them. No less was she pleased to take in Mr. Splitfoot.

To the contrary. Karen Abbott writes; "Rochester was a hotbed for reform and religious activity . . . Community leaders Isaac and Amy Post were intrigued by the Fox sisters' story, and by the subsequent report spreading from Hydesville that the spirit likely belonged to a peddler who had been murdered in the farmhouse five years beforehand. A group of Rochester residents had examined the cellar of the Fox's home, uncovering strands of hair and what appeared to be bone fragments."[****]

[****] Raymond Fitzsimmons, a biographer of the escape artist Harry Houdini, writes that "[a] search [of the Fox basement] was made but had to be abandoned. because the ground under the cellar was waterlogged." According to Sir Arthur Conan Doyle, not the most trustworthy of sources in matters of the paranormal, a later examination, in 1904, discovered an entire human skeleton buried in a cellar wall. A doctor who supposedly examined the bones said they were about fifty years old.

On November 7, 1849, Maggie began a series of appearances at Corinthian Hall, Rochester's largest, gaudiest auditorium, which was like no place that any of the Foxes had ever experienced before. "WONDER-FUL PHENOMENA," read the banner outside the building, which Kate, for some reason, never saw. She had not joined Maggie in Rochester. It was thought that she was in Auburn, New York, at the time, although history does not record why, nor what she was doing there. Kate did not accompany Maggie at future Corinthian Hall performances either. Perhaps Leah believed it was too intimidating a venue for so young a person.

Whatever the reason, Leah took her place, although at first, rather than accompanying Maggie onstage, she stood in the wings, providing moral support and ready to assist if needed.

The starting time for the Foxes' debut performance: 7 pm.

Admission fee: 25 cents.

The reception: bafflingly hostile.

The audience, according to local newspaper reports, greeted Maggie with hisses as she walked out onstage and took her chair in the middle. She did not understand such animosity and looked around her in fright. It was all she could do not to flee. She dropped her eyes for a few moments, and when she raised them again, she barely had the energy to speak. The audience's hisses soon turned to laughter.

Maggie froze, staring out at the largest crowd she had ever confronted with an expression so horrifyingly blank that it could not help but reveal the turmoil within. She soon felt herself trembling. When the audience's derision reached a peak, Leah dashed onstage, putting

---

Interestingly, Houdini would one day develop a strong but adversarial position toward the notion of communing with the dead. Extremely close to his mother, he was bereft when she passed away, even giving up his career for a few years to mourn. Then he started attending séances, trying to re-establish the bonds with his beloved. Instead, as an illusionist himself, he found illusions in the methods of mediums. None could really enable him to talk to his mother, despite their claims--and so upset was he by their chicanery that he turned his grief into a productive anger, becoming the country's foremost--if not learned--critic of psychic practices early in the twentieth century.

an arm around her sister and glaring out at those who dared to treat so innocent a child in so dreadful a manner. She might even have cursed them; there are conflicting reports.

Mr. Splitfoot, however, remained undaunted, and reports from the evening indicate that he was his usual accurate self--he knew so many details of, and offered so much advice from, loved ones no longer alive. Of course, this should have established his credibility, making those in attendance ooh and aah, applaud and cheer, and respond to Maggie with a warmer welcome. But again their behavior was a puzzle, for the result was just the opposite. Mr. Splitfoot's accuracy led to further rage, as those listening to him apparently believed he could have obtained the correct answers only through deceitfulness. It was bad enough, they seemed to think, that they were being fooled; worse was that they had no idea how it was being done.

By the time Maggie's opening night performance finally ended, the spectators had reached a boil. There were demands that both she and Leah be examined for evidence of fraud. The girls were too terrified to refuse. A panel of worthy Rochester citizens, plucked from the audience, was given the assignment. They rose from their seats, climbed up to the stage, and terrified the girls with their thoroughness.

But to no avail. Their efforts satisfied no one, not even the panelists themselves. They "remained perplexed," *American History* reported. "That Thursday night a committee representative confessed to a restive audience their inability to explain the phenomenon. Desperately, still other committees attempted to test Maggie and Leah--placing them on glass, on pillows, and even appointing a subcommittee of ladies to discover if they had hidden any machinery in their underclothes." A strip search, we would call it today.

Nothing was found amiss. The sisters' underclothes contained no foreign devices. The Foxes should have been vindicated, and would *be* vindicated time and again in the future, when some of the most perceptive men and women in the field of psychic studies investigated the girls after their demonstrations.

Against all visible evidence, though, Maggie and Kate had *not* been absolved that night in Rochester. The people in the audience, having already reached an apex of animosity, lost their collective minds at the panel's final findings. "Blinding cascades of light from firecrackers lit by raucous nonbelievers exploded in the back of the auditorium...Thanks to police intervention, Maggie, Leah...and other terrified spiritualists were whisked out of the building."

Despite such an unpromising start, the Foxes and Mr. Splitfoot, troopers all, continued their Corinthian Hall engagement until its scheduled end. Gradually, Maggie began to win over the people of Rochester, her youthfulness conveying a naïve trust, her courage in facing a hostile audience turning that hostility to admiration. Leah, however, was not so fortunate. Author and social critic Gilbert Seldes relates the following:

> This eldest sister was eventually to be accused of being the evil genius of the younger ones. She claimed that, before Maggie and Katie were born, she had received messages promising great things for them and, when the young children, became the medium for the first communications with the other world, Mrs. Fish formed the rather grand project of founding a new religion.

More likely, what Mrs. Leah Fox Fish had in mind was the revival of an old religion, albeit seeking to steer it along a new path. Perhaps the Second Great Awakening could remain awake after all, but rather than focusing on the Almighty, it would now seek contact with those whom the Almighty had already claimed for His Eternal Kingdom. With Leah providing all the assistance she could, with Kate having rejoined her sister, and with apple-tapping now having become a thing of the past for the girls, they were taking a huge and inexplicable leap toward respectability. They were "inventing" what became known as Spiritualism.

Most people who knew of it would think of it as flimflam. But some would regard it as a religion, some as a philosophy, and some as both. Psychic researcher Peter Aykroyd, the father of comedian and Ghostbuster Dan (who is also a student of the supernatural) believed that the foundation of the faith was the belief "that the human personality survives after bodily death and . . . those with biological life have the ability to communicate with those who appear to be minds without bodies. The uncertainty about what happens to us when we die and, even more important, whether we here on earth can communicate with those who have passed on, drew people together to pursue the mysteries of the supernatural spirit."

And is it, in the most general of terms, so extraordinary a notion? Most Spiritualists think not, and have reasoned in a manner that will seem blasphemous to others, but to them seems only logical. It is as follows: Christians insist on the premise that one does not have to see an entity for that entity to exist, nor to hear actual words for there to be a dialogue. They believe the dialogue can be felt if not heard. Spiritualists "preach" the same. The Christian entity is God. To Spiritualists, the entities, plural, are deceased mortals. Christians accept God on faith. Spiritualists accept deceased mortals on the same basis. Christians employ priests or ministers to serve as intermediaries to God. Spiritualists employ mediums, or psychics, to facilitate communication with the departed. The Christian God resides in heaven. Those on whom Spiritualists rely reside in the after*life*, accent on the life.

And as the nineteenth century lurched forward, more and more people, albeit never a majority, began to wonder whether mediums might actually provide more verifiable truths than ministers.

Chapter 2

THE LOUDEST JOINTS

Although Maggie and Leah Fox were not received as they had hoped to be in Rochester, they did manage to impress someone who was unable to attend any of the Corinthian Hall performances. Because of "[h]is purported ability to diagnose clairvoyantly and to prescribe for disease, in addition to a reputation for prophecy," Andrew Jackson Davis was sometimes referred to, after a nearby New York city, as the "Poughkeepsie Seer," and some who celebrated him elevated to the position of "John the Baptist of Modern Spiritualism." Others, though, thought differently. To them he was "the feeble-bodied, untutored son of a drunken cobbler and a superstitious uneducated mother." The truth might have lain somewhere in between.

Conducting a séance one day when he was only eighteen years old, Davis supposedly channeled a highly sophisticated fellow, a gentleman far more eloquent, more deeply resonant and precise in his enunciation, than Davis could ever be. His tonal quality, in other words, was one that Davis was said to be incapable of producing himself. Dr. George Bush, a professor of Hebrew at New York University, attended the séance and listened to Davis speak in that atypical voice. Amazed by what he heard, Bush explained that there was no way Davis's own vocal cords could have produced such sounds. Someone else, Bush concluded, someone not only educated but, given his old-fashioned vocabulary, probably having lived earlier in the century, was using the rube as his mouthpiece.

> The circumference of [Davis's] head is unusually small. If size is the measure of power, then this youth's mental capacity is unusually limited. His lungs are weak and unexpanded. He had not dwelt amid refining influences--manners ungentle and and awkward. He has not read a book save one [the Bible]. He knows nothing of grammar or the rules of language, nor associated with literary or scientific persons.

Furthermore, at a previous séance, Bush swore that he had heard Davis converse flawlessly in the professor's own tongue, Hebrew, covering such unlikely topics as chemistry, geology and mythology. Bush passed beyond amazement to stupefaction. He doubted that Davis had ever heard Hebrew spoken before, and even more that he could spell the names of the sciences with which he had suddenly become conversant. As for analyzing the tenets on which they were based, which Davis began to do, Bush could not even consider the possibility.

Despite having little acquaintance with Spiritualism, the professor decided he had no choice other than to conclude that Davis had somehow become the intermediary through which a human being no longer living and completely unlike himself, was able to make contact with those still enjoying mortality. Bush was simply not able to come up with a more satisfactory explanation.

Davis had heard of Maggie and Kate's exploits in Hydesville, as well as the investigations in Rochester that had turned up no fakery. This, as far as the seer was concerned, suggested that the girls were members in good standing of paranormal practice. He had also heard of their friend Mr. Splitfoot--a catchy name, he thought. Always on the lookout for new talent, he began to consider taking the Foxes under his tutelage and introducing them to a larger public.

In 1850, two years after the first apple had hit the floor in upstate New York, Andrew Jackson Davis invited the three Fox sisters to visit him in Manhattan, the talented girls from the barrens being summoned for their chance at the big time. We do not know what they did in their private audition for Davis, but that they did it well seems obvious. Receiving the master's imprimatur, "Maggie, Kate, and Leah Fox embarked on a professional tour to spread the word of the spirits, booking a suite, fittingly, at Barnum's Hotel on the corner of Broadway and Maiden Lane, an establishment owned by a cousin of the famed showman."

By this time, the girls had varied their act, making it even more otherworldly. "In addition to the rappings," reported Raymond Fitzsimmons, "new phenomena occurred [at Fox séances]--people were caressed by invisible hands, untouched musical instruments played, and the table [at which séance-goers sat] not only tilted in various directions but even rose from the floor." The first, it was thought by skeptics, could be attributed to power of suggestion; the second to someone's playing the same instrument offstage; the third to the girls' lifting the table with their knees. Or, in the surmise of the famed British scientist Michael Faraday, "the force moving the tables was the result of involuntary contractions of the muscles of sitters who wanted to see the table move."

Did anyone check to see whether any of the preceding might have occurred? It does not seem so. The opinions were offered from afar, in Faraday's case from the other side of the Atlantic. There had been far closer investigation of the girls in Rochester than in Manhattan. Perhaps in part for this reason, and in part because the New York audience was more interested in being entertained than in attesting to the validity of occult experiments, the Foxes' new set of feats turned into one of the city's longest-running shows, rivaling the musical *She's Come! Jenny's Come!* and the drama *King Rene's Daughter*.

And the *New-York Tribune*, surprising many, gave the girls a critical seal of approval. "All this sounds sufficiently ridiculous and amusing," the paper reported, "yet the men [seated around the table] are parties of high intelligence and respectability."

At first, the sessions were conducted in the parlor of Barnum's Hotel, a large room but more intimate by far than the sprawling Corinthian Hall. For the general public, Maggie and Kate--Leah had returned to Rochester and slipped behind the scenes again--performed thrice daily, at 10 a.m., 5 p.m. and 8 p.m. A large table had been constructed for the girls, capable of seating as many as thirty people at once. For certain individuals, though, private sessions were offered, the fee unknown; those who could not afford them and sat in the parlor were charged a dollar. It was expensive for the time, but Maggie and Kate worked hard for whatever portion of their earnings that Davis, now their manager, allowed them to keep. "The sisters went to bed each night exhausted but during their long working hours found the crowds generally courteous."

There were no hostile reactions toward the Foxes in New York; virtually without exception, audiences seemed to love them. Furthermore, according to biographer Barbara Weisberg, "So popular were the séances that a well-known singer [Mary Taylor] incorporated a new song, 'The Rochester Knockings at Barnum's Hotel,' into her Broadway act."

Fortunately, no copy of the lyrics exists anymore.

And as recently as 2020, theatregoers in London could see a one-man-dressed-as-a-woman play about Kate called *The Fabulist Fox Sister*. The play was subtitled *A Musical Lie*.

The most famous of the Foxes' New York City séances was not held at the Barnum Hotel, but

> at the home of the prominent author and minister Rufus Griswold, [and] was attended by members of the nation's intellectual elite. Among others, Griswold hosted James Fenimore Cooper, author of the *Leatherstocking Tales*; George Ripley, the [New-York] *Tribune's* literary critic . . . George Bancroft, former secretary of the navy, historian, and statesman; the poet William Cullen Bryant; and N.P. Willis, editor of the *Home Journal*, a magazine that kept the fashioned apprised of what was "new, charming or instructive in the brilliant circle of city life."

Cooper was the most esteemed of Griswold's guests. It was also he whose experience was the most extraordinary. His sister had died half a century ago, something that was not generally known, and so much time had passed that even some who *did* know of the young lady's death had forgotten the details. Cooper, though, would never forget them--such a freak accident had it been, so much had they reverberated through his life. But although he thought of her often, he almost never discussed her with others.

At the Griswold's house, he made an exception. A friend had prompted Cooper to attend the séance with him and, knowing of his sister's fate, urged the author to find out whether Maggie and Kate also knew. At first he refused; then, reluctantly, he asked the girls how long his sister had been gone. Fifty time-consuming but suspenseful raps followed. Then, according to professor of science journalism Deborah Blum, the questioning went as follows:

"Had she died of illness? No answer.

"An accident?

"Yes.

"Was she killed by lightning? Was she shot? Did she fall from a carriage? Was she lost at sea?

"No answer. No answer. No answer. No answer.

"'Was she thrown by a horse?'

"Two knocks. Yes.

"Definitely.

"After he left, Cooper told his companions that every answer had been correct. Making his experience all the eerier, he had been thinking about his sister, who, fifty years ago that month, had been killed when her horse reared unexpectedly.

"Cooper decided not to return. He was spooked."

And he remained spooked. He would never be able to understand how two callow girls from the benighted western corner of New York, two girls who had probably never heard of him and surely never read one of his books or known about his sister. He felt as if a fog of some sort had descended on him, a hallucinatory fog, cocooning him and making escape impossible. James Fenimore Cooper had a year left to live. In that time he would be as unwilling to talk about the séance as he was to discuss young Miss Cooper's demise.

It is possible that prominent figures in addition to those previously mentioned had joined the assemblage at Griswold's house. It is certain that they attended at least one Fox séance some place at some time.

They included the former governor of Wisconsin, Nathaniel Tallmadge; Arctic explorer Elisha Kent Kane who, although believing the sisters' exhibition to be tomfoolery, would end up marrying Maggie; and the abolitionist leader William Lloyd Garrison, who "witnessed a [Fox] session in which the spirits rapped in time to a popular song and spelled out a message: 'Spiritualism will work miracles in the cause of reform.'"

Also falling victim to the Maggie-and-Kate spell was Horace Greeley. He is known today (if at all) for having uttered the phrase, "Go West, young man, go West," which was actually spoken by someone else and rephrased by Greeley as, "Go West, young man, and grow up with the country." But it was Greeley who got credit for the sentiment. At the time, he was the editor of the *New-York Tribune* and, as such, one of our nation's leading opinion makers.

If he witnessed the Foxes at their Griswold forum, it was probably his second encounter with them. His first would have been a private session at the Barnum, where "Greeley had heard the raps, felt the vibrations, and received correct answers to his questions, but he left the Fox sisters' rooms as baffled and curious as he was when he entered. He had gone there with a friend who received only one correct answer to his six different questions. The whole 'curious and puzzling affair,' Greeley concluded, could be 'stripped of all supernatural interest' and still merit further investigation."

Before long, those further investigations would be conducted by associates of Greeley, men of solid professional achievements, their backgrounds as impressive as his, in some cases even more so. Without exception, they entered their sessions with the Fox girls--most of them at the Barnum--in a mocking frame of mind. More often than not, it seems, they did not depart the same way. Rather, they emerged from the hotel sharing Greeley's mystification.

"The production of the sounds is hard to explain, and still stranger," mused the [famed diarist and] lawyer George Templeton Strong, "is the accuracy with which the ghost guesses of whom one is thinking--his age, his residence, vocation and the like." After carefully weighing different possibilities, such as the sisters' ability to use sleight of hand or to read clues from facial expressions, he eliminated the notion of trickery and "deliberate legerdemain." He was inclined to believe that a mysterious but natural cause was at work, "some magnetic or electrical or mesmeric agency" that propelled the young mediums, a power that they themselves couldn't explain.

Soon, however, Greeley became more decisive than Strong about Maggie and Kate. And more decisive than he himself had been previously. By the time he had submerged himself in a few more séances with Maggie and Kate, including a private sitting at his home in Manhattan, Greeley had shed his earlier doubts and leaped onto the Spiritualist soap box. "Whatever may be the origin or cause of the 'rappings,'" Greeley proclaimed, although erroneously, "the ladies in whose presence they occur do not make them. We tested this thoroughly, and to our entire satisfaction. Their conduct and bearing is as unlike that of deceivers as possible; and we think no one acquainted with them could believe them at all capable of engaging in so daring, impious, and shameful a juggle as this would be if they caused the sounds. And it is not possible that such a juggle should have been so long perpetuated in public."

Although Greeley was wrong about the source of the sounds, he was not wrong in believing the information that the sounds related. Or so he concluded, and a conclusion reached by Horace Greeley was not one to be taken lightly.

Even before such a benediction, the Fox girls were "arousing national interest" and emulation. "All over America mediums began surfacing." In fact, by one estimate, there were 30,000 mediums in the United States by 1853. "To believers this was the time of a new Revelation, a new Pentecost; God manifesting himself through certain chosen people."

The author of the preceding, Houdini biographer Fitzsimmons, does not exaggerate. As Karen Abbott and others had posited, Spiritualism became more religious in nature as the late nineteenth century sped forward, in part because the Fox girls and many of the mediums who followed them had added yet another twist to their repertoire, one that gave the séance a more official, less casual air.

Instead of communicating directly with the deceased at séances, more and more mediums began to deal with intermediaries, citizens of the spirit world who acted as interpreters of a sort. They were known as controls. The mediums asked questions of the controls, who in turn relayed them to the deceased. Then the process was reversed: the deceased gave their replies to the controls, who provided the information to the mediums, who, in turn, sent it along to the sitters who had begun the process in the first place.

To some people, controls seemed unnecessary. Rather than being facilitators, they were a layer of bureaucracy between séance-holder and sitter, and, as such, only slowed the process of communing. Surely, thought doubters, mediums could continue as they had always been doing, querying the spirit world directly. If it ain't broke . . .

But those who favored controls explained that they made the mediums' job easier, speaking, as they did, the specific language of the afterlife and thereby serving as a kind of priesthood, members of an elite group with more direct access to the apparitions, like Mr. Splitfoot, who were the "gods" of the séance. This, in turn, gave the séance some of the pomp of a church service. It was also claimed that the new and increasing role of controls was "giving their trances a rather eerie suggestion of possession."

Unarguably, Spiritualism came along at just the right time. "By the 1840s," according to historian Nancy Rubin, "America's preoccupation with death was widespread. The nation's new cities were expanding. Immigration was at an all-time high and its factories and ports were booming, all of which contributed to urban overcrowding and poor sanitation, which spawned epidemics of cholera, whooping cough, cholera, and diphtheria. Mortality was on the rise. Nearly one-third of all city-born infants died before reaching their first birthdays, and young mothers--bearing an average of five children each--were often fatally struck with puerperal fever. Death thus touched all families, leaving behind memories of those who had passed to the other side."

In Europe at the time, there might not have been a preoccupation with death, but there did seem to be a spreading dubiety about religion in Western cultures. As Tom Wolfe writes, "Well educated, would-be sophisticated people . . . had begun to reject the magical, miraculous, superstitious, logically implausible doctrines of religion, such as the Virgin Birth of Christ, the Creation (of the world in seven days), Christ's Resurrection, the power of prayer, the omnipotence of God, and a thousand other notions that were irrational by their very nature."

There was, thus, an increasing vacuum in the soul of this age of invention in the United States, which was the Victorian era in England and a variety of other eras across the Channel. To many, Spiritualism seemed both as plausible and as unlikely as the religions that had for so long occupied the space. And as if they were the greatest inventors of all in this great age of invention--this age of Bell and Burbank, Morse and Edison, Elisha Otis, Cyrus McCormick and George Eastman, France's Louis Daguerre (photography) and Louis Pasteur (pasteurization, vaccination), Italy's Guglielmo Marconi (wireless telegraphy), Germany's Karl Benz (the gasoline-powered automobile), Croatia's Nikola Tesla (alternating current), and Brits like Richard Trevithick (the steam railway), Henry Bessemer (steel-making improvements), and Sir Francis Galton (eugenics)--as if they were like these men, people identified as psychically gifted were reputed to have made the greatest discovery in the history of mankind, a means of crossing the world's most insurmountable frontier, passing behind the black curtain that separates life from death. Initially, none of the people who facilitated these journeys attracted more attention than Maggie and Kate Fox.

From New York, Andrew Jackson Davis sent the girls on the road. According to one biography of the Foxes' early years, "they left behind dozens of circles for spiritual communication, hundreds of men and women who believed they were in contact with their ancestors, thousands of people who were curious and interested, and a few wealthy believers who . . . would be willing to devote their lives and their fortunes to spiritual investigation."

Departing from Manhattan, Maggie, Kate, and Mr. Splitfoot were dispatched to Washington, D.C., St. Louis, Cleveland, and Cincinnati, among other cities. And it was in Buffalo, one night in 1831, that the apples' replacement was finally confirmed and revealed. Three physicians, medical professors at the University of Buffalo, were watching Maggie and Kate on that occasion, and in a letter to a local newspaper a few days later, they announced their findings.

> "Reasoning by way of exclusion," the doctors wrote, they had gone into the meeting having agreed in advance that a spiritual explanation for the raps couldn't be considered until all possible physiological explanations had been eliminated. And the gentlemen had emerged from the meeting convinced, after careful observation, that Maggie's barely perceptible bodily movements produced the noises.

More specifically, the doctors determined that Maggie and Kate had a remarkable ability to crack their joints: knees and knuckles, ankles and toes. And they could do so without being noticed. They could sit right next to someone and reconfigure their joints without anyone's detecting movement. The doctors also found that "the raps did not occur if the sisters were placed on a couch with cushions under their feet."

To many it seemed absurd. Conventional joint-cracking could barely be heard from one end of the room in a house to the other, and certainly not from the front of a theatre to the back row. Nor could the gentle snapping of joints be repeated often and quickly enough to constitute a "conversation" with a medium. But journalist Nancy Rubin Stuart concluded that there was nothing in the least normal about the Fox girls' anatomy. After a while, she says, they became "so adept that they performed the trick in their stocking feet and even while standing in shoes. These rapidly repeated sounds were allegedly so loud that the elder Foxes had been awakened from their sleep." And the sounds were so easily mastered, Kate insisted, that she was able to teach an in-law, Mrs. Norman Culver, how to turn up the volume on her own toes, "explaining that it helped to place the feet in warm water before a demonstration. After a week of practice Mrs. Culver was able to produce raps with all the toes on both of her feet and to make as many as 150 raps in a row."

Those who continued to trust Maggie and Kate as conduits to the afterlife were not dissuaded by reports of the girls' sonically-enhanced bone structure. Nor should they have been. For the sounds were but the means. How to explain the ends; i.e., the fact that the sounds of bones provided so many correct responses to so many queries on so many subjects?

Asking this question does not reveal authorial bias. It is a logical, even objective, reaction to the fact that so many non-believers are so feeble in their rebuttals to Spiritualism. It is one thing to disagree, quite another to disprove. Surely if something that *seems* as preposterous as mortals communing with the dead really *is* preposterous, there ought to be ways to prove it. If not, there at least ought to be effective arguments to make against the premise. But with the exception of numerous cases of obvious, amateurish chicanery, this is simply not so.

For instance, if Maggie and Kate were nothing more than simple frauds . . .

How did they know Mrs. Redfield's age?

How did they know the details of the murder in their former home, many of which were never made public, including the name of the victim?

How did they know about the horse-riding accident that had killed James Fenimore Cooper's sister long before they were born?

How did they know the correct answers to so many of Horace Greeley's questions?

How did they know they accuracy of the responses to which George Templeton Strong had alluded?

And how did they manage to be so accurate so often as they toured, leaving audiences far more engaged than disappointed?

The counter-arguments to these to these examples are unsatisfactory. The girls were lucky, say non-believers. Or they had been told the answers beforehand or received them via silent signals from someone tucked into theatre wings, or a dark corner of the séance site or had had their legs tapped a certain number of times by a co-conspirator seated nearby. There is an off-the-top-of-the-head quality to these denials; they are hardly thoughtful, and raise as many questions as they purport to answer.

Especially the point about Maggie and Kate having been provided with answers prior to the séance. This was probably the charge made most often against the girls, but it is also the least likely. Actually, it truly *is* preposterous. How can replies be provided before the questions are even known?

Some skeptics are ready with an answer. They assert that the sisters were inundated with so many facts and figures about those who sat before them at séances and in auditoriums that at least some of the answers were bound to be covered by the information. The key word in the preceding is "inundated." How could two young girls possibly commit to memory the massive amounts of knowledge that would be required to pull off such a hoax?

And not just massive, but constantly changing amounts. Different sitters would ask Maggie and Kate different questions, and there was no possible way for them to know who would comprise their audiences from one performance to the next. Especially when they were contacting the afterlife in Cleveland one night, Cincinnati the next, and someplace else after that. It is simply not conceivable. The girls would have to have memorized entire libraries: shelves of biographies, scores of encyclopedias, and the complete contents of newspaper morgues. Not to mention the smaller details of everyday lives excluded in biographies, encyclopedias and newspapers--and how would they even be able to procure such information?

The human mind is simply not equipped for a feat like this. It is not even certain to me that a computer is capable. The people who make the accusation of information-in-advance simply do not think through their charge.

Further, if further refutation is even necessary, who would be providing this information? It would take an army of researchers and detectives with their own set of supernatural powers to gather facts without number, especially since--But enough. It is too weak an argument to deserve this much refutation.

As for the notions of people relaying information by hand, or of other people sitting next to the psychics providing information via leg-tapping, these too can be easily dismissed. In Rochester and other places, such possibilities were examined, always carefully and usually more than once, as trustworthy men and women were recruited to act as spies, hidden out of sight and stationed at various observation points during séances. Never was an accomplice found.

Even after thirty-seven years had passed, when Maggie and Kate made the most surprising statements of their lives, detonating bombshells in the temple of their faith by confessing to deceitful behavior in their séances, it would not be clear *how* they acted deceitfully. If there were tricks to their trade, other than noisy joints, they never revealed them and, more important, they never answered the fundamental question of their trade: how did they know what they knew when they knew it? In fact, the manner in which the sisters explained their apostasy solved none of Spiritualism's many puzzles; rather, it created new ones, more vexing than ever. Believers continued to believe, cynics to doubt, and investigators to remain unsatisfied, often bewildered, with their findings. As for the temple of faith that the girls created, it continued to remain upright, with barely a scratch upon it.

The youngest of the Fox sisters was fifty-one when she claimed to have spent virtually all of her life promoting falsehood. It was early in

October, 1888, and Kate startled believers in the afterworld by making a public admission of remorse, denouncing her career in no uncertain terms. "Spiritualism is a humbug from beginning to end," she said. "It is the greatest humbug of the century."

Perhaps Kate believed her confession. Or perhaps she recanted in the hope that her comments would quiet the controversy that had swirled around Maggie and her for so long. There was no gainsaying that the two of them had been wearied to the point of exhaustion, perhaps even mental imbalance, by the bizarre lives they had led, while at the same time having had their names both exalted and tarnished beyond repair.

Still, Kate's diatribe was big news. When her sister made a similar, more detailed profession of guilt later in the same month, it would be even bigger news. "I do this," Maggie said to a reporter from the *New York World* in advance of a formal presentation the same night, "because I consider it my duty . . . I want to see the day when [Spiritualism] is entirely done away with. . . . I was the first in the field and I have a right to expose it."

And expose it she did, forty years after Mr. Splitfoot had first made a splash in Hydesville, New York.

> On October 21, 1888, the . . . *World* published an interview with Maggie Fox in anticipation of her appearance that evening at the New York Academy of Music, where she would publicly denounce Spiritualism. She was paid $1,500 for the exclusive. Her main motivation, however, was rage at her sister Leah and other leading Spiritualists who had publicly chastised Kate for her drinking and accused her of being unable to care for her two young children. Kate planned to be in the audience when Maggie gave her speech, lending her tacit support.

When Maggie took the stage on the twenty-first, with Kate sitting in the front row, she appeared calm but spoke with a noticeable edginess, something of a rasp.

She began by telling the packed house at the Academy of Music that she and her sister were young and playful when "this horrible deception began." They had intended no harm, and had certainly not intended a career. Now fifty-five years old and "a black-robed, sharp-faced" woman, Maggie told her audience about the apples bouncing on the floor, and the discovery the sisters had made afterward that they could make a similar noise when they shifted the positions of their joints, realigning the tectonic plates of their bodies.

And then Maggie gave a demonstration. According to the *World*, "The entire house became breathlessly still and was rewarded by a number of little short, sharp raps--those mysterious sounds which have for forty years frightened and bewildered hundreds of thousands of people in this country and in Europe." As the raps resounded through the theatre, several doctors hovered around Maggie, studying her foot as carefully as if it were a new form of life. They "agreed that the sounds were made by the action of the first joint of her large toe."

Maggie also displayed the auditory capacity of her other joints; these, too, were verified by the doctors. "Like most perplexing things when made clear," Maggie said, after giving her lesson in skeletal flukes, "it is astonishing how easily it is done. The rappings are simply the result of a perfect control of the muscles of the leg below the knee, which govern the tendons of the foot and allow action of the toe and ankle bones." She went on to explain that this perfect control can only be achieved by one's starting to practice as early in life as possible. "A child at twelve is almost too old."

It might have been Maggie Fox's most remarkable performance ever, at least until the last words she uttered on her death bed five years later.

Yet, as before, remaining unmentioned was the question of how the snapping joints, and before that the ricocheting apples, knew what to say.

To Spiritualists, the Fox sisters were now blasphemers, turncoats, and it might be thought that the effect of the girls' treason on their previous "ism" would be fatal, or at least permanently disabling. After all, newspapers devoted more space to Maggie's speech than they had ever devoted to Spiritualism before, and many of them used the term "death-blow." So did the author of a book published shortly afterward: *The Death-Blow to Spiritualism: Being the Story of the Fox Sisters, As Revealed by Authority of Margaret Fox Kane and Catherine Fox Jencken.* And in Rochester, the Burned-over District's megalopolis, a billboard was erected at roadside in the manner of a gravestone.

MODERN SPIRITUALISM

Born March 31, 1848

Died at Rochester, Nov. 15, 1888

Aged 40 years, 7 months and 15 Days

Born of Mischief and Gone to Mischief

But Spiritualism had not passed away. Far from it. Believers had not flinched from the challenges posed by the report of the medical professors in Buffalo and the Fox girls' later departure from their ranks. In fact, reasons Raymond Fitzsimmons, these two events, and others of similar negation demonstrated clearly where the strength of the movement lay. The faithful believed that they had got hold of a fundamental truth in the proven fact that man survives death and can communicate with the living. No matter how loudly skeptics shouted and materialists denied, no matter how scientifically their claims were investigated and dismissed, no matter how many fraudulent mediums were exposed, the spiritualists continued to believe, for their conviction once gained was unshakeable. In any case, *Margaret later retracted her confession* [italics added], stating that she had only made it because she was desperate for money and the New York *World* had offered her fifteen hundred dollars. This retraction boosted the movement. In New York and in every city and town throughout America mediums prospered. Spiritualism, like the American economy, was booming.

As strange as it sounds, the boom in Spiritualism, so ethereal a school of thought by nature, was aided by comparison to the nuts-and-bolts of science; and although spectral at its core, Spiritualism was also given a boost by being analogized to its antithesis: machinery. "The desire to establish proof of spirit communication," writes Fox biographer Barbara Weisberg, "found a hopeful symbol in a great technological achievement of the age, the telegraph"--not Marconi's wireless, but its predecessor, Samuel F.B. Morse's wired version.

Weisberg makes her assertion all the more plausible, and certainly all the more tantalizing to contemplate, by quoting from "[o]ne of the first individuals to draw the analogy, the Reverend Ashahel H. Jervis," who had once shared a stage with the Foxes.

It seems that a friend of Jervis named Pickard was attending a séance in which the taps he heard, as translated by the medium from her control, revealed the tragic news that his son had died. Pickard had never been to a séance before; he had, in fact, long sneered at the notion of life after death, much less the possibility of setting up lines of communication thereto. Still, he was jolted by the pronouncement. How did the medium or the control even know that he *had* a son? Excusing himself, he raced home in a panic.

That night, thanks to Morse's version of the telegraph, Pickard sent a message to Jervis. The spirit world, he was aggrieved to state, had reported accurately. Pickard's son, a healthy young man as far as anyone knew, had passed away of unknown causes. Jervis told his wife the news, and after giving her a few moments to digest it, said "God's telegraph has outdone Morse's altogether."

The name, or at least the idea, caught on. God's telegraph, a means of communicating with a realm that had previously been shrouded in silence. At the time, Thomas Alva Edison, who would later seek to build such a machine, albeit in the most bizarre method imaginable, was but an adolescent.

Chapter 3

THE BOOM, PART ONE

As the nineteenth century entered its final decade, as more and more people followed the girls' lead and became interested in the prospect of sending a telegraph of sorts to the afterlife, and as "popular fascination with the spirit world began to spread like a grass fire," the Fox sisters found themselves in an unusual position. Because of their confessions, they had been reduced to spectators more than participants in their otherworldly pageant, the one they had created. But they were uncomfortable on the sidelines, lonely in their exile. Having disbarred themselves from Spiritualism, they now wrestled with the effects of their decision. The result was change of heart number two. Maggie Fox decided they were Spiritualists after all.

Within a year of her appearance at the New York Academy of Music, and sounding every bit as sincere as she had when expressing the opposite sentiments, Maggie announced her old, now new, position. "Would to God," she said, "that I could undo the injustice I did the cause of Spiritualism under the strong psychological influence of persons who were opposed to it. I gave expression to utterances that had no foundation in fact and that would at the time throw discredit on the Spiritual phenomena."

But what to believe? Had Maggie recanted because she was truly "under the strong psychological influence" of Spiritualism's foes, as she claimed? Had she really made her initial confession, as had been claimed, because of the $1,500 she had been paid by the New York *World*? And, if so, had she then disavowed her disavowal because, if she hadn't, she would no longer have been able to support herself with séances after the *World*'s payment ran out? Or was the surface meaning of her words the true meaning after all; i.e., had she decided, after a period of doubt and confusion, that she was indeed a genuine believer? Could the same be said of Kate, who followed her sister's lead back to Spiritualism?

These and other questions kept being asked of the women, bedeviling them as, with their reputations corrupted now regardless of what they espoused, they were reduced to Spiritualistic bit players rather than the stars they had once been.

As a result, Maggie became a part-time medium and lecturer, insisting, as she had done in the past, that she had the power to make contact with the dearly departed. But the audiences she now attracted were not as large as they had once been, nor was the impact of her séances or the amounts of her paychecks.

She and Kate were reduced to playing second-rate venues that provided enough money for them to live on, but just barely, and not in the manner to which they had previously been accustomed. The Foxes sometimes appeared individually, sometimes together, doubling their appeal, such as it was. But they had been too scarred by their wavering, their having made the transit from mediums to atheists to mediums again. Would the real Maggie and Kate Fox please stand up?

That there was still an afterlife for them as mediums, and for others who followed in their footsteps, seemed surprising to many, but in retrospect is easily explained. And not just, as Raymond Fitzsimmons posited above, because "[t]he faithful believed they had got hold of a fundamental truth . . . that man survives death and can communicate with the living." An even more fundamental truth is that human beings, then as now, fear they do *not* survive death in any form, a fear that only increases with age and the passing of family and friends who were once responsible for the fullness of our lives. To some in the Fox girls' waning days, Spiritualism spoke poignantly to such dread. It spoke poignantly of the need for a palliative to the loneliness that is at the core of the human condition. And it spoke poignantly to the fear of those who doubt the efficacy of institutionalized religion's promises of life everlasting.

As Maggie and Kate made their intermittent appearances in the second act of American Spiritualism, traditional religion in America was gradually becoming less influential than it had been in the past. In 1859, Charles Darwin published *On the Origin of Species*, and copies of the book had no sooner been shipped from London to the United States than it began chipping away at the beliefs of many, the beliefs that had been the foundation upon which they had so confidently stood in the past. In time, according to historian Randall Fuller, "Darwinian theory [would] become an indisputable aspect of American cultural life, widely accepted by scientists, sociologists, novelists, businessmen, and even mainline Protestant denominations." As it eroded reliance on conventional religion, Darwin's theory simultaneously provided a handhold for Spiritualism.

It was also in this era, 1886 to be specific, that Friedrich Nietzsche made perhaps the most famous, and damning, of his utterances. "The great event of recent times," he wrote, "is that 'God is Dead', that the belief in the Christian God is no longer tenable." Of course, Nietzsche's statement was not the definitive obituary he meant it to be; still, if one knew of it, one was likely to ponder it.*****

No less damaging to the cause of organized worship in the United States was the Civil War, the first shots of which were fired in 1861. By the time the guns had been put aside, more Americans lay dead than had been killed in all other previous U.S. combat efforts combined. The lowest estimate of fatalities that I could find is 620,000, the highest 750,000. Add to the deaths the number of soldiers who were injured or victimized by disease, unsanitary living conditions and insufficient nutrition, and the number skyrockets. And once those who were indirectly affected are added to the total, the entire nation may be seen as casualties of the brutality.

Death on so massive a scale could not help but weaken--if not shatter confidence in a benevolent God, resulting in a kind of "lost generation," like that which followed World War I and led to startling revolutions in our country's art and philosophy. But the Civil War also led to an increasing desire, an ache, on the part of survivors to commune with their deceased loved ones. So many people, in all likelihood more than ever before, longed for the continued presence of so many other people.

***** As late as April 8, 1966, *Time* magazine's cover headline was "God Is Dead," the first *Time* cover ever devoted solely to words, unaccompanied by a photo or illustration of any sort.

William Wallace "Willie" Lincoln, the president's son, was not a fatality of the North-South carnage, but died during the war's second year. His cause of death is not certain, but was probably typhoid fever, the result of a contaminated water supply at the White House. Nonetheless, cried his father, "my boy is gone--he is actually gone!" His mother Mary seemed even more inconsolable than his father, and was drawn to the spiritualist world. . . . [S]he was introduced to a celebrated medium who helped her, said Mary, pierce the "veil" that "separates us from the 'loved & lost.'" During several séances, some conducted at the White House, she believed she was able to see Willie. Spiritualism would reach epic proportions during the Civil War. . . . Mediums could offer comfort to the bereaved, assuring them "the spirits of the dead do not pass from this earth, but remain here amongst us unseen." One contemporary commented that it seemed as if "one heard of nothing but of spirits and of mediums. All tables and other furniture seemed to have become alive."

A lesser contribution to the woes of organized faith, but still a further weakening of opposition to Spiritualism, was made by men from Mars, whose existence was posited by Percival Lowell, one of the wealthy Lowells of Massachusetts. And verified by a headline in the *New York Times*. "MARS INHABITED, SAYS PROFESSOR LOWELL," the paper declared, and there were those--although, granted, only a few-- who could not help but wonder. After all, astronomers were beginning to believe that canals existed on the planet; Lowell simply went a giant step further. In *Mars*, a highly successful book of 1895, and one that led to an equally successful lecture series, more books, and scores of newspapers articles, Lowell speculated that the canals were not natural phenomena but rather the products of life forms unknown to humans. He further speculated that these life forms might still be alive, making use of the canals for a purpose not visible to earthlings.

Nina Sankovitch, the biographer of four hundred years' worth of Lowells, tells us that Percival was vilified by scientists for his utterances. He "was also criticized by many religious leaders. In their view, God had created life on Earth, and on Earth alone." If, in truth, there was also life on Mars, Western religion would have to be rewritten from Genesis to last Sunday's sermon.

In 1897, the British science fiction writer H.G. Wells published his novel *The War of the Worlds*. He imagined a Martian civilization sufficiently advanced to attack our planet and wreak destruction on conventional religious teachings about the universe. *The War of the Worlds* was fiction, of course, but fiction by a reputable author that was published while Lowell's "factual" observations of the red planet still resonated with some.

There was, however, more to Spiritualism's rise than Darwin, Nietzsche, the Civil War, and Martians. The United States had been changing ever since the Fox sisters made their own change from apples to body parts, giving itself what amounted to a complete makeover. Steamboats crowded the rivers more than ever before; railroads crossed and criss-crossed the land in crazy geometric patterns. Refrigerated cars on the latter made it possible for recently-slaughtered beef from the Midwest and fresh fruit from California to be consumed at homes in Boston and restaurants in Philadelphia, sometimes throughout the winter. Another improvement in transportation, the trolley car, began to change the patterns of intra-city transportation, as did the trains that thundered ominously over people's heads, and then the subways, rumbling beneath their feet.

It was, after all, the age of invention, and with the exception of Sigmund Freud, who was taking the first few steps in the process of befuddling everyone who hoped to understand himself better, those responsible for the innovations of the time often created din and dirt and a greatly-altered landscape. As a result, to Americans of a certain age, their country was no longer recognizable as the one in which they had grown up. The Industrial Revolution scorched the earth, and machines seemed in many cases to be the victor over human beings.

As a result, people sought familiarity, consolation, ease. They sought new beliefs, or at least new questions, to replace the ones that had fallen prey to all the noisy novelties of speeding nineteenth-century life. To many, the tenets of old-time religion seemed suddenly anachronistic. Some began to wonder about heaven; perhaps it was not a celestial aerie after all; perhaps it was a place--a waiting room, where those no longer living congregated, hoping to hear from those they had left behind. If so, the new question was how to contact them. Says scholar Frank Miller Turner, not only summing up the American psyche of the era but adding a note of specificity to the topic, "Spiritualism often attracted the attention of upper middle-class men and women . . . who, having lost faith in Christianity, still retained yearnings for some variety of religious experience."

One of the men attracted by Spiritualism was one of the few who could afford to look down upon the upper middle-class. His perch, one that he shared with John D. Rockefeller and a very few others, was the highest in the nation, with Commodore Cornelius Vanderbilt eventually amassing a fortune of $185 million which, at the time this book was written and adjusted for inflation, would be $216 billion. The money came from railroads, shipping, and some of the most vicious business practices of an age when wealth and viciousness were virtual partners in the debasement of capitalism.

On one occasion, he was asked how he had managed to accumulate such wealth. He did not say that paying his employees poverty-level wages was a factor. He did not admit to working them six or seven days a week, sometimes for such long, backbreaking hours that they barely recognized daylight on the few occasions when they saw it. What he *did* say about his fortune was that he had had paranormal help. "Do as I do," Vanderbilt advised his interviewer. "Consult the spirits."

All of this notwithstanding, most Americans still identified themselves as members of various established churches. But there was a more meaningful statistic to consider: the number of people who, regardless of their affiliations, actually attended the church to which they nominally belonged. In 1874, a mere twenty percent of Americans were sliding into church pews every Sunday; by the late 1880s the percentage had climbed to thirty, but then began a gradual decline that leveled out at about ten percent, where it remains, at least according to some sources, in the twenty-first century.

Spiritualism, of course, did not have traditional churches or official memberships. But in 1897, it was estimated that more than eight million people in the United States and Europe identified themselves as Spiritualists. Perhaps as many as ten million. By way of comparison, in America alone, 10,775,000 men and women were Roman Catholics, a million and a half were Jewish, nineteen million were non-affiliated, and thirty-five million were Protestants.

The latter figure, though, is misleading. The tally of Protestants makes an important omission. It does not break down the total into its sub-divisions: Presbyterians, Episcopalians, Methodists, Baptists and Lutherans, all of which may be considered major houses of worship. Thus the number of Spiritualists compares more favorably than it initially seems to those in any individual Protestant faith.

And there were, at the time, more Spiritualists in the United States than either Christian Scientists or Mormons. Theirs might not have been a mainstream religion, and to most Americans was not a religion at all; neither, though, can it be dismissed as merely a secular fad.

Well before the Fox sisters reached their peak, even before Kate had caught up to Maggie as a teenager, they were the leaders of a movement entering the biggest growth spurt it had ever known. "According to the *New Haven* (Conn.) *Journal* of October 1850," author Trevor Hall tells us, "knockings and other phenomena were reported by seven families in Bridgeport [also Connecticut], forty families in Rochester, New York, and 'some two hundred' in Ohio, New Jersey, and in more distant places, such as Hartford, Springfield and Charleston. A year later, it was reported in the newly established *Spiritual World*, that there were over one hundred mediums in New York alone, and fifty or sixty 'private circles' of spiritualists in Philadelphia."

Psychic researcher Peter Aykroyd claims that by 1853, a mere five years after the Fox phenomenon began, there were more than 30,000 mediums in the United States. At the same time, the esteemed Ralph Waldo Emerson announced that "medium" must now be considered an official occupation, "along with railroad man and landscape gardener." And historian Elaine M. Kuzneskas reports that "[t]he 1880 census listed occupations of clairvoyant, spirit medium, psychometrist, [and] trance lecturer." According to the United States Census Bureau, none of those careers had ever existed before.

It did not take long for Spiritualism to become an international religion--or a substitute for it or addition to it. It proved "a warmly satisfying and eminently democratic view of immortality. It answered the prayers of the whole generation of evangelists by inaugurating the millennium on earth."

And in addition to the progress it made in America, it began to attract followers in Europe, especially England. Further--and farther--away a number of Russians were now taking it seriously, in part because their greatest writer, Leo Tolstoy, was explaining and supporting it in a number of literary forums.

In fact, as late as 1882, Kate Fox, long mired in has-been status in the United States, received a letter from someone named A. Aksakoff, "a Russian bureaucrat and a dedicated investigator of Spiritualist phenomena." Kate had recently lost her husband, and Aksakoff, who had also lost his mate at about the same time, believed it would be beneficial for Kate to visit his country. She would do so, Aksakoff explained, "on a mission: to convert skeptics through her mediumship and in consultation with the spirits, to design safety measures for the coronation of Czar Alexander III, thereby enabling the new ruler to avoid his father's fate of assassination."

At first Kate was reluctant. Russia was a long way off; to the loneliness of widowhood would now be added the rigors of travel. Eventually she agreed on the journey, but only after Aksakoff allowed her to bring her two children as companions. "She couldn't bear to be parted from Ferdie and Henry so soon after their father's death."

Few details of the trip are available, but it must, one supposes, must be judged a success. There is no way to know how many skeptics she converted, but Czar Alexander III was not assassinated on Kate Fox's watch, the monarch dying eight years later of nephritis, or kidney disease. Hardly Kate's fault.

By this time, the lives of the Fox girls were as imbalanced as their legacy. Having started out as mischievous children, they were now becoming woeful and embittered old women, far from the spotlight they had once known, never having decided quite what to make of themselves.

In time, Kate became addicted to the bottle, perhaps even to drugs. There had long been rumors to this effect, but it wasn't until she reached her mid-forties and was arrested several times for public drunkenness that her condition was confirmed. Her efforts to rehabilitate herself failed, and in 1888 she was found to be such an unfit mother that her two boys were taken from her by the Society for the Prevention of Cruelty to Children. Kate Fox died of "end-stage alcoholism" in 1892; her "body, reeking of old dirt and cheap gin, had been found on a sidewalk [in New York]. Maggie died in a tenement house in lower Manhattan, virtually alone," less than a year later, aged sixty, although in appearance much older. It is believed that she, too, had begun to rely on spirituous liquids to get her through the spiritless nights.******

But it was in her final week on earth that perhaps the strangest of all the strange events in the widow Maggie Fox Kane's life occurred. Or is reported to have occurred. In her book *Ghost Hunters: William James and the Search for Scientific Proof of Life After Death*, University of Wisconsin professor Deborah Blum, reveals that as Maggie lay on a

---

****** Leah Fox Fish, who became Leah Fox Brown after Bowman Fox left her, then Leah Fox Underhill after Calvin Brown died, herself passed away in 1890. For a time, she claimed to be a medium, but attracted little attention in that role. After he experience in Rochester, she occasionally toured with both sisters, but remained offstage. Until, that is, Maggie and Kate rocked the Spiritualist world with their claims of fraud, when Leah became estranged from them and set about living a more normal life.

foul-smelling mattress in her tiny room, virtually paralyzed by rheumatism and fever, she was softly mumbling, as if trying to communicate with someone who could not be seen. And there were other sounds in the room, barely audible, that might have come under the category of responses. Rappings of some sort? But they did not come from Maggie; so weak was she by this time that she could barely roll over in bed or muster the energy to eat, much less crack her joints. No, the noises did not come from the woman who had once made them for a living.

Blum attributes the following quotation to a neighbor who had helped nurse Maggie Fox Kane through her last days and spoke afterward to a reporter from the *New York Times*.

> "One day, as Mrs. Kane felt somewhat improved, she unexpectedly asked for paper and a pencil. She had a small table standing by the side of the bed. Placing the paper I handed her on the table she began to write feverishly and kept this up till she had filled some twenty pages with rapid scrawling. I did not know what she was doing until she had finished and handed me the pages. I found that she had written down a detailed story of my life." The woman's mother had died earlier that year, apparently without writing a will. The message scribbled by Maggie Fox Kane not only claimed that a will existed but gave directions to it, in a desk at the home of some friends.

The neighbor wrote to her brother, who dispatched a friend to search for the will. He knocked on the door of a house whose residents claimed not to know anything about such a document, but were trusting enough to allow the friend to enter and look through the desk. He did just that, and found the will precisely where Maggie had said it was. She died without offering an explanation, and perhaps could not have done so anyhow. Maggie and Kate ended their lives as mysteries to themselves as much as they had long been to others.

Chapter 4

THE BOOM, PART TWO

Almost three decades after the Foxes had departed from their first American home, the "Burned-over District" was no longer recognizable. "The religious and quasi-religious fervor [they left behind] gave way to a complete and utter transformation in upper New York State. It became a haven for spiritualists, and in 1879, Lily Dale came into existence."

It started out as a small scattering of shacks on Lake Cassadaga, sixty miles southwest of Buffalo. But by 1893, Lily Dale had grown to a collection of more than two hundred cottages, forty of which were occupied year-round. Soon an auditorium was added to the grounds, and as more and more people came to visit, hotels and restaurants sprang up to accommodate them. It was the beginning of a new social tradition among Spiritualists: rustic resorts for instruction and immersion in their belief--primarily, of course, to attempt communication with the departed.

Thanks to Thomas Edison, Lily Dale was the first community in the United States to be electrified, and for that reason was known for a time as the City of Light. The name was an especially appropriate one, as a long-ago believer pointed out, because the lights were more than just illumination; they were like stars in the sky of another realm of existence.

But the place also had names other than Lily Dale. Those who did not believe in correspondence with the dead called the village "Silly Dale," "Spooksville," and worse. But names alone could never hurt it. The town's mission was clear, the dedication of its adherents unwavering. And, says Christine Wicker, who wrote a history of Lily Dale, "It was so popular that as many as four thousand people would show up for a lecture."

As for its regular services, Lily Dale's equivalent of a Sunday mass, they were quite different from those of more widely-accepted faiths.

> Spiritualist religious practice includes giving messages from the dearly departed, which is called "serving spirit." These services contain no offering and no sermon, only spirit messages. They begin with a prayer asking that only the "biggest

and best" spirits be present. Mediums, who often say they must turn off the spirit voices or go crazy from all the chatter in their heads, want to make sure that not just any errant spirit comes beaming in when they open the channel.

Typically mediums stand before the group, scanning the crowd. Then they pick someone and ask permission to give a message.

Most often they ask, "May I come to you?" Some mediums prefer more flamboyant phraseology. "May I step into your vibrations?" Or "May I touch in with you, my friend."

Thus, in summary, the Spiritualist liturgy.

Smaller gatherings were conducted by "[n]onresident mediums and others concerned with spiritual matters." These were individuals who "visit from around the world to socialize, study, and attend seminars and séances in a peaceful lakeside setting." In fact, so lovely was the setting, so bucolic its ambience, that early in the twentieth century the community also became an upper-crust vacation spot for nonbelievers as well as a Spiritual haven. Hotels were built on the grounds to house them, restaurants to feed them. These "heathen" were always welcome, no matter what their beliefs; it was required only that they respect the convictions upon which Lily Dale had been founded. There was to be no mockery, no distraction. They could even partake of the settlement's activities, including attendance at the séances; but they were more often drawn to attractions of a more secular nature that the Spiritualists provided for them, as well as for themselves. These included a bowling alley and a ballroom where guests in their dressiest attire danced to the music of the big bands.

Ronald Skowronski, a retired psychic who once practiced at Lily Dale, afterward managed one of the hotels at which visitors to the camp were accommodated. He believed that "Spiritualism is the most comforting of religions because it holds that death is only a transformation from the material to the spiritual world, communication between the two is possible and there is no hell or damnation. He also thinks it is the most open to fraud. 'Unquestionably it has attracted con artists who prey on vulnerable people,' he said. He believes, however, that self-delusion is far more common than outright fraud."

Self-delusion is not an easily treatable ailment. Fraud, however, can be prevented--and at Lily Dale rigid guidelines were enforced to make devious practices hard to engage in, although never impossible. As Wicker writes,

> To hang a shingle in Lily Dale, mediums must pass a test. They are required to give individual readings to three members of the Lily Dale board and then give a public reading to an audience made up of the entire board. Although as many as a dozen mediums take the test every year, only thirty-six mediums were registered and able to give readings in Lily Dale the first year I was there [circa 2000]. The low number is a matter of great pride among some people in the Dale. They think it speaks to the community's high standards, a notion they pass on to outsiders.

After all these years, Lily Dale still exists, even thrives, trying to keep its standards high, maintaining the proper atmosphere for communication with those who have passed into the Great Beyond.¨¨¨¨ Now, however, it does not just do so in the summer; it has become a year-round haven. Much of the architecture remains charmingly Victorian, and the mood cheerfully creepy. The National Spiritualist Association of Churches is headquartered here, as it always has been, and it still swears by the statement upon which it was founded more than a century earlier.

¨¨¨¨ At one time, there were numerous Spiritualist communities in the United States; it is not certain exactly how many. As of this writing, only four remain. In addition to Lily Dale, there are Cassadaga, Florida; Wonewoc, Wisconsin; and Chesterfield, Indiana.

We affirm that communication with the so-called dead is a fact, scientifically Proven by the phenomena of Spiritualism.

Lily Dale is not quite the same place it used to be, however. Something that was once an important part of it is missing. "In 1916," Barbara Weisberg tells us, "the Hydesville house [of the Foxes] was dismantled, loaded onto a barge, and floated west along the Erie Canal to the town of Lily Dale. After being reassembled, the house was inhabited by a medium who claimed to be in frequent contact with the Fox sisters, and some Lily Dale residents can still recall hearing the girls' spirit rap messages. Then, in the 1950s, the house burned to the ground in what was called a mysterious fire."

Also aiding the late nineteenth-century boom in Spiritualism, serving as both cause and effect, were printed works, scores of them, the majority published in the years when the Foxes were still alive. As a result, the deceased began to play a larger role than ever before in the culture from which they had corporeally departed. It was not true just in the United States.

According to Lara Baker Whelan, population shifts in England were one of the reasons for the new literary genre of "ghost fiction." City-dwellers were moving out to newly-created suburbs, hoping for more space, better views, and a cleaner environment. But: "Public sanitation codes were rarely enforced, drains and sewers were poorly built and sometimes backed up into areas and gardens. The homes themselves were shoddily constructed and poorly planned." In fact, living conditions were so poor in the suburbs, Whelan says, that they shattered the dreams of those who resided there, leaving them "frustrated, disappointed and sometimes fearful."

As a result, she writes, "[a] significant portion of popular fiction written primarily for the middle classes appealed to these emotions in ghost stories set in suburban environments."

More broadly, it is said in the volume *Nineteenth Century Literary Criticism* that "the supernatural was used regularly as a device to examine any number of social and cultural trends in Great Britain and the United States."

But it was a device whose primary purpose was to entertain. Both newspapers and magazines published ghost fiction, sometimes in serialized form--and entertain it seems to have done, although it was usually devoid of literary merit.

Some newspapers, though, did more than just publish tales of the continuing existence of the deceased; they devoted themselves almost entirely to life beyond life. In 1851, there were seven Spiritualist-oriented newspapers in the United States. Six years later, according to historian Whitney R. Cross, they totaled sixty-seven. Before the yellow press was yellow, much of it was an eerie, diaphanous shade of white.

But, on the other hand, just as the masses were pondering the notion of communicating with the dead for amusement and diversion, and as scores of far more eminent individuals were trying to bring the supernatural into the realm of science, an equally impressive assembly of artists began to introduce the subject into literature.

A partial list of eminent authors and works includes the following:

> 1833: Numerous short stories and poems, through the 1840s, Edgar Allan Poe.
>
> 1843: *A Christmas Carol* (novella), Charles Dickens.
>
> 1847: *Wuthering Heights*, Emily Bronte.
>
> 1851: *The House of the Seven Gables*, Nathaniel Hawthorne.********
>
> 1852: *Uncle Tom's Cabin*, Harriett Beecher Stowe.
>
> 1855: *Stanzas from the Grand Chartreuse* (poetry), Matthew Arnold.

******** Hawthorne said, "There remains, of course, a great deal for which I cannot account, and I cannot wonder at the pig-headedness both of metaphysicians and physiologists, in not accepting the phenomena so far as to make them the subject of investigation."

1884: *The Body Snatcher*, Robert Louis Stevenson.

1887: *The Canterville Ghost*, Oscar Wilde.

1888: *The Phantom Rickshaw*, Rudyard Kipling.

1904: "The Lady's Maid's Bell," one of eleven stories collected in *The Ghost Stories of Edith Wharton*.

Another classic tale of the supernatural was published in the decade between Kipling's work and Wharton's. But to discuss it now is to get ahead of our story.

Some books that were not classics, their titles never heard today, were ostensibly works of nonfiction about life meeting death, and were far bigger sellers than other supernatural books of the time. None was more popular than a volume by Catherine Crowe, an Englishwoman known primarily for her novels, short stories, plays, and children's tales. But later in life, she began a gradual turn toward the spirit world. In 1848, the same year that Mr. Splitfoot made his debut in Hydesville, Crowe published *The Night Side of Nature Or Ghosts and Ghost Seers*. Although first released in England, the book was quickly exported to America, where its reception was the same: a large, captivated readership, spellbound and curious and consisting of many people who had previously been dubious about Spiritualism but were beginning to doubt their previous doubts.

To skim through the volume is to understand why. At first. The book contains one eerie, often unbelievable account after another-- page after page, chapter after chapter of them. The tales grip the reader at first, so inexplicably chilling do they seem. But after a while the hold loosens. The stories begin to sound alike, reading predictably, formulaically, and as a result, tediously. One can become numb even to the fantastic. *The Night Side* is, in fact, rather an artless collection, and totally lacking in attribution; it cannot, for that reason, be taken seriously, and almost certainly does not deserve to be considered nonfiction. But it was one of the first collections of supposedly true ghost stories ever to reach the marketplace, and thus a classic in its own low-cultural way.

For this reason I present, in necessarily abbreviated form, one of the accounts that made Catherine Crowe's volume such irresistible reading to so many. It calls to mind, in fact, what happened to Maggie Fox Kane in her last days.

> Some years ago, during the war, when Sir Robert H.E. was in the Netherlands, he happened to be quartered with two other officers, one of whom was dispatched into Holland on an expedition. One night, during his absence, Sir. R.H.E. awoke and, to his great surprise, saw this absent friend sitting on the bed, which he used to occupy, with a wound in his breast. Sir R. immediately awoke his companion, who saw the spectre also. The latter then addressed them, saying, that he had been killed that day in a skirmish, and that he had died in great anxiety about his family, wherefore he had come to communicate that there was a deed of much consequence to them deposited in the hands of a certain lawyer in London . . . [whose] honesty was not to be altogether relied on. He therefore requested that, on their return to England, they . . . demand the deed, but that, if he denied the possession of it, they were to seek it in a certain drawer in his office, which he described to them. . . . Some time afterwards, however, it happened that [Sir R.H.E. and his soldiering companion] both met in London, and they then requested an interview [with the lawyer], and demanded the deed, the possession of which he denied; but their eyes were upon the drawer that had described to them; where they asserted it to be; and being there discovered, it was delivered into [the family's] hands. Here, also, the soul had passed from the body, whilst the memory of the

past and an anxiety for the worldly prosperity of those left behind, survived. . . . [C]ertain it is, that man's freedom, as a moral agent, would be in a great degree abrogated, were the barriers that impede our intercourse with the spiritual world removed.

According to literary scholar Peter G. Beidler, *The Night Side of Nature* was "the most influential single book about ghosts in the second half of the nineteenth century." And, as he might have added, it maintained its stature well into the twentieth.

Numerous other volumes were also written about Spiritualism, and two of them--less popular than *The Night Side of Nature* but more influential to an educated audience--were published in 1863, also in Britain.

From Matter to Spirit was the product of Mrs. Augustus De Morgan, with an introduction--which is to say, a sanction--from her husband, a highly-regarded gentleman in his country's academic world, a mathematician and the secretary of the Royal Astronomical Society. "Professor De Morgan," it has been said, "was willing to concede that phenomena had occurred for which no known rational explanation, including fraud, was possible, and he anticipated the later view that they were due to the exteriorization of the medium's energy, by some as yet undiscovered process."

The second 1863 tome of note was *The History of the Supernatural in all Ages and Nations, and in all Churches, Christian and Pagan, demonstrating a Universal Faith.* A book even more massive as its title suggests, it is as hard to comprehend in places as it is to handle. The author, William Howitt, was a historian and educator, accomplished in both fields, with at least one of his fifty books earning the praise of his idol, Karl Marx. His wife, even more prolific, turned out a hundred volumes, including translations. As of this writing, the school that the two of them founded, the Howitt Primary School in Heanor, Derbyshire, is still open for business, although not preaching the gospel of Spiritualism.

But no book on the afterlife had a pedigree to match *Phantasms of the Living*, which reached the public in 1886. Like the preceding two volumes, it was introduced in England, and also like the others, it was buried by the sales of *Night Side*. Another massive collection of pages, examples and explanations, *Phantasms* is "a pioneering effort to explain ghost-seeing through the idea of telepathy, by the analysis of over 700 case studies." The book was published by the most prominent assembly of scholars ever to turn its attention to such a topic, although not all of them had a direct role in the volume.

It was, however, "criticized by a number of [other] scholars when it appeared, one ground for attack being the lack of written testimony regarding the apparitions composed shortly after they had been seen. In many instances several years had elapsed between the occurrence and a report of it being made to the investigators from the SPR." (The initials stand for the Society for Psychical Research, which will play a major role in the following chapters of this volume.)

More commonly, still others found fault with *Phantasms*, as well as the previously published books, for a different reason. Why, they asked, had so many respected individuals devoted themselves to so unworthy a topic? It was as if members of today's MENSA had pooled their resources for a volume on UFOs, including interviews with those who had undergone alien impregnation.

Yet it was the very fact that academics, men and a very few women at academia's peak, possessors of impeccable credentials, had found the topic of psychic research worth their while, that made *Phantasms* so remarkable. It was the work of sages, not dilettantes; thinkers, not sensationalists, honest and intelligent scientists, not charlatans. As such, they knew enough to reject most mediums as the latter, worthy of no heed. But there was the occasional medium, the academics believed, who seemed curiously authentic, and for that reason deserved attention that had never been paid to them before. Certainly not homage, but at least attention. In fact by now it was beginning to happen. As Peter Aykroyd put it, "Fraud had already created a whole new science: psychic investigation."

Part Two

THE SCIENTISTS

Chapter 5

HIGH SOCIETIES

The first of the nineteenth century's geniuses to take the afterlife seriously, to dedicate himself to its study, might have been Oliver Lodge, later *Sir* Oliver Lodge, and in the opinion of Guglielmo Marconi, the very embodiment of British science. At one point, in fact, Lodge was ahead of Marconi in the race to develop a wireless telegraph. But his attention wandered; he was too interested in too many things, and as a result Marconi caught up with and then surpassed him.

But as a result of Lodge's intellectual meandering, his resume [accent over the second "e"] was a more varied document than Marconi's. He discovered electromagnetic radiation. He held patents for a type of loudspeaker, that would one day make radio possible, and another for a means of electric spark ignition, which would make the internal combustion engine possible. In addition, Lodge invented something called a coherer, without which Marconi's wireless telegraph could not have existed. Oliver Lodge was among the countless wise men who marched through history unremembered and indispensable.

Most photographs showed a man whose heavy beard was misted with gray, and his head--"'the great head,' as a friend put it--was eggshell bald to a point just above his ears . . . He stood six feet three inches tall and weighed about 210 pounds. A young woman once reported that the experience of dancing with Lodge had been akin to dancing with the dome of St. Paul's cathedral."

But it was many years earlier, shortly after he turned thirty-two and had settled into an assistant professorship in mathematics at University College London, that he set out on the most important quest of his life, this time finding a subject upon which his intellect would finally settle.

> In 1883 he became interested in psychical research and began attending a few séances, but his early work was limited to experiments in thought transference. Like a number of his colleagues in the early years, Lodge did not yet entertain the question of spirit communication as a plausible explanation

for the manifestations he witnessed. His investigations were little more than cursory until 1889, when he began to take an active role as an observer and reporter at séances. Even then, psychic investigation remained a sideline for him while he concentrated his intellectual efforts on academic pursuits.********

Lodge's first inquiries into thought transference required the assistance of "[t]wo young female shop-assistants . . . In these tests the sender would make a drawing and the receiver would try to reproduce what she thought had been drawn. Encouraging results were recorded."

Long regarded as a prodigy, Lodge was still a young man when offered the chair of University College's physics department. He accepted the offer only on the condition that he be allowed to continue his research into the paranormal. It was a strange request for an academic to make, and it even gave pause to Lodge. "I knew it would be unpopular," he admitted, but his resolve was unshaken. He awaited the administration's response anxiously.

It was affirmative.

Lodge's first inquiries into thought transference required the assistance of "[t]wo young female shop-assistants . . . In these tests the sender would make a drawing and the receiver would try to reproduce what she thought had been drawn. Encouraging results were recorded."

In 1900, the newly-opened University of Birmingham welcomed both its first class and Oliver Lodge as its first principal, another word for president. Again he had insisted on time and support for his controversial avocation. Again his employer acceded.

******** It was in this year that Lodge signed up with an organization called The Ghost Club. Founded in London in 1862, with Charles Dickens, Sir Arthur Conan Doyle and William Butler Yeats among its most prominent members, the club continues to hold meetings today, primarily dedicated to investigating haunted houses and the apparitions responsible for them. In short time, Lodge became president of the group.

By now, Lodge had put the Ghost Club behind him. Instead, he had become a prominent member of another assembly with supernatural interests, the most prestigious ever to associate itself with the study of what most scientists regarded as the least prestigious field ever to enlist the brainpower of such learned individuals. It that had been founded primarily by three men with credentials no less impressive than Lodge's own.

Henry Sidgwick taught classics at Cambridge University's Trinity College. A poet and philologist, he was perhaps best known among his colleagues for his book *Methods of Ethics*, "hailed as a major work of moral philosophy in the tradition of John Stuart Mill and Immanuel Kant." For the most part, Sidgwick was a man of traditional academic interests, but superior in accomplishment to virtually all with whom he worked.

But there was another side to him, or as might better be said, a greater range to his interests than just moral philosophy and verse. Henry Sidgwick was curious about immortality. Actually, he was more than merely curious, and not persuaded by the promises of organized religion that eternal life awaited him, he began looking into Spiritualism, wondering if perhaps the latter was as close as humans could ever come to life everlasting. A member of the Cambridge Ghost Society--another of whose members would one day become the Archbishop of Canterbury--Sidgwick's goal was one to which few of his fellow Cambridge faculty members would ever aspire; he wanted to prove, through empirical means and thus beyond doubt, that life in the spirit world either did or did not exist. He was leaning toward the former, but far from certain.

The title of one of Sidgwick's later books, *Human Personality and Its Survival of Bodily Death*, makes it sound as if he came to believe in eternal existence of some sort. He did not. Not, at least, as he began his investigations. His book was speculative in nature, not conclusive. He never gathered what he believed to be sufficient evidence to make his case one way or the other. "However," we learn from scholar Frank Miller Turner, "he did accept the validity of telepathy. That conviction encouraged him to feel the course of investigation still held out hope for further discovery." When he died in 1901, Sidgwick was partway along the road toward a definitive statement about an afterlife, and at the rate he was progressing, he almost certainly would have counter-signed for it.

Still, he was disappointed that he had not proceeded further. He took what consolation he could from the fact that he had tried, but it was not enough to quiet his restless mind. His duties at Trinity, as had been the case with Lodge's at University College, did not offer the stimulating challenges of his ventures into the paranormal.

Frederic Myers was a student of Sidgwick, one of the few who shared his enthusiasm for inquiries into the possibility of life after death. And, eventually, he would share Sidgwick's rejection of the church's con-fidence in such a thing. To those who knew him as a youngster, his eventual atheism was a surprise. "Myers was, like Sidgwick, the son of a well-to-do Yorkshire clergyman and an unusually clever child. Myers first expressed doubts about his qualifications for heaven at the age of two, yet went on to write his first sermon at five, and to enter Cam-bridge when he was seventeen, still fired with faith, praying to be stron-ger, wiser, to 'have a strength not my own infused into me.'"

But by the time he had graduated from university, only embers of his childhood beliefs remained, and they resisted any attempt to stir them into a flame again. For a few years, rather than trying to find a substitute for the religion his father had taught him, he turned his atten-tion to other matters. He "earned a reputation as a brilliant psycholo-gist, erudite lecturer, versatile author, and energetic psychic explorer. His early writings spanned the genres from poetry to biography (on poet William Wordsworth in 1881) and essays."

Then he began seeking his theological substitute. Whereas Sidg-wick simply wanted an answer to questions about immortality, his pupil developed a more specific, yet broader and more ambitious goal. As was said of Leah Fox, Myers wanted to do no less than establish a new religion based on what he was learning in his newly-entered field of the paranormal. "He expected psychical research to furnish data that would lead to 'the discovery by scientific methods of a spiritual world' and eventually to a religion according to which neither the life nor the love of human beings could ever become extinct."

But Myers, too, would be disappointed in the outcome of his efforts. Not, however, in the demands he imposed on his research. He might have set for himself the grandiose goal of developing a new religion but, even though he failed, he refused to compromise the standards of strictness and accuracy that science imposed on his search.

Myers died in 1901, the same year as Sidgwick. But Myers had attracted more of a following than his mentor, and there were people who believed that he tried to make contact with them after his passing, that "he now seemed to be engaged in a piece of posthumous research of a kind which he could not have carried out when he was alive." He had, after all, told a few intimates that he would get in touch, if possible, from the other side of life's final barrier, and that they should be attentive for his summons. He did not know precisely what form this communication would take, but would be eager to learn.

No proof was ever adduced that Myers had been successful in conversing posthumously. But there were former colleagues who thought that they might have heard a few whispers from their departed friend once or twice in the thickness of night. If pressed, however, they might also have admitted that they heard nothing more than the whispers of wishful thinking.

It is hard to think of Edward Gurney as a single human being. Also a graduate of Trinity College, Cambridge, although not enrolled at the same time as Sidgwick or Myers, Gurney envisioned a career as a classical pianist. Instead, accepting his limitations at the keyboard, he wrote *The Power of Sound*, which examined the philosophy of music. Many there were who could play music; few, if any, could analyze it so thoroughly as Gurney.

Afterward, although he had no intention of practicing, he studied medicine; his primary interests at the time were the staples of the field: chemistry, physics and physiology. Nonetheless, Gurney passed his medical examination at Cambridge, whereupon he changed his mind again and took up the study of law. Then he decided not to practice that, either. So little time, Gurney must have thought, so much to learn.

It is not known what attracted such a polymath to the realm of psychic studies, but once attracted, his intellectual focus finally became specific. He began to devote most of his attention to the possibility of otherworldly communication. That he believed it was possible, if not certain, is evident from his favorite ghost story, told to him by an English squire who swore to its veracity, despite its resemblance to one of Catherine Crowe's yarns.

It seems that the squire had a neighbor to whom he was not very close, but would speak occasionally, but briefly, when they happened upon each other. One day in March, 1876, the two men met as they were traipsing their lands, combining an evening stroll with inspection of their fences. The neighbor surprised the squire by asking him to his manor house for a cigar; never before had he shown an interest in socializing. The squire, although pleased, had to decline the invitation, citing a dinner engagement.

But the neighbor, who seemed in an unusually agitated state that night, would not take no for an answer. He repeated his request several times, then began to plead, finally reaching a point at which he seemed so desperate to have company upon returning home that he might have dragged the squire along behind him. Such behavior did not make sense to the squire, and in fact put him off. He continued to insist on the plans he had already made, growing more adamant as his companion grew more imploring; the dinner was one to which he had long been looking forward and it was too late for him to change his mind, even if he had been so inclined. Finally, having no choice, the neighbor *did* take no for an answer, and the two men parted awkwardly, the squire feeling decidedly uncomfortable at such an emotional encounter over what struck him as so minor an issue.

The meal was a delight for the squire, and after he finished his food and a post-prandial brandy, he returned home and, as was his custom, nestled into his library, book in hand. According to his watch, it was ten o'clock. Suddenly he heard his front gate open, followed by the sound of footsteps, unusually loud and hasty. They were approaching his door. "And then a scream, a wail of horror, fading into sobs of agony."

Gurney continued with his story, quoting the squire:

"Of my fright and horror I can say nothing--increased tenfold when I walked into the dining room and found my wife sitting quietly at her work close to the window." He asked her about the noises, but she didn't know what he was talking about, and wondered why her husband seemed so querulous, insistent. The squire shook his head, asking himself how he could have heard such terrible emanations while on the second floor of his manse when his wife, on the first floor and blessed with perfect hearing, was oblivious to them.

The next morning, after a restless night's sleep, the squire went outside to look for footprints or any other sign of last night's anguished visitor. He found nothing. Nor had his gate been left open; it was, as he had left it, tightly closed. He remained puzzled, and yet, his curiosity still nagging at him, could think of no way to satisfy it.

Later that morning, though, it was satisfied in the worst of ways by a friend, a gentleman of the vicinity who stopped by for one of his occasional visits. He had some unfortunate news. It seems that the squire's neighbor, the very man who had wanted to smoke with him last night, had committed suicide. Returning from his visit with the squire, he had drunk a glass of prussic acid, a powerful distillation that caused "a terrible death, rackingly painful. The body looked as if the young man had died screaming. The county coroner thought perhaps the death had occurred after ten or so, the previous night."

After recovering his wits, the squire came to a startling conclusion. What he had heard, the terrible emanations, were the sounds of his neighbor's agony, sounds that were actually uttered but that he could *not* have heard from so far away. But he had listened to his gate squeak open, followed by footsteps aimed at his front door, and neither of those had happened either. Or had they? Had his neighbor sought out the squire in a frantic search for help after help was no longer a possibility. The squire was dumbfounded.

So was Edward Gurney. The story was a riddle that the scholar could never solve. It was also one that he never doubted.

In 1888, at the age of forty-one, Gurney himself passed away. He had been taking small doses of chloroform for his neuralgia, and one night seems to have consumed too much. His death was ruled accidental, but Gurney was not the type to be careless about a matter like this. At least a few of his colleagues believed that, like the squire's neighbor, he had committed suicide; he had, after all, been depressed recently, having learned that two men whose alleged psychic powers he had been scrutinizing, and in whom he had begun to believe, were in fact impostors.

It was a crushing blow. Gurney had so wanted to believe otherwise.

Six years earlier, in 1882, the three men--Henry Sidgwick, Frederic Myers and Edward Gurney--had been the principal figures in forming the Society for Psychical, Research, a group which assembled on an irregular basis for the most irregular of studies among all of London's academic community. Among those who joined the SPR, were Alfred, Lord Tennyson, the British poet laureate; Charles L. Dodgson, who had attached the pseudonym Lewis Carroll to the classics *Alice in Wonderland* and *Through the Looking Glass*; H.G. Wells, whose *The War of the Worlds* is among most of his other novels which are still in print today; John Ruskin, author, philosopher, art critic and the Victorian polymath who continues to inspire thoughtful students of society in the present; William E. Gladstone, the only man to serve four terms as Great Britain's Prime Minister; future Prime Minister, and later Foreign Secretary Arthur Balfour; and Alfred Russel Wallace, who had developed a theory of evolution even before Charles Darwin. Yet despite his dryly scientific manner, Wallace, like his fellows in the SPR, believed in "some kind of fourth dimension, the unearthly domain of a force, a spirit, that ordinary mortals couldn't comprehend."

In addition, other original members of the group included "a physiologist from France who would win the Nobel Prize in Medicine, an Australian who became a founding member of the American Anthropological Society, a female mathematician who became principal of Cambridge University's first college for women, a pioneer in British utilitarian philosophy, and a trio of respected physicists," the most esteemed of whom was Oliver Lodge.

In all, it is said that more than seven hundred men""""""" joined the SPR at various times, "including sixty academics, many of them from Cambridge, fifty clergymen, members of the armed forces . . . eight Fellows of the Royal Society, and scientists with an interest in electromagnetism." It was the most illustrious of assemblies, not a single quack or mediocrity among them.

The group's guiding precept, published in each issue of its *Journal*, was "to examine without prejudice or prepossession and in a scientific spirit, those Faculties of man, real or supposed, which appear to be inexplicable on any generally recognized hypothesis."

It was for this reason that Frederic Myers was so important a member of the SPR, often serving as its spokesman.

""""""" There were also a few, very few, female members. Marie Curie was not one of them, but she did belong to the Groupe d'Etude des Phenomenes Psychiques (group for the Study of Psychic Phenomena), which, in its goals and methods, patterned itself after the SPR. Nor was Queen Victoria a member, but the subject of paranormality interested her greatly, and she is known to have attended at least one séance in her life.

His ardent yet rational approach was a refreshing attitude in a discipline that had its share of scoffing, cynical skeptics on the one side and defensive, unquestioning believers on the other. With one foot in each camp, Myers was able to distinguish for the avid public the differences between theory and proof and between speculation and confirmation. He did so wisely, without entering into the argument of what was or was not possible. Interestingly, his own convictions appear to have had more to do with survival after bodily death than with communication from the spirit world.

Myers had been one of the co-authors of *Phantasms of the Living*, and it was the Society for Psychic Research that published it.

It is impossible to say how many people read *Phantasms*, more useless to state whether or not they were influenced by the book, and to what degree. Yet, although the book was written for a scholarly audience, there were general readers, non-academics, who also found it compelling (if more than a little dense at times), an enlightening introduction to a world they had never known existed, outside of stories told by parents to frighten their children cozily to sleep. Although it did not compare with *Night Side* in popularity, the *Phantasms* was a best-seller from 1886 through the rest of the nineteenth century and, like Crowe's less reputable volume, attracted readers well after the turn of the century.

In large part, the two books were similar in format; that is, they were collections of reports that could not be analyzed--nor believed--by conventional means. What was different about the books was that *Phantasms* tried to probe both the reasons for the episodes it cited and verification of them. The volume included footnotes, the names of witnesses; it was an approach in keeping with the principles of traditional science, but one that, if successful, would compel traditional science to almost entirely redefine itself. As the psychic researchers would learn, though, the formally-schooled scientific mind would prove to be an immovable object, and psychic research much less than an irresistible force.

A few Americans also joined the SPR, although it was their names and prestige they provided, not--except on rare occasions--their presence at meetings across the ocean. The most famous of these was the former Sam Clemens and present Mark Twain. He had recently written *Tom Sawyer* and, although previous volumes had won him a degree of fame, it was the adventures of the wayward lad from St. Petersburg, Missouri, that had made him a true celebrity. But his brother's death was still on his mind, and would in fact never depart; he had been waiting a long time for the SPR to come into existence, and finally it did. "Truth is stranger than fiction," he had once observed, "because fiction is obliged to stick to possibilities; truth isn't." His fellow members of the SPR would have agreed.

In 1891, Twain would show his gratitude for the commitment of intellectuals to the paranormal--not only in England but, a few years later, in the United States --by picking up his pen. He wrote an article unlike any ever published before by one of America's most highly-regarded magazines, both then and now. In *Harper's*, he eschewed his frequent raillery to opine on the scientific study of the supernatural.

> Further, Twain said, the SPR pioneers had freed people like himself to speak out on such subjects, in this case, on telepathy (which he liked to call mental telegraphy). He had tried to write about it earlier, he said, figuring that his own reputation would be enough to sell such a piece. But his editor had flatly refused to glorify the occasional "coincidence" as telepathy. Now, he wrote, the hard workers of the SPR had "succeeded in doing, by their great credit and influence, what I could never have done--they have convinced the world that mental telegraphy is not just a jest, but a fact, and that it is a thing not rare but exceedingly common. They have done our age a service--and a very great service, I think."

Twain was overly optimistic. "The hard workers of the SPR" struggled, both to have their mission accepted as valid, and, in some cases, their conclusions accepted as accurate. The world would remain, as it had been in the past, far from convinced that telepathic studies rose above the level of jest or deception. Or perhaps honest mistakes. But never before had telepathic studies attracted men of the caliber of those who had pledged their intellects to the Society for Psychic Research. To use a term from a hundred years in the future, they were the otherworldly Dream Team.

It was crucial to the members of the SPR that those who learned of their group not misunderstand it. As its founding precept tried to make clear, the group had not set out to verify the truth of Spiritualism. Rather, it dedicated itself to discovering the truth *regardless* of its effect on Spiritualism. In other words, it would be as conscientious in its standards for judging psychic experience as it was in judging more conventional fields of study. As a result, the SPR was able to uncover numerous techniques of fraud in the conducting of seances: subtle signaling, verbal codes, secret compartments, wires, or even human hairs that were used to make objects move in without apparent human contact, trap doors, panels hidden in the back walls of closets, and more devices that are today for sale in second-rate magic stores.

But the SPR also found the occasional medium who stumped them, seeming to be precisely what he or she claimed to be, rather than a practitioner of sophisticated skullduggery. When this happened the investigators shifted into their highest gear--conducting further tests, sometimes attending dozens of a single medium's séances, studying them from every angle, every perspective, every point of view. In one case, it was reported, a single SPR member sat in on more than a hundred of the same psychic's séance! And so there remained--and still remain--a number of cases that no one in the group could dismiss, instances in which there was no evidence of fraud, no explanation for what had happened that adhered to the known rules of any recognized science. The members of the SPR, many of them at least, came to believe they had no choice other to search for new definitions of reality.

Guglielmo Marconi never went to a séance, never met a medium. If he knew anything at all about Spiritualism, and that is far from certain, he disdained it. But his name keeps coming up in the history of psychic research. After all, both he and the SPR--at least in the most general of terms--were trying to do the same thing: utilize invisible waves to communicate in ways, and over distances, that had never been traversed before. Historian Ruth Brandon tells us that

> [t]he society's official aim was to examine "in a scientific spirit those faculties of man, real or supposed, which appear to be inexplicable." One of the attraction of psychical research (or what we now call parapsychology) was that it offered a secular alternative to religious explanations of scientifically unexplainable phenomena. When Marconi said he couldn't explain the scientific basis for how his airwaves worked, psychical research had an answer: telepathy.

Marconi biographer Marc Raboy goes further: "With the discovery of 'communication via waves,' even serious journalists . . . made a link between Marconi's work and psychic phenomena, such as séances, concluding that underlying it all was 'the mystery of the ether,' and evoking a connection to 'thought waves,' impulses from one person's brain affecting others over distance."

Marconi would have been appalled by the comparison.

Like Oliver Lodge, SPR member Sir William Crookes also pre-dated Marconi in understanding the power of invisible waves. It was in 1892, when Crookes served as president of the SPR and Marconi had not achieved meaningful success in communicating wirelessly with the living, that he wrote the following in the *Fortnightly Review*:

> Rays of light will not pierce through a wall, nor, as we know only too well, through a London fog; but electrical vibrations

of a yard or more in wave-length will easily pierce such *media*, which to them will be transparent. Here is revealed the bewildering possibility of telegraphy without wires, posts, cables, or any of our present day appliances . . . an experimentalist at a distance can receive some, if not all, of these rays on a properly constituted instrument, and by concerted signal messages in the Morse code can thus pass from one operator to another.

It is a document of great foresight. But Sir William, like Sir Oliver, was a man of theoretical bent more than the practical, and not particularly interested in converting his ideas to practicality and his practicality into income. Which is to say that he was not the conventional scientist that he seemed to be. He believed there was something odd going on in the universe--new comparisons were being made, new studies were producing unexpected results, relationships were discovered that did not seem accurate, sensible, or possible even a few decades earlier. Secrets were on the verge of being revealed, and Crookes was captivated by the prospect. A historian of technology named Sungook Hong stated that "before Marconi, Crookes was sneered at or neglected; after Marconi, Crookes was considered a visionary."

If only the invisible waves that the SPR investigated could turn out to be as efficacious as those that Marconi would soon invent.

In 1885, three years after the Society for Psychical Research was founded in England, an identical organization came into being in the United States, one whose leading figure was probably the most distinguished of all intellectuals in either country ever to have dedicated himself, at least in part, to study of the supernatural. Which made him, surely, the most controversial intellectual ever to do so.

But the U.S. group was founded, or, as has been said, was "excited into being," by a Britisher, the physicist Sir William Fletcher Barrett. The first publication of the American Society for Psychical Research acknowledged the importance of its forerunner in London. "The evidence published by the English society is of a nature not to be ignored by scientific men," Barrett wrote, urging on the smartest minds on the other side of the Atlantic.

Which wasn't really necessary. The ASPR and the SPR were fated to be collaborators from the outset. They shared notes on séances, background information on mediums and their subjects, and sometimes even personnel. It was in 1896 that Crookes was elected president of the British society. Under his aegis, the two SPRs would eventually, and officially, join forces--among other reasons, to study a prim, proper, and sometimes persnickety American woman named Leonora Piper, who is still regarded by many as the most perplexingly legitimate practitioner of paranormal activity ever known. In fact, studies of Piper had already begun, but only at a preliminary level; they had not yet reached their unforeseen apex.

The American Society for Psychical Research set up shop in a three-story brownstone on what is today New York's Upper West Side, a stroll of but a few minutes from Central Park. It is still there at present, housing the largest collection of materials of its kind in the United States and, as I had occasion to discover while educating myself in its library, the ASPR, like the tenders of Lily Dale throughout its history, is as wary of charlatans infiltrating the field today as it was at its founding.

Among others, the original members of the American branch of psychic analysts were publishers Henry Holt and Charles Putnam; the famed biologist Asa Gray; Andrew D. White, the president of Cornell; the future founder of the National Geographic Society, Gardiner Hubbard; Charles Everett, the dean of Harvard's Divinity School; University of Pennsylvania philosophy professor George Fullerton; Minot Savage, a Boston clergyman and author of *The Religion of Evolution*, and the noted Asian scholar Crawford Toy.

Others affiliated with the Society, although not in all cases card-carriers, were Theodore Roosevelt; abolitionist leader Frederick Douglass;

Simon Newcomb, "the head of the astronomy department at Johns Hopkins and arguably the nation's most famous scientist"; G. Stanley Hall, one of the nation's leading psychologists, also at Johns Hopkins; the head of Harvard's Astronomical Observatory; a Harvard professor of anthropology, and the dean of Harvard's medical school.

Also from Harvard came the ASPR's most esteemed member, its leader, and arguably the most learned and objective man ever to approach the paranormal thoughtfully, the scholar William James.

To his friends, James's decision to study the possible existence of an afterlife was a startling one. He is, after all, regarded as a founder of the Pragmatic School of Thought, which teaches "that only principles that can be demonstrated not only theoretically, by deduction, but practically, by use, deserve intelligent consideration." In other words, pragmatism is the glorification of logic, of sensory experience rather than theory or faith. Paranormalism would seem to be its antithesis. And yet James, this unbending empiricist, was converted--albeit in small, gradual steps--to a belief in the possibility of psychic phenomena, and to such an extent that he became not just a member of the ASPR, but one of its initial members, and without question its conscience. With apologies to William Fletcher Barrett, it is probably accurate to say that there would have been no ASPR had it not been for James. His membership helped to draw other members of distinction, at the same time commanding attention for the society, if seldom as much respect as he believed it deserved.

Like Edward Gurney, James was trained as a physician but never earned a living with a stethoscope or scalpel. Instead, he turned his attention from the body to the mind, and it remained there for the rest of his life. At Harvard, he taught the first psychology course ever offered by an American institution of higher learning, and eventually became recognized as the "Father of American psychology." In 1890, after causing Henry Holt to fume at his delays for more than a decade, James delivered for publication his magnum opus, two volumes entitled *The Principles of Psychology*, a book still considered a classic today.

Actually, it is two books, a two-volume set that0 has become known as the *James*. There is also a one-volume edition as well. It is the *Jimmy*.

At any rate, a case can also be made for James's being the father of American philosophy as well as psychology; he was, without question, one of the most influential men our country has ever produced in that realm, and the first to achieve (relatively) significant public notice. In addition, he was a thinker with an unusual approach to his field. "He'd developed an innovative approach to philosophy, rattling elitist traditions by linking every day, real-life experience to intellectual exploration." Of course, not all American philosophers appreciated having their traditions rattled; then again, America had produced so few philosophers from its founding through James's era that the rattling could barely be heard. Regardless, it is no wonder that he was "considered one of the most influential thinkers of his time."

In recognition of this and other achievements of a mind constantly swirling, constantly operating at peak efficiency, James would eventually receive honorary degrees from Princeton, Harvard, and the Universities of Edinburgh and Padua, among others.

He was, thus, hardly a soft touch for the paranormal. In fact, his earliest reaction was to denounce it. A "camp meeting" of believers that he attended in 1884 was "extremely depressing," he wrote to his wife. "We spent the evening at a rather striking circle in which a man told lots of definite things to about 6 other sitters. This A.M. I saw 3 other performances, one of mesmerism, the others of so called spiritualism--nauseous!"

Although his brilliance could be intimidating, his physique was not. "James had never been a physically imposing man. He stood just five feet eight inches tall, fine-boned, and high strung. As a young medical student with a barely suppressed preference for art, he'd sketched himself as a dreamer--sharp cheekbones, sensitive mouth, flowing hair, drooping mustache, shadowed eyes. Over the years, he'd shed the soft look but not the inner, idiosyncratic dreamer."

A scion of one of the first families of cerebral attainment in the United States, James was the son of Henry James, Sr., a minister more intellectually acute than most, and a follower of the famous Swedish clergyman and mystic, Emanuel Swedenborg, a radical who believed strongly in the afterlife. And William was the brother of the diarist Alice and the novelist Henry, considered one of the great purveyors of prose in American history.

It was under William's leadership that the Americans joined the British in investigating extra-sensory phenomena, examining the claims made on its behalf, publishing the results of their examinations, and, in ever-growing frustration, sharing the abuse that rained down on them from the majority of their associates.

Chapter 6

THE JAMES BOYS

Although William James was older than Henry, albeit by little more than a year, William was usually identified in relation to his more famous sibling. It was true when the two were alive, and is just as true now. That is, when William is identified at all.

Both men stood at the top of their fields, but Henry's field stood more clearly visible in the public eye. By 1894, he had written *Roderick Hudson, Daisy Miller, The Europeans, The Bostonians, The Portrait of a Lady* and *Washington Square.* More classic novels would follow--*The Ambassadors, The Wings of the Dove* and *The Golden Bowl* among them. As for William, he had published his epic *The Principles of Psychology.* But like *Essays in Radical Empiricism, The Meaning of Truth* and other works of his authorship, *Principles* was intended for an academic audience, not a literary one. Most people did not even know the title of a William James opus, much less having read one.

Despite his position on the Harvard faculty, his presidency of the ASPR, and the inconvenient presence of the Atlantic Ocean, Henry's brother accepted the top position in Britain's Society for Psychic Research in 1894. The group was by this time twelve years into its existence, but as Henry Sidgwick had said to Frederic Myers, the SPR "had yet to accomplish its most basic goal, convincing the scientific community to consider telepathy with a little respect." Even though James would head the British group largely in absentia, his prestige, it was hoped, would bring more than just a little respect to the goal of legitimate psychic research. It was certainly James's intention. He sailed to London only a few times, but corresponded with the SPR's leaders frequently, as they corresponded with him, each keeping the other apprised of their work and its conclusions.

The timing for James's presidency was fortuitous. As has been previously pointed out, there seemed a receptivity in the air for psychic studies that had never existed before.

Spiritualism in the mid- and late nineteenth century... pulsed with the high voltage of a religious revival. It swept through

Europe, where it remained a perennial and iconic feature of aristocratic eccentricity long into the twentieth century--as exampled by the clairvoyant and Tarot-reading Madame Sosostris of T.S. Eliot's *Waste Land* (1922) and the feckless Madame Arcati of Noel Coward's *Blithe Spirit* (1941). But, strangely enough, this "modern" spiritualism actually came originally from the United States—from the Jameses' own back-yard. Another fiery product of the burned-over district . . . it burgeoned into a full-scale cultural fad--an irrepressible parlor entertainment, a vast snake-oil industry, and (as psychologists like William began to investigate it) a blistering scientific wrangle.

According to Paul Fisher, who accomplished the daunting feat of producing a single-volume biography of the entire James family, "William plunged on into the fringe world of mediums," quickly becoming a central figure in the blistering wrangle. Unlike Sidgwick, he was not troubled by the fact that the SPRs had not won more converts from the academe in its years of existence. What *did* trouble him was what had troubled him from the beginning: a fear that the reputations of those who joined the bands of researchers, both in London and the United States, would be forever stained by their association with a cause that so many believed to be beneath the dignity of science.

In fact, it had already happened to James. "Psychical research," it has been written, "was clearly costing William James academic prestige and political capital among his fellow scientists. Privately, he confessed some regrets over it. Publicly, James responded as if he didn't care." He was wasting his time studying "wild facts," it was said. But, at least at the beginning of his association with supernatural studies, James was less a believer than a man whose goal was to find out whether belief was justified; the supernatural was a field that he believed deserved investigation, not mindless dismissal. His attitude, in other words, was one of open-mindedness; it was met, for the most part, with minds that were sealed shut against him.

Several years earlier, speaking in opposition to James, the estimable British pioneer of electromagnetism Michael Faraday had declared that he and his fellow scientists must determine "what is possible and what impossible, and not waste time in trying to look for the impossible." Since then, Faraday had passed away, but his quote was cited again and again when James was being criticized for indulging himself with the paranormal. James gnashed his teeth with each repetition. How, he asked himself--and it seemed to him the most reasonable of questions--was one to know the difference between the possible and the impossible unless research was done, experiments conducted, findings shared and dissected? As James's biographer Linda Simon has stated, "To scientific men such as James, psychic phenomena were no less 'real' than invisible natural forces--gravity or electricity, for example--and no less worthy of intellectual inquiry." But the number of scientific men in the world was a small one.

Faraday's comment might have served as the rallying cry for scientists who disparaged James's efforts. On the other hand, James provided his own rallying cries for those who joined him in his efforts, constantly insisting on a place in university curricula for the supernatural. James feared a negative reply. Almost unanimously, he received a negative reply. Nonetheless, the labors required to answer the question seemed worthy to him, seemed *necessary* to him, and he undertook them expecting reprisal, but not fearing it.

Normally an even-tempered man, more prone to depression than anger, James sometimes responded to foes with a previously un-James-like spurt of temper to his critics. On one occasion he said, "It is not a scientific way of dealing with a mass of testimony to explain what you can, and say that the rest is untrue. It may be common-sense, but it is not science." And on another occasion: "Hardly, as yet, has the surface of the facts called 'psychic' begun to be scratched for scientific purposes. It is through following these facts, I am persuaded, that the greatest scientific conquests of the coming generation will be achieved." And yet another time, with a twinge of sadness, one imagines: "Are the much despised 'spiritualism' & the 'Society for Psychical Research' the[n] to be the chosen instruments of a new era of faith? It would surely be strange if they were, but if they are not, I see no other age[n]cy that can do the work."**********

Comments like these were not as vitriolic as many that James tried to counter but it was not in his nature to lack civility, no matter how indignant he was, either aloud or on paper.

It was as well his nature to admit, in response to censure, that the majority of so-called supernatural events were scams, the product of second-rate showmen and masters of deceit rather than those of genuinely paranormal abilities. But this, he insisted to his critics, was hardly the same as claiming that the paranormal did not exist at all; that "paranormal" was but a word to mask the shenanigans of mountebanks. And so "he worried that [if] scientists stayed deliberately blind to the rare credible [occurrences] . . . researchers might be ignoring 'a natural kind of fact of which we do not yet know the full extent.'"

On occasion, James placed his supernatural inquiries into a broader context, going back over the eons, referring to "every book of human history" and asserting that, "No matter where you open its pages, you find things recorded under the name of divinations, inspirations, demoniacal possessions, apparitions, trances, ecstasies, miraculous healings and products of disease." In other words, the paranormal had been a topic of concern for humankind since its earliest days. It was, according to the *World History Encyclopedia*,

> central to every major civilization of the ancient world and
> this encouraged the recognition of the reality of ghosts as the

---

********** And yet, perhaps in an attempt to cover all of his bases, James insisted that his sons attend Harvard's non-denominational, but conventional, morning church services.

spirits of the departed who, for one reason or another, either returned from the realm of the dead or refused to leave the land of the living.

So much of contemporary American culture was based on the beliefs of Plato and Aristotle and other ancient Greeks, of Lucretius and Pliny the Elder and other ancient Romans, beliefs in gods and goddesses, who never existed as we understand the term today--why, then, were James's fellows in the academe so unwilling to consider their views of the supernatural?

Another reasonable question, he thought.

Sometimes James felt as if his only support was coming from fellow members of the two SPRs. He worried that they were exerting no influence outside the narrow bounds of their own rosters. Many members of the groups agreed. Especially Edmund Gurney.

No one in the British Society was a greater ally of James than Gurney. The two men had felt a natural affinity for each other from their first meeting, as well the highest regard for the other's achievements in orthodox realms of academic inquiry. And each was equally disgusted by the attitude of colleagues whose breadth of learning could not atone for what Gurney and James believed to be its shallowness. In fact, the former wrote to the latter on one occasion to bemoan "this perpetual association [of the SPRs] in the eyes of the world with 'intellectual whoredom.'"

It was, perhaps, a term that might have been used by many clergymen to refer to psychic studies. The Church was well aware of the two Societies and of the cachet of their members. And now, still reeling from the effects of the Darwinian view of creation, organized religion had to contend with things that went bump in the night. Behind those nocturnal rumblings, clerics believed, could be none other than the devil, engaged in his typically nefarious activity--the corrupting of souls, the thwarting of heavenly aspirations. As Professor Blum points out:

> Not all churches could be judged as one, of course, but James found himself dissatisfied with so many aspects of Victorian religiosity. The Catholics, steadfast in faith, seemed to him determined to pretend that scientific discoveries were meaningless. At the other end of the spectrum, however, he deplored the "bloodless pallor" of the Unitarians' careful open-mindedness. "Of all the senseless babble I have ever had occasion to read, the demonstrations of these philosophers who undertake to tell us all about the nature of God would be the worst, if they were not surpassed by the still greater absurdities of the philosophers who try to prove that there is no God."

Frederic Myers might have been even more frustrated than James about religion's attitude toward the supernatural. Granted, these studies were a risk to men of the cloth, Myers conceded, but it was one that they had to take given the temper of the times, the skepticism of so many (although it bears repeating, these were always a minority). Myers believed that "if chemistry and physics and astronomy all together stumbled, the faithful would in no way suffer. But if he and his colleagues failed, if they could find no evidence of an afterlife, no proof of otherworldly powers, they might further undermine the church's promises of immortality. And there, indeed, was the risk: he and his colleagues might find the evidence for 'the independence of man's spiritual nature and its persistence after death'--or they might confirm the existence of nothing, no promise beyond that of a quiet grave."

But if instead the SPRs *did* discover the persistence of man's spiritual nature after death, then the promises of the church became strengthened, perhaps even proven. Why couldn't clerics understand this? Why were they unwilling to roll the dice on the tenets of what was not only their own system of beliefs but the the ultimate vindication of that system? They had, after all, dedicated their lives to the certainty of a seven or eleven.********

Yale's Jon Butler, one of the late twentieth century's most highly regarded professors of religious studies, went even further. He believed that "the laity and some ministers who joined the [Spiritualist] movement saw it as an extension of Christianity. Episcopal, Presbyterian, and Methodist laypersons adopted spiritualist views because they believed spiritualism represented the most perfect expression of Christianity yet revealed."

And, after all, wasn't organized religion, by its very definition, supernatural? If it were not, wouldn't its purpose be obliterated?

In addition to what he believed were practical reasons for his role in the field of psychic studies, James had personal reasons. And in all likelihood, it was these that gave him the strongest push, providing the final impetus, toward broadening his definition of pragmatism.

At a séance that James did not attend, according to biographer Linda Simon, "a table, encircled by a brass rail, exhibited some strange movements. It seems that the brass rail slid around from no physical cause, first when the sitters' hands or wrists were placed upon it and then by itself. One sitter went so far as to put a piece of chewing gum on the rail to follow its movements. James concluded that 'no room for fakery seemed possible' and hoped that 'this is the crack in the levee of scientific routing through which the whole Mississippi of supernaturalism may pour in."

It didn't turn out that way.

But, undeterred, James had an even more meaningful reason for his Spiritualistic curiosity. It was a séance that changed his life evermore, even though he was not there. But his wife Alice was one of the sitters, as was James's youngest brother Robertson, commonly called

---

******** The author readily and with a certain embarrassment acknowledges the inappropriateness of the gambling metaphor.

Bob. The medium was Leonora Piper, who awaits her later role in the spotlight of this book.

Alice's sister Kate had been ill recently and Alice asked Mrs. Piper about her health. "She is poorly," said a certain Dr. Phinuit, the medium's control, and then, a few minutes later, Alice and Bob were told by Mrs. Piper, through Phinuit, that, early the same morning, about 2 a.m., Kate had died.

Horrified by the statement, if not certain of its veracity, Bob dashed out of the séance to find his brother. William, in a faculty meeting at Harvard when he arrived, had heard nothing about Kate for several days; there were no mass media at the time to relay news of her passing, if in fact that had really been her fate. Neither the James family nor Mrs. Piper could yet verify Phinuit's declaration.

When the Harvard meeting broke up, William and Bob dashed home, Alice trailing behind them as closely as she could. The three of them fell into living room chairs, nervous and edgy but not certain what to think. A few hours later they found out. A knock came at the door, and a nervous young man in a uniform handed them a telegram. Their aunt Kate had passed away early that morning, at some point after midnight. Perhaps at 2 a.m.

How, the three Jameses asked as one, could Phinuit possibly have given Mrs. Piper the news? Through his sorrow, William James might have wondered not only why science would not ask the same question, but would not even seek an answer, would instead disregard an incident like this, rejecting it, with bias and bias alone motivating the reaction. It was willful ignorance, James decided, and he was appalled that such a thing existed in the academic world to which he had devoted his entire professional life.

So many stories of this kind, like that of Sam Clemens, like that of Maggie Fox Kane on her death bed, like that of Edward Gurney's squire; so many eerie events having been attested to as fact on the one hand, denied as absurdity on the other; so much being discussed, argued about, written about--and on at least one occasion, filling the pages of New York's leading newspapers, all of them, not just the *Times*, as was the case with Maggie Fox and the missing will.

It seems that George Funk, the co-publisher of *Funk & Wagnall's Dictionary*, was told by a medium that he had a valuable coin in his possession. Known as the Widow's Mite, a name biblical in origin, it had been borrowed by Funk some years earlier to be copied for an illustration in his book. Attending a séance some months afterward, Funk swore to the medium that he no longer possessed the item, that he had returned it to its owner after it had been photographed. The medium disagreed. She told the lexicographer that he had forgotten to return the coin, and told him to look in his safe. Finally yielding, although certain he was wasting his time, Funk ordered his cashier to conduct the search, with several assistants serving as witnesses. "In a small drawer, in a dirty envelope, pushed under a muddle of papers, they found the coin."

Funk was astonished. But he was a man of precise definitions, and in thinking about the matter, he came up with four possible explanations: "fraud, coincidence, telepathy, or spirit communication." Only one of those, he was certain, could account for the Widow Mite's being situated in a place where Funk knew it could not be.

To find out which of the possibilities was most likely, Funk wrote to more than three dozen scholars of one stripe or another, explaining what had happened, asking for their conclusions. As might have been expected, he received such a variety of replies that the mystery remained unsolved. "'Spirits,' replied [Alfred Russel] Wallace and Sir William Crookes. 'Possibly spirits,' answered William James, as well as [Columbia University professor of ethics and logic William Hervey] Hyslop and James. The rest of the scientists queried, to a man, voted for either fraud or mental illness," the latter of which was the most useless of conjectures. The synapses in Funk's brain were making their connections just fine, thank you; it would be difficult for one with mental deficiencies to supervise the tasks of compiling and constantly updating a dictionary.

And as far as the votes for fraud were concerned, they were, like so many explanations for supernatural events, less replies than gateways to more queries. What kind of fraud? How was it perpetrated? Who was responsible for the deed? For what possible reason? None of those who believed that fraud was behind Funk's dilemma could provide an answer to any of these questions.

Coincidence is an even more meaningless term than fraud. It is surprising that Funk even put it on his list, and impossible to know what he meant by it. Did he believe there were two coins, and that the coincidence was their placement in both the possession of the owner as well as in Funk's safe? It was, at any rate, a possibility--more like an *im*possibility--ignored by the respondents.

That left telepathy and spirit communication from Funk's original list. It also left Funk shaking his head. None of his three dozen experts chose either of them, either.

Because of the lexicographer's renown, and the unusual nature of the case, "the Widow's Mite was front-page news in New York, jostling for space with accounts of the trans-Pacific telephone line connecting Canada and Australia, President Roosevelt's successful move to take over the Panama Canal, and an extraordinary decision in Australia to allow women to vote."

All in all, it had been a remarkable, and remarkably quick, transit for Spiritualism from cultural footnote in the backwoods to newspaper headlines in the country's largest city.

Perhaps as a result of all the attention being paid to the paranormal, the most admired American novelist at the turn of the twentieth century decided to try his hand at some ghost stories. He had never written this kind of fiction before, and some of his readers found it to be beneath his dignity, just as so many others found the topic to be beneath the dignity of scholars like William James. Regardless, many found the author's tales of the supernatural more accessible reading than his novels, the latter always composed with masterful but sometimes dense prose piled atop more prose, casual observations being analyzed like major plot points.

The author published his first tale of the supernatural a few years after the end of the Civil War. In "The Romance of Certain Old Clothes," a ghost turns out to be a murderer, as the apparition of a deceased first wife kills a man's second wife, the latter happening to be the first wife's vile sister. It is as clever a plot as it is ghastly, more originally conceived than the typical tale of its kind.

"The Third Person," when alive, was a smuggler; now become a spirit, he begins to torment two spinster ancestors of his. The women find that they can rid themselves of his spectral presence only by smuggling something themselves. The "something" leads to consequences that are dire, if not as surprising as one might hope.

And "Sir Edmund Orme," who is the ghost of a jilted lover, does his best, or worst, to make sure that the daughter of the woman who broke his heart does not break the heart of another young man. These and other fictions, such as "Owen Wingrave," "The Private Life," and "The Ghostly Rental," to name but a few, chilled readers at the time and have been collected in various volumes that still sell modestly today, more than a century later.

The author's most famous tale of otherworldly occurrence was published in 1898. In the novella *The Turn of the Screw*, a governess is hired to supervise two children, one of whom has been mysteriously expelled from school. Both children, she comes to believe, are consorting with unearthly presences: the ghost of the previous governess and an evil spirit with whom she associates. The pair of them roam the family property unacknowledged. The governess fears that her young charges are in danger. Specifically, she "is certain that the two sinister visitants . . . are in demonic pursuit of the children." She does what she can to understand the reasons and alter the outcome. It is not enough.

The story ends with the governess trying to save one of the children from hurtling over an abyss. "I caught him," she says, "yes, I held him--it may be imagined with what a passion; but at the end of a minute I began to feel what it truly was that I held. We were alone with the quiet day, and his little heart, dispossessed, had stopped."

The plot does not resolve all of the possibilities it raises. Solutions dangle before the reader, twisting around each other, allowing--or forcing--him to make his own decisions. In fact, says literary critic Martin Habegger, the plot is "an entire oeuvre . . . that leaves us mesmerized by its ambiguity."

The novella has been published separately a number of times, both by itself and in collected editions with the short stories. In 2009, the BBC made *The Turn of the Screw* into a television movie, and the play *The Innocents*, based on the novella and having been performed on Broadway 141 times in 1950, led to a 1961 British theatrical film. Prior to this, Benjamin Britten had turned the story into the libretto for an opera, and years afterward, the words somehow inspiring music, the tale was converted into the score of a ballet. In between came several theatrical movies based on the novella, some of them loosely and others more loosely.

The *Turn of the Screw* and the other ghost fictions were written by Henry James.

William's brother.

Chapter 7

THE PEASANT VAMP

Eusapia Palladino was born in poverty in 1854 near Italy's Adri-atic shore. She never knew her mother, who reportedly died in childbirth, and as for her father, he was said to have been slain by bandits when she was twelve. But there is no establishing the truth of these accounts; in Italy, as in other countries at the time, records were not kept of early events in lives as unpromising as Eusapia's seemed to be.

Some other stories about her childhood, however, stories that seem far less believable than the preceding, were supposedly witnessed by many and sworn to be true. Certain people who knew the youngster believed that there was always something mystical about her. "As a little girl," it was said, "she heard raps on the furniture against which she was leaning, she saw eyes glaring at her in the darkness and was frequently frightened in the night when invisible hands stripped off her bedclothes." Further, it was stated that if there was a guitar nearby and she looked at it, its strings would start thrumming without being plucked by fingers. Lights would suddenly flicker in her presence, although it is not certain that she wanted them to. She *did* want tables to rise from the floor, though, and as attested to by Sir Arthur Conan Doyle, an advocate of Spiritualism no less than of intellectually devil-ish mysteries, Eusapia was also capable of making tables elevate, turn and slide across the floor. In addition, he insisted, "the chairs began to dance, the curtains in the room to swell, and glasses and bottles to move about."

Further, Doyle would claim, at a séance of Eusapia's that he once attended, he felt a woman rest her head on his shoulder, and she was "sobbing violently, so that those present could hear the sobs: [she] kissed me repeatedly." At first, he had no idea who she was, but eventu-ally, Doyle said, he got a good look at the woman's features, and could not have been more surprised. It was a woman he knew, although not well, who had died several years before. Her tears, he believed, were the result of an argument the two of them had had shortly before her pass-ing, an argument they never had a chance to resolve. Later in the séance,

Eusapia spoke the woman's name aloud; Doyle said it was correct. He was certain that no one could have identified her to the medium; she had been too remote a figure in his life.

The stories of Eusapia Palladino are so extreme as to sound cartoonish. One wishes that Sherlock Holmes had not been a fictional character, but rather a detective of flesh and bone, capable of investigating the claims made by his creator on the psychic's behalf. The author was an intelligent man, artistically gifted and respected by most. But to many, he could not be trusted about matters paranormal; he was simply too rabid a believer, too undiscriminating. Holmes could not be fooled; Sir Arthur, it might be said, fooled himself. That, at least, is history's verdict.

It is likely that poor Eusapia never went to school; nearly, if not completely illiterate, she could find no position other than that of housemaid for a family of the "upper bourgeoisie" in Naples. But it was also a family of strong Spiritualist leanings, and once it discovered what it believed to be the young woman's talents, the family provided not only encouragement, but training for her eventual life in the world behind the black curtain. Eusapia was introduced to séances at a young age, and they held her in thrall. Soon it was she who held the sitters in thrall. The mediums who were willing to serve as her mentors did so eagerly; she was said by all of them to be a quick learner.

And perhaps, odd though it sounds, she might have been prepared in yet another way for her future career. "Eusapia had a peculiar depression of her parietal bone [one of two in the head that help to form the cranium], due, it is said, to some accident in her childhood. Such physical defects are very often associated with strong mediumship." So proclaims Doyle, without explaining the how or why of his claim. But it does seem that a disproportionate number of at least partially-successful mediums were afflicted in one way or another; the reader will remember the severe headaches suffered by Maggie and Kate Fox in their youth.

Regardless, whether Eusapia was helped, hindered or not affected at all by the dent in her head, by the time she became a young woman, "short, heavyset . . . with charm of neither face nor personality," she was a one-person carnival, and the most famous psychic in all of Europe. She had been observed at work by such accomplished individuals as Pierre and Marie Curie, Nobel-laureates in physics, and the influential philosopher Henri Bergson, who taught, among other things, that intuition is a more effective means of understanding reality than rationalism or even, in some cases, science.

Also taking note of Eusapia's trance-state behavior were the Director of the Observatory of Milan and the Councillor of State to the Emperor of Russia. Some of them spotted occasional signs of trickery and outright deceit during Palladino séances, "but they could not explain all of the phenomena." She seemed to go back and forth between hucksterism and sincere Spiritualism, almost always cantankerously, making her a source of foaming-at-the-mouth frustration for those who wished to understand what lay behind her apparent abilities.

The University of Edinburgh's Dr. Peter Lamont agreed. "Palladino," he wrote, "was no simple case: on the one hand, she was regularly caught cheating, even by those who continued to express belief." At times, for instance, she would employ the second-rate scam of making a table "levitate" by slipping her foot under one of the legs and slowly lifting it. "Afterward the participants would swear that the table soared up by astral power alone--and it rose higher with each retelling."

Then again, "she was reported to have produced genuine phenomena, in front of experienced and (previously) skeptical observers." She was, perhaps, given the lack of structure in her childhood, just an untamed sort of individual, taking as much pleasure in mocking her sitters as she did confounding them.

Cesare Lombroso was no less respected in his field than Bergson and the Curies were in theirs. For several years, at least. Then, among academics, he became as much a laughingstock as one of those mediums who, in a later time, set up shop in an urban storefront and, for twenty-five dollars a sitting, says things like, "I see a tall, dark, handsome stranger in your future . . ."

As the founder of the Italian School of Positivist Criminology, Lombroso was once hailed as one of his nation's most original thinkers. But that was the problem; he was *too* original. Even fanciful. Lombroso taught, in effect, that criminals were not made (through familial and cultural influences), but rather were born (because of genetically inherited traits). Further, he insisted that those genetically inherited traits took a physical form, actually a number of physical forms. Most prominent among them were the size and shape of the skull, the slope of the forehead, the configuration of the ears, the length and width of the face. Lombroso believed that all human beings, in all countries, should be subject to cranial measurement, or craniometry, the moment their heads stopped growing. Calipers, in other words, could be the most effective of crime-stoppers.

It is all silly to us now. Well-educated men and women found Lombroso's teachings silly even then. But people of such background were, as they have always been, a minority, and despite his mistaken views of anti-social behavior, Lombroso continued to be well-respected by large numbers of his countrymen. He was, after all, an intelligent fellow, a gentleman, one with serious interests and noble intentions. His most commonly reproduced photograph shows a visage with stern expression, eyes narrowed into an almost accusatory glare, a full mustache, and a high forehead, dominating the features below. He did not fit the description of a criminal. Nor did he seem the kind of man to indulge in nonsense. He did not believe in such a thing as Spiritualism. Peter Aykroyd identifies him as an "avowed skeptic."

He had, thus, the perfect background to take on Eusapia Palladino, and was asked to study her methods after a fellow scientist, Dr. Ercole Chiaia, saw her in action and, flabbergasted by her results, wrote to Lombroso. He described Eusapia as "an invalid woman who belongs to the humblest class of society. She is nearly thirty years old and very ignorant; her appearance is neither fascinating nor endowed with the power which modern criminologists call irresistible."

Then Chiaia--describing a hallucination, some believed--told Lombroso what he saw at a séance over which Eusapia presided:

> She seems to lie upon the empty air, as on a couch, contrary to all the laws of gravity; she plays on musical instruments--organs, bells, tambourines--as if they had been touched by her hands or moved by the breath of invisible gnomes. The woman at times can increase her stature by more than four inches.

> She is like an India rubber doll, like an automaton of a new kind; she takes strange forms. How many legs and arms has she? We do not know. While her limbs are being held by incredulous spectators, we see other limbs coming into view, without knowing where they come from. Her shoes are too small to fit these witch-feet of hers, and this particular circumstance gives rise to the suspicion of the intervention of mysterious power.

Lombroso hardly knew what to think. The claims made by Chiaia were ludicrous, would have been risible even as a chapter in a dime novel. Yet although not as well-known a figure in Italian science as Lombroso, Chiaia was at least a fellow academic, and a respected one at that. His missive could not be readily dismissed.

But Lombroso continued to hesitate. William James had not yet warned that reputations would be smirched by taking Spiritualism seriously enough even to renounce it, and Lombroso seemed to sense the danger. In fact, two years passed without any word of assent from him. But Chiaia kept imploring--he was a friend, after all--and finally, if for no other reason than to put an end to his pleas, Lombroso agreed to attend his first séance.

He expected to see right through Eusapia, to figure out how she produced her special effects by applying the same kinds of quantifiable logic he had applied to the criminal mind. And he did just that, easily identifying the con woman that was part of Eusapia's makeup. But only a part, for Lombroso also found himself stumped by some of Eusapia's apparent shows of sorcery, and it was these that intrigued him. This time, at the end of the séance, when Chiaia asked him to attend another, Lombroso needed no persuasion. He not only showed up for it, but for another, and another after that.

Still, he wavered on the veracity of what his eyes were telling him. Although there was no denying that his interest had been piqued, he continued to tell those who asked about Eusapia that she was probably a skilled entertainer more than the possessor of extra-sensory ability. Her repertoire, Lombroso felt certain, was hardly proof of "the intervention of mysterious power," as Chiaia believed.

Lombroso explained further: "Many are the crafty tricks she plays, both in the state of trance (unconsciously) and out of it--for example, freeing one of her two hands, held by . . . [investigators], for the sake of moving objects near her; making touches . . . and feigning to adjust her hair and then slyly pulling out one hair and putting it over the little balance tray of a letter-weigher in order to lower it."

Lombroso's analysis was not without merit, especially when he espied her lighting the edge of her table with her knee. Still, there was something in the woman's methods that baffled him. Actually, several somethings. How did she manage to free one of her hands if men were holding both of them, and then somehow slip the hand up to her scalp to pull out a hair? How did she then slide her hand over to a postal scale, tie the strand securely to it, and then tug on it to make the scale move, all of this without being detected? And even if she could do it, was a single human hair strong enough to propel the scale? And how did she lift her table on the occasions, several of them, when spectators claimed her knees did not so much as budge?

And, and, and . . .

Lombroso's inability to understand Eusapia began to play on him. Perhaps, having been persuaded to grasp one of her hands himself during a séance, his doubts about Eusapia's authenticity were further weakened when he found that she had actually been able to free her hand without his feeling it; Lombroso ended up grasping the man who sat on Eusapia's other side. And, it is said, Lombroso went further in verifying the medium's legitimacy. He subjected her "to urine tests, x-ray imaging during séances, photographic samples, cardiographs, and other sophisticated measures, and time and again he reported that she was genuine."

But it was charged that something entirely different was at work here. Perhaps, at least to an extent, sins of the flesh had overwhelmed the rectitude of science. Authors William Kalush and Larry Sloman have written that Eusapia was "[t]he most notorious medium" of them all, one who, despite her lack of physical charms, "had no qualms" about sleeping with the men who studied her, nor they with her. Lombroso, the two men charge, was one of them, falling under the spell of her "truly feminine languor." Perhaps he allowed her "strange and feeling passion" to muddle his perceptions. Or to deliberately commit fraud in his analyses.

Whatever the reasons, the famed criminologist finally pronounced that Eusapia Palladino truly *was* supernatural, and expressed his repentance for not having realized it sooner. "I am filled with confusion and regret," he is quoted as saying, "that I combatted with so much persistence the possibility of the facts called Spiritualistic."

The community of Italian science was shaken by the verdict. Chiaia was astonished. True, a few praised him for his courage. But most others derided him for his gullibility.

Lombroso seemed impervious to either reaction. Having bestowed his imprimatur on Eusapio, he simply stood back and allowed the storm to swirl around him, a storm that swirled even outside of his country's borders. "Lombroso's subsequent conversion was reported by the press in Italy and the world," we are told, "becoming instrumental for

Palladino's reaching the status of a veritable celebrity at the turn of the century."

Lombroso's daughter was embarrassed by her father's conclusion. Some years later, she offered her own explanation for the riddle that was Eusapia, revealing that her father had been suffering from arteriosclerosis when he observed her. This, she believed, had adversely affected both his mental and physical health for much of his life. (In particular, she conjectured, the malady might have enabled Eusapia to release her father's hand without his feeling it. And it might, as well, have affected his vision.)

At the time, though, no one suggested that Lombroso's condition might have influenced his judgment, and there is no way of knowing, either then or now. Nor was it known to what extent, if any, his peers were aware of his affliction. But that didn't matter. To much of the public at large, what Cesare Lombroso did for Eusapia was what an appearance on *The Ed Sullivan Show* would do for many another career midway through the following century.

Among the handful of researchers who detected occasional traces of legitimacy in Eusapia's work were men with a much more impressive imprimatur to bestow than Lombroso could, even at his peak. The most investigated medium to which Spiritualism had yet applied itself was about to be held under the microscope of the most qualified of inquisitors, the members of London's Society for Psychical Research. For the SPR, there had been no more important undertaking in its decade-long existence; it was one that would do as much to establish its own legitimacy, or lack thereof, as it would Eusapia's. The assignment fell to Sir Oliver Lodge, Frederic Myers, and a man named Charles Richet, "an esteemed bacteriologist, psychologist, and pathologist" who would go on to win the Nobel Prize for his work in anaphylaxis, a word of Richet's own coinage that refers to acute allergic responses, such as those to a bee sting.

The three men were nothing if not thorough. At one of Eusapia's séances that they attended, Myers sat on her immediate left and took her hand while Richet, on her other side, took the right, the two of them immobilizing her like a set of handcuffs. It is not certain what Lodge did, except that he proved to be the man most affected by what was about to happen, as well as the amanuensis who provided the later accounts.

Still, Eusapia seemed to ignore the pressure and slip into a trance. Once there, she summoned her control, whom she called John King. According to Lodge, who swore that he actually saw him, King was "a big powerful man." And after a few minutes, Lodge said he did more than see him. He felt his touch. He looked at Eusapia; her eyes were closed and her hands, both left and right, remained in the white-knuckled clench of Myers and Richet. The hands of others at the séance were clearly visible, either atop the table or in their laps. So who could be nudging him other than the spirit called John King?

Unless Lodge was imagining it all. Unless, perhaps, his fixation on Eusapia's hands had somehow translated to King's illusory gripping.

But he did not think so. Lodge trusted his cognition more than that. "It was as if there was something or someone in the room," he would later write, "which could go about and seize people's arms or the back of their necks, and give a grip; just as anybody who was free to move about. These grips were very frequent, and everyone at the table felt them sooner or later."

Lodge also claimed that a beard brushed against him, "and the feeling was certainly eerie on my head, which even then was incipiently bald." John King, he would later be told by Eusapia, had not shaved his chin for a year or more. His beard, she said, was a soft one. Lodge agreed.

Later in the séance, after the medium's hands had been released, she poked out a fingertip and wiggled it in the direction of a writing desk across the room. Myers, Richet, and Lodge all looked toward it. Lodge testified that, with each wiggle Eusapia made, and there were three of them, the desk "tilted back against the wall, just as if she had a stick in her hand and was pushing it." The desk's movements, Lodge felt certain, were the result of some kind of "mechanical connexion" between the finger and the furniture. He did not explain what he meant by the term.

He was becoming more of a believer in the paranormal with each example Eusapia provided. Still, among other reservations, he could not make himself accept the notion of the mind moving a physical object. Lodge was a scientist, after all, and scientists did not believe in telekinesis. Then again, he had not previously believed in invisible beards or unseen hands making contact with him.

But his academic grounding was about to be tested, his credibility strained, even further. After a few minutes, he saw a third arm poking through Eusapia's blouse. He counted. He was sure of it. There was the left, which was back under Myers's control; the right, secured again by Richet, and now all of a sudden . . . *the middle!* Secured by no one! Oliver Lodge, sitting in a "dark and hot and very still" room, situated somewhere between life and the afterlife, was looking at a freak of nature or an exception to nature and could not for the life of him decide which it was.

At yet another of Eusapia's séances, a man identified as Professor Galeotti swore that he too saw the medium with an additional arm. "One is on the little table . . . the other seems to come out of her shoulder--to approach [a female sitter], and touch her, and then return and melt into her body again. This is not an hallucination." Later in this same passage, the reader is assured that "[m]uch similar testimony might be given."

Perhaps. But by whom? Credible observers? Lodge, Myers, and Richet certainly qualified, as might be the case with some of the laymen who sat around Eusapia's table. But the likelihood was that all were fooled. In the darkness of the medium's chamber, what seemed to be a third limb was probably nothing more than the stuffed sleeve of a shirt or blouse clumsily attached to her own garment and tucked under it for most of the séance. Photographs of three-armed mediums actually exist, but there is an undeniable air of fakery to them. And they are in no cases accompanied by an explanation of how the medium managed to pull the extra arm out of hiding and into sight without being detected.

On one occasion, after Eusapia's third arm popped into view, it began to slither across the table in the direction of Frederic Myers. Lodge watched the hand at the end of the arm as it approached him--wondering, perhaps, whether it was a stuffed glove sewn onto the end of a stuffed sleeve. But the "hand," Myers swore, actually attached itself to him, with Lodge swearing that he saw the fingers curl into his colleague's ribs. How do fingers that are packed with fabric or paper or sand manage to bend themselves onto the human anatomy?

There was no time to answer the question. Myers shrieked, afraid to touch the hand and brush it away. "History is silent," Sir Arthur Conan Doyle, is reported to have said, "on why Myers did not leap from his chair and run screaming into the night."

Richard Hodgson had earned a law degree in 1878 at the University of Melbourne in Australia, then decided to pursue a different course in life, enrolling in literature courses at St. John's College, Cambridge. It was there that he met Henry Sidgwick, and soon became a student of the paranormal, as well as poetry. He joined the SPR, and quickly won a name for himself by exposing at least some of the practices of the notorious psychic-cum-guru, Madame Helena Blavatsky. His next assignment, following up on the work of Myers, Lodge, and Richet, was Eusapia Palladino.

He began by studying her as if she were a subject in which he hoped to earn a post-doctoral degree. He went to her séances, talked to numerous people who had sat in on them, and, alone in his room, pored over accounts of still more sessions so intently that he could almost feel himself a part of the assemblies around her table. He even conducted a few crude experiments of his own, trying to replicate Eusapia's effects with methods he devised himself. He was in training, so it seemed, preparing himself for contact with the lady herself, building up his defenses against even the most sophisticated of her trickeries.

He began to suspect that, despite their seeming conscientiousness, the methods employed by his SPR predecessors to espy deception had been inadequate. Arranging further performances which Eusapia conducted solely for Hodgson's benefit in a Cambridge laboratory, he soon concluded that he had been correct. His subject *was* a mountebank, superbly gifted but an imposter nonetheless. He admitted that her maneuverings were deftly executed, but found them falling far short of the supernatural, especially in the dim lighting upon which virtually all mediums insisted.

Although he does not explain how she could have been so dexterous as to perform the feat, Hodgson claims that Eusapia was able to free herself from the grasp of the investigators on either side of her in such a way that the two men ended up holding each other's hands instead of the medium's. The lack of an explanation is a major flaw in his expose, [accent over last letter in "expose"] but let us accept him at his word. With her hands now at liberty, she could perform all manner of tricks, ruses and miracles. Lodge's "mechanical connexion," Hodgson then explained, was really a wire running under her table that Eusapia used to jiggle the writing desk. As for what appeared to be her second arm, it was in fact her third; she had slipped a dummy arm into position before the séance so that it looked like one of her real limbs, sprouting from her shoulder and resting without moving, not so much as a twitch, at her side. Thus her "third arm," which was the real thing, rested unnoticed between her rather large breasts until she called upon it to move about freely to dazzle her sitters.

But it was all theory, all supposition on Hodgson's part. So sure of it was he that he did not bother to conduct a hands-on search for either a wire or a fake arm, nor did he address the issue how one of her three limbs could possibly have slid across the table to latch onto Myers's ribcage. More notable flaws in his debunking, and they suggest a certain lack of commitment on his part, a laziness in his methods.

Nonetheless, perhaps because of all the time he had devoted to his research on Eusapia, and the earnest manner in which he had presented his findings, he had established himself as the SPR's primary authority on the woman. Agreeing with Hodgson's conclusions, at least in general terms, was a magician named John Nevil Maskelyne, who published a lengthy critique of the medium in the British newspaper, the *Daily Chronicle*. Summarizing Maskelyne's findings, author Ruth Brandon wrote "that everything rested on the question whether Eusapia could get a hand or foot free occasionally. She wriggled so much that it was impossible to control her properly . . . If she could get one hand, and sometimes a foot, free, everything could be explained."

Despite their condemnation of Eusapia, the two men elicited the same old song of objection from its foes. Leading the way was the *British Medical Journal*, which surprised no one by criticizing the Society for applying itself to such a person as Eusapia in the first place. Sensible men of science had already concluded that the woman was a con artist, the *Journal* contended, and yet their nonsensical brethren in the SPR had devoted so much time establishing the obvious that they seemed at best to be wasting their energy, at worst to be denigrating the very principles of their professional lives.

William James expected such reactions. Not just because he had heard so many of them in the past, but, in this case, because he thought the *Journal* might have a point in its criticism. He had been dubious about probing Eusapia in the first place, excusing himself from personally inspecting her practices because he feared "that associating with the slippery Palladino would make him appear foolish." He never attended one of her séances, and did not discuss her with Hodgson. But it was James whose name was most publicly attached to the group, even in London; he was, thus, the member most tarred by its insistence on making Eusapia one of its subjects.

Still, Henry Sidgwick wrote to the *British Medical Journal* on the SPR's behalf, once again justifying its purposes, its methods, and both the soundness and value of its examinations of Eusapia. But, as James might have warned him, his defense would only bring forth more attacks, further questioning why the SPR had paid so much attention to so obvious a quack. And, in fact, even one of Eusapia's supporters, a so-called psychic detective named Hereward Carrington, who had also examined her at the request of the SPR, joined the chorus of those who admitted that she was not always to be trusted. Although he had to concede that sometimes, just sometimes, all might not be the "jugglery and imposture" it seemed.

> The mystery of Eusapia Palladino's mediumship is a many-faceted one. Carrington wrote, for example, that she was often caught attempting the most crude kind of trickery--pranks that even the most inexperienced psychical researcher would be certain to catch. Her nature was permeated with mischief and guile, and she would try to cheat at card games or even croquet. Carrington felt that she did these things to those who would test her to see how far she might go in taunting them--or because she was basically a lazy person, to see if she could fool them with a few tricks so that she might be spared the effort of going into a trance. When she found that she could not deceive the knowledgeable investigators from the various research committees . . . Palladino would settle down to producing some of the most remarkable psychic phenomena ever recorded and witnessed by an investigating body of skeptics.

Carrington, like Maskelyne, was a magician, and like Hodgson, he was confident he could explain how Eusapia had performed some of her supposed wonders. For instance, he revealed that she could have simulated a baby's fingers and palm, which occasionally appeared at her sittings, by using "a piece of cheesecloth dusted with phosphorus."

On the other hand, Carrington continued, and with Eusapia there was always another hand (and often, of course, a third), "I have always said that she will resort to trickery if she can," Carrington continued, "but if she was carefully watched she still performs the most marvelous acts and some of these acts I can explain only on supernatural grounds."

In time, James seemed to agree, or at least to modify his disdain for Eusapia. But was careful not to advertise the opinion. To him, the lady was a fraud, all right, but perhaps only part-time.

Intricate, so very intricate, this Palladino puzzle.

To the surprise of many, the most tenacious supporter of Eusapia was a man who did not belong to the Society for Psychic Research. Frank Podmore was, rather, a founder of the most influential of Britain's socialist organizations, the Fabian Society, which counted George Bernard Shaw among its members. But he was also a respected student of the paranormal, although less known for a neutral stance on the subject than for outright disbelief. Known, in fact, in the words of Sir William Fletcher Barrett, for "his usual prejudice against any supernatural explanation." Of anything.

Yet somehow, Eusapia managed not only to attract Podmore's attention but to penetrate his defenses--this even though he had read a report about her, prepared by an SPR committee that was so scathing it resulted in the group's formally disassociating itself from her in 1895.******** Podmore did not find the report scathing at all. "Here, for the first time perhaps in the history of modern spiritualism," he wrote, "we seem to find the issue put squarely before us. It is difficult for any man who reads the Committee's report to dismiss the whole business as mere vulgar cheating."

Within the SPR, Sir Oliver agreed--and vociferously. He *had* felt his hand being squeezed at a séance; he was sure of it. He *had* felt a beard tickle his pate. He *had* seen a desk move and an arm appear from a body at a place where arms were not normally to be found. A *real*

******** Podmore's opinion seems to have been instrumental in the eventual discounting of the SPR report. The group would *re*-associate itself with her, which is to say that it would once against deem her worthy of study, more than a decade later.

arm, not something that could be purchased at a magic shop or stitched by a needle and thread at home. He fumed at the report's questioning of his perceptions. With Podmore's encouragement, as well as that of Frederic Myers, who also thought that rays of legitimacy sometimes peeked through the fog of Eugenia's deceits, Lodge proposed writing an article extolling her and submitting it to the prestigious *Science* magazine. He was still a towering figure in the British academe, and Myers no less highly respected; surely, they believed, *Science* would publish their conclusions

James tried to persuade his friends across the Atlantic that *Science* would do no such thing. The article, no matter how well written and reasoned, would only stir the hornets' nest again, James wrote to them, and the SPR's work would be further denigrated, its time wasted. Hodgson agreed, and joined James in his opposition.

But Lodge would not be dissuaded. He knew what he knew and wanted to proclaim it--damn the ignorance of others, their unfounded scorn. And so, without Myers's assistance or James's sanction, Lodge committed his beliefs to paper. But instead of dispatching them to *Science*, he sent his report to a publication much more likely to print them and least likely to stir controversy, the house organ known as the *Journal of the Society for Psychical Research*. It appeared in 1894, a year before the SPR sentenced Eusapia to her thirteen years of perdition.

> However the facts are to be explained, the possibility of the facts I am constrained to admit. There is no further room in my mind for doubt. Any person without invincible prejudice who had had the same experience would have come to the same broad conclusion, viz.: that things hitherto held impossible do actually occur. The result of my experience is to convince me that certain phenomena usually considered abnormal do belong to the order of nature, and, as a corollary from this, that these phenomena ought to be investigated and recorded by persons and societies interested in natural knowledge.

Lodge's report in the SPR journal was probably the most important document in his undoing as far as the history of science is concerned. His name remained a notable one among his colleagues, and he would in fact go on to win a number of awards and make a number advances in his various fields, but some of the luster was gone and would never return. For the most part, the British public would never know him, and people who did would not hold him in sufficient regard. Of all the scientists who found their reputations blemished by their belief in the paranormal, it is likely that none was damaged more than Sir Oliver's.

And it would get worse. Two decades later, the first World War would erupt and his son would enlist and be killed in the fighting. Lodge was, of course, bereft. But at some point after his son's demise, he would find a particle of consolation by conversing with him--actually communicating with the beloved lad who was no longer among the living. That is what he told a few friends and colleagues. As a result, he was more convinced than ever before of the integrity of Eusapia's psychic powers; certain that, however briefly, Raymond Lodge had actually gotten in touch with him from behind the veil of mortality.

Chapter 8

THE INCREDIBLE
FLYING MEDIUM

In addition to being the most body-bending of all the acts described in this book, it is also the most truth-stretching. There were witnesses to this most extraordinary of demonstrations but, given the nature of what they saw, or claim to have seen, can they be believed? It would seem that no person with his cranial synapses properly attached to one another could possibly answer in the affirmative. Yet the witnesses were rational people, solid citizens, men and women who had never before shown themselves to be subject to flights of fancy.

But even if what I am about to write is not true, it *is* part of the historical record of supernatural occurrences and thus deserves mention in this most recent of records. Yes, it reads like one of the chimerical tales of an Arabian night, like one of the Roadrunner's stunts in his pursuit of Bugs Bunny, like one of the special effects in a Marvel Comics movie. It does not just defy common sense; it defies gravity.

But then what about those witnesses, the people who swear they saw the medium fly? Or perhaps float is a better word. They were more than just rational; some of them were eminent. Why would they make a sudden descent into balderdash? There is no apparent reason for them to have lied, nothing for them to have gained.

At the risk of making my own descent, I will tell the most amazing of the many amazing stories of the man known to some as the wizard.*********

The year was 1867. The place: London. A thirty-four-year-old man had decided to display this remarkably ability of his in front of a small audience--three men, all friends, who had gathered in a third-story sitting room, probably at an elegant residence known as Ashley House. The wizard began by lying on the rug in his sitting room and slipping into a trance as comfortably as if it were a favorite dressing gown. As his

---

********* He is referred to as a "wizard" in the titles of two biographies, and is the only psychic practitioner I have come across to be so identified. See the works of Jean Burton and Peter Lamont in the bibliography.

concentration grew deeper, his body elongated itself--by four inches, six inches, eight inches. Nobody knows for certain. Nobody measured. But all three of his guests were unanimous in agreeing that he was a taller man on the floor than he had been seconds earlier when upright. Perhaps it was an illusion of some sort--but three men sharing the same illusion simultaneously? There were other occasions, or illusions, also witnessed by small gatherings in which the gentleman was said to have reversed directions, shrinking himself by half a foot or so.

Whatever his length on this particular night, after he achieved it he began to speak in a voice barely above a whisper, telling his companions not to be afraid and not to leave their places; it was important that they sit where they were and remain perfectly still until the medium returned. He would be back in mere moments, but in the interim would change locations, moving about in a manner his friends had never seen before. The wizard might have been quiet, but he was also confident, as if he knew there was secret at the core of all paranormal experience, that the world as most people perceive it is not the real world in its entirety. Or, to put it another way, it was as if he knew that reality, common usage notwithstanding, is not a singular noun; that there are different realities, several of them, and he was the master of at least one of them.

After having extended himself in a supine position on the rug, the man began to rise slowly up toward the ceiling, levitating, just lying there upon the empty air, as Dr. Ercole Chiaia said that Eusapia Palladino had done. But that was all she had done, just lie there, with no visible means of support. The wizard, though, also unsupported, achieved a greater height than Eusapia, somewhere between five and seven feet, thereby reaching his cruising altitude. And cruise is precisely what he began to do, sliding horizontally through the air over to the room's sole window. Then, leaning down to open it, he disappeared outside into the night. He was a bird sailing smoothly on a sea of soft breezes. A later measurement would indicate that the man did his flying somewhere between seventy and eighty-five feet above the ground. The distance of his flight: seven and a half feet.

At which point the elongated one eased himself back into his apartment through a window, already opened, in the dining room, which adjoined his point of departure. There he came to rest again on the floor, breathing loudly and regularly, and slowly beginning to shrink back to his normal height. Once having attained it, he stood slowly and a bit unsteadily, as if recovering from a bout of dizziness. Returning to the sitting room, he presented himself again to the three gentlemen awaiting his arrival. It took him a while to shake himself totally out of his trance and return to normal.

If, that is, the word "normal" could ever apply to this man.

And so it was that he completed what is known as either "The Great Levitation" or "The Great Fraud."

The three witnesses to this dazzling exhibition of sorcery were Lord Lindsay, who would later be the Earl of Crawford; Viscount Adare, who would be the fourth Earl of Dunraven; and a cousin of Adare named Captain Charles Wynne, a member of Parliament. In addition to being suitably titled and "of high social standing," little else is known about the trio, and nothing that would undermine their credibility as onlookers.

Adare was the first to raise a question about what they had just seen. The window through which the medium had re-entered Ashley House had been pulled up eighteen inches above the sill, and Adare "expressed his wonder how [the medium] had been taken through so narrow an aperture." It does not, however, seem a vexing question. Surely a slender man could slide through a gap of a foot and a half. And our man was indeed slender, even without having to rely on extending himself.

More questions followed: Did the medium really fly seven and a half feet from room to room, or did he shift from one to the other by walking on the window ledges? After all, he had insisted that his three friends were to remain in place during his brief journey; they were not to shift positions and look outside at his transit.

But, *were* there ledges beneath the two windows? And was the distance between the ledges small enough so that a person could jump from one to the other--supposing that the ledges were wide enough to support such a maneuver in the first place? These questions should have been easy to answer, but for some reason reports of the incident from the period do not agree.

Adare said there *were* ledges and that they were about four inches wide, barely enough so that a man could keep his balance on them, while Lindsay agreed there were ledges, but claimed their width was an inch and a half, unable to have supported any footsteps at all.

If there *weren't* ledges, but only a sill extending from each window, the kind of base upon which flowerpots could be placed, their width would have been no more than about six inches, enough for a man to keep his footing but with no room for error. A ballet dancer might have jeted [accent over the second "e"] from one to the other, but it is unlikely that anyone else could have managed it. "I very much doubt," said Lord Lindsay well after the fact, "whether any skillful rope-dancer would like to attempt a feat of this description, where the only means of crossing would be a perilous leap."

And, of course, there were questions even before the leap: How did the psychic increase his height? How did he raise himself from the floor? How did he manage to float? What in the hell, if anything, had really happened in that apartment on that occasion?

Actually, the men could not even agree on where the apartment was. Adare insisted that Ashley Place was the correct site, but Lindsay claimed it was a residence on Victoria Street. Nor, in retrospect, could the men settle on the date: Was it December thirteenth or the sixteenth? Was the night moonlit, as all three witness claimed, or black, as an almanac was said to have stated?

As expected, Sir Arthur Conan Doyle dismissed the disagreements as petty and declared that only the big picture mattered. He quoted Professor James Challis, a clergyman, physicist, and astronomer, who supposedly said, "Either the facts must be admitted to be such as are reported, or the possibility of certifying facts by human testimony must be given up." The comment is, of course, so general as to be specious, and so specious as to be meaningless. It hardly constitutes an explanation in a case like this.

But are we then to believe that Adare, Lindsay, and Wynne consciously lied about what they saw? If so, we must ask why. We must ask whether they had anything to gain by lying. The answers seem to be (a) no, (b) there is no way of knowing, and (c) no.

Trevor Hall, who wrote a critical biography of the incredible flying medium, although not anointing him a wizard, provided the closest thing to a reasonable analysis that I could find, declaring

> that the observers must have been in a mildly abnormal state throughout the sitting and generally during their association with [the medium], who was one of those rare individuals who possess the power of imposing suggestion upon others to a marked degree. If this theory is accepted, it is not difficult to understand why the observers believed that they had witnessed a miracle but were quite incapable afterward of giving a coherent account of what they thought they had seen.

Still, Hall's version of events also contains loopholes. He refers to "the power of imposing suggestion on others to a marked degree," and this is surely something that can certainly occur verbally. But visually? The latter is much more difficult to accomplish, especially when the "others" number three, all of them men in good societal standing and, at least up to the night in question, of sound mental functioning. It is also worth considering that, like members of the SPR, the witnesses risked the scorn of their peers for attesting to the events of the night if they did not occur as described. Why would they put their reputations at risk if not convinced of what they saw?

Not only do Hall's comments fail to satisfy, so too does the laughable explanation of Frank Podmore, who found the "The Great Levitation" easy to understand and thus to dismiss. He attributed the initial part of the performance to trickery with curtains extending from the sitting room window partway across the floor, giving the illusions of both elongation and elevation when the wizard lay on the floor. Ostensibly, flickering candles, with shadows of flames dancing on the curtains, also contributed to the legerdemain. Podmore does *not* say how curtains and candles could be used for such illusory purposes, and an answer does not come readily to mind. It is a self-defeating omission.

As for the short journey outside from sitting room window to dining room window, Podmore, one of the authors of *Phantasms of the Living*, proposed a phantasm of his own. Remarkably, he suggested that there might have been a hot-air balloon hovering outside the apartment building, awaiting its passenger. Whether or not he did so with a straight face is a mystery, although it seems so. If the medium *did* make use of a balloon, it seems reasonable to assume that such a contraption would be clearly visible from the street and thus ruin the ruse. And what if the wind started to blow in an unforeseen direction? A passenger in the balloon might end up hanging from the hour hand of Big Ben rather than entering his intended destination? And finally, wouldn't the three witnesses have caught a glimpse of something so large and unwieldy as a hot air balloon, or heard it as night breezes slapped it against the building?

The most reasonable of all explanations for the otherwise inexplicable flight came from a psychic researcher named Guy William Lambert, "who suggested that [the wizard] had attached a rope to the chimneys of the building and hung the rope down unseen to the third floor. During the alleged levitation [the medium] 'swung out and in the room' by using a double rope maneuver." A few other critics agreed with Lambert, but not many; his solution was apparently too simple a solution to appeal to those examining so complex a stunt. Most naysayers, especially those with inherent biases against the SPR seemed more content to vilify the midnight flight than to seek an explanation for how it might actually have been achieved.

Many attempts were made over the years by the SPR to authenticate or disprove various feats attributed to the incredible flying medium. One of the tests to which he was subjected, and to which he agreed without hesitation, called for him to be "placed against a wall. Someone was to be posted to hold his feet and make sure he was not standing on tip-toe; another watched his waist, another his face . . . another his arms; another stood by with a pencil to trace his growth on the wall." And a good thing too, because despite all of the restraints on him, the fellow was reported to have sprouted several inches.

At a later time, an audience of prominent academics and authors gathered at the home of Rufus Elmer in Springfield, Massachusetts, for another display of wizardry.

> Among these visitors were a Harvard professor, David Wells, and the poet and editor of the *New York Evening Post*, William Cullen Bryant. Along with two other people, they . . . witnessed the violent movements of [a] table. They saw it levitate off the floor and experienced, "a powerful shock, which produced a vibratory motion of the floor . . . like the motion occasioned by distant thunder." They were so impressed that they wrote to the *Springfield Republican*, stating in the clearest terms that all this happened while "the room was well lighted, the lamp was frequently placed on and under the table, and every opportunity was afforded us for the closest inspection, and we admit this one emphatic declaration: *We know that we were not deceived.* [Italics in original.]

They also knew they were not deceived when, according to a published account, five men "whose united weight *was eight hundred and fifty pounds*, stood on a table." [Italics in original.] The medium positioned himself some distance away. No matter--the table rose from the floor. At the same time, "a tremulous phosphorescent light gleam [appeared] over the walls."

The psychic of whom I write "was investigated by physicians and chemists, by Professor [Robert] Hare, the inventor of the oxy-hydrogen blowpipe, and by J.W. Edmonds, a legal scholar and member of the New York State Supreme Court. Both Hare and Edmonds started out as doubters and then publicly stated their conviction that these feats were the work of spirits." Hare was later accused in a publication called *English Mechanic* of having lost his mind.

Daniel Dunglas Home. That is how history refers to him. It does not, however, refer to him very much. This even though Peter Lamont's biography of him, *The First Psychic: The Peculiar Mystery of a Notorious Victorian Wizard*, labeled him "one of the most famous men of his era." It was surely among the least disputed statements ever made about Home.

His name is, perhaps fittingly, misleading in two ways. He was not born with the "Dunglas"; rather, he wedged it in between his other appellations because it belonged to a royal clan in Scotland, and he wanted to affix some prestige to himself before his paranormal exploits earned it for him. As for the "Home," it *is* his real surname, but for no reason ever made clear, he chose to pronounce it "Hume." Later in life, he took to spelling it "Hume," but for the sake of consistency, I will use the initial spelling throughout this chapter.

Born near Edinburgh, Scotland in 1833, Home was the son of a mother so sickly and a father so destitute that they could not afford to keep him. The boy's mother Elizabeth, turned over his reins to her sister, the devoutly Christian Mary Cook, and at the beginning, Mrs. Cook and her husband were delighted with the arrangement. But only at the beginning. In his autobiography, Home tells how their attitude began to change.

> I was very delicate as a child, and of a highly nervous temperament; so much so that it was not thought that I could be reared. I cannot remember when I first became subject to the

curious phenomena which have now for so long attended me, but my aunt and others have told me that when I was a baby my cradle was frequently rocked, as if some kind of guardian spirit was tending me in my slumbers. My aunt has also told me that when I was about four years old, I had a vision of the circumstances attending the passing from earth of a little cousin . . .

The cousin lived many miles from Home. As was true of William James and his aunt, Home could not have known of the death as early as he did by any terrestrial means. When people came to his house to pay their respects, the little boy had been well-dressed and propped up in a chair where all could see him. He sat still, composed, his feet not quite reaching the floor. He did not know the identities of the mourners. He had never seen them before. And, to repeat, he was but four years old. Yet it is said that Daniel called most of the people by name, both impressing them and surprising them eerily.

Before long, Mary Cook and her husband also began to feel a certain eeriness, becoming wary of their boy and the strange powers he seemed to possess. Like Daniel, they too developed a highly nervous temperament, and began to think that rearing the boy might be a task beyond their abilities, as well as beyond their desire. At the least, they feared they would have to resort to unusual means, and they were not unusual people. But Daniel was, after all, the Cooks' nephew, and they owed him their best efforts.

When the child was nine, the family immigrated to the United States, settling in a Connecticut town known today as Norwich. There, among his playmates, he acquired the nickname "Scotchy," which makes it sound as if Daniel had become a Danny, one of the boys.

But he hadn't. Far from it. He didn't play with the boys and didn't dress as sloppily as the boys did and seldom shared his pastimes with the boys. He much preferred solitary activities, like his piano lessons, and was as diligent with them as he was his lessons in school. "In his lighter moods he could be playful and sometimes distressingly arch," says biographer Burton, "but it was characteristic of both Daniel and the period that one of his favourite diversions was to stroll in the woods, 'silently contemplating the beauties of the springing vegetation and pondering upon death.' He was not precisely morbid, however; merely curious."

At the age of thirteen, Daniel finally made a friend, beginning to share his curiosities with a boy named Edwin. Unfortunately, Daniel would soon play Sam Clemens to Edwin's Henry.

The two of them often went for walks through the woods together; they would read the Bible to each other and, one afternoon, Edwin told his new friend about a story he had come across in another book about two lovers. So deeply in love were they, Edwin related, that they made a vow, swearing that, if there were such a thing as life after death, the first of them to pass away "would visit the other in spirit form." Edwin, touched by such commitment, suggested that he and Daniel make the same vow. Daniel agreed. The agreement was sealed.

"About a month from this time," Home later wrote, "I went with my family to reside at Troy in the State of New York, a distance from Norwich [and from Edwin] . . . of nearly three hundred miles."

One night, however, the distance was, in a manner of speaking, surmounted. It was a night when the sky was a deeper, more starless black than usual; it "grew more dense," Daniel later wrote, "until through the darkness there seemed to be a gleam of light, which I cannot describe, but it was similar to those which I and many others have since seen when the room has been illuminated by spiritual presence. This light increased, and my attention was drawn to the foot of the bed, where stood my friend Edwin. He appeared as in a cloud of brightness, illuminating his face with a distinctness more than mortal."

From this vision Daniel deduced that Edwin was dead.

The information was confirmed three days later, with Edwin having passed away at the precise time of night that he appeared before the friend he had left behind.

It was at this time that Daniel knew his life would be guided ever-more by his visions. Scotchy would never be one of the boys, and upon growing up would never be one of the men.

The story of Daniel and Edwin began to spread among the Cook's Troy neighbors. Some didn't believe it and wondered why Daniel would make up such a story. Others did believe it, and were intimidated more than impressed. Who *was* this newcomer among them? If his psychic skills were real, what was their source? If they were some sort of scam, what was its purpose? Regardless of the answer, the neighbors did not believe that the young medium belonged among them, and before long, according to him, they

> laid siege to the [Cook] house "in a way that did not tend to soothe the religious susceptibilities of my aunt." By this time, everyone knew that questions could be answered by the raps And within a week after Daniel's gift was officially established they were told where to find so many long-lost relatives, title-deeds, and misplaced brooches, and so many striking proofs of spirit identity were obtained, as would be tedious to enumerate.

Mrs. Cook, however, did not find her adoptive son's proofs tedious. She found them perverse, frightening, and worse, un-Christian. Noth-ing in the Bible, she believed, accounted for a decent, God-fearing man--the Almighty's own son, excepted, of course--possessing such miraculous powers as Daniel claimed. She and her husband began to contemplate drastic action. At the same time, Daniel gave them reason to think even more drastically.

Soon, despite his youth, he had begun to conduct the occasional séance in Troy and vicinity. Those who attended them were spellbound; others, who simply knew about them, were appalled. Mrs. Cook looked in on what might have been the first of them, and heard Daniel claim that, for the first time, he had made contact with his mother. He did not expect it, had not been trying to contact her, but heard a rapping previously unknown to him, sounds that he somehow knew could only be a message from Elizabeth Home, now several years deceased. "Daniel," she said, according to her son's translation of the raps, "fear not, my child, . . . seek to do good, be truthful and truth-loving, and you will prosper . . . Yours is a glorious mission--you will convince the infidel, cure the sick and console the weeping."

It seems to have been the only séance that Mrs. Cook could bring herself to observe.

At a later séance, a sitter named Mr. Brittan swore that boy-wonder medium had managed to put him in touch with a woman named Hannah, a relative of his who had become insane a full twelve years before Daniel was born. "I see no way out," was Hannah's message to Mr. Brittan. "There's no light! The clouds roll in upon me, the darkness deepens! My head is whirling!"

By this time, heads were whirling all about Troy. Future séances were quickly scheduled, almost all of them in neighboring communities. Some of those who sat around Daniel's table claimed they felt both feminine and masculine hands take hold of them in the boy's presence, and, on at least one occasion, the sensation of iron hands squeezing into flesh was reported. Furthermore: "When an invisible hand gave Mrs. Howitt [the same Mrs. Howitt referred to earlier, the wife of supernatural author William and an author herself] a sprig of geranium, they planted it and it *grew*: 'so it was no delusion.'" [Italics in original.]

For Mr. and Mrs. Cook, so committed to their faith, these reports on Daniel's séances were the end of parenthood. Accounts vary, but when Mrs. Home's son was either thirteen or seventeen, "the staunch Presbyterians promptly disowned him and turned him out to his own devices." He was to leave the Cook residence immediately and never darken its doorway again. He packed a bag--all of his possessions fitting into just one--and, without even knowing where he would sleep that night, the boy stepped out into an unsheltered world.

It sounds cruel, and easily could have been. But Daniel's devices proved to be more than sufficient to carry him through the remaining years of childhood and into adulthood. Whether he was a wizard, a fraud, a freak, or some combination of all three, he had acquired enough of a reputation before his expulsion by the Cooks to be offered room and board by numerous believers. In return, they simply wanted the gift of his stupefying services. They wanted to watch him, to listen to his utterings to the afterlife and marvel at them. They attended him in small groups, which he seems to have insisted upon, and were, for the most part, the leading citizens of their communities, "gentlemen of education and means."

At one of his early séances in Springfield, Massachusetts, a New York clergyman named S.B. Brittan asked to commune with his deceased wife. After a few minutes, Home said that he had reached her. "Hannah Brittan is here!" he announced, although perhaps she wasn't; perhaps she had employed one of his friends in the afterlife to relay a message to her husband. "[T]he spirit has ... informed me that her present life is calm, peaceful, and beautiful." That was the reverend's report.

Later, at séances in Boston, "Spirits were seen distinctly by all present in the room, and more than once they kissed persons present so as to be both felt and heard."

For several years Home remained in the United States, moving randomly through New England. In 1855, at the age of twenty-two and feeling restless, he went to England where he expanded his repertoire. No longer content to specialize in communication with the deceased, he began to conduct séances that "featured raps, strains of ghostly music, and the sight of spectral hands, often with the gaslights turned up in the séance room. He also had exhibited, according to many witnesses, a startling ability to levitate as well as to shrink and elongate his body."

And, as if that were not enough, "strong men blanched the day Home in a trance walked up to an open fireplace, and then, 'kneeling down, placed his face right among the burning coals, moving it about as though bathing in water.' Awestruck, [observers] examined him. Not a hair of his head was singed."

Then there was the night when, reportedly, Home was handed a letter by a servant as he returned to the house where he was staying. "As Home took it from the man's hand, standing in the dark at the street door, vivid sparks shot from his fingers, and the servant fled, uttering cries of terror." He was now, apparently, a magician as much as a medium.

It is possible to believe in the paranormal and not believe in Daniel Dunglas Home. He simply takes the unbelievable too far, further than the vast majority of mortals could believe in those days. Or, of course, today. One who reads of what he is supposed to have done is much more likely to believe he is reading fiction, rather than history, and yet all that he did was witnessed, verified--by different people, at different times, in different places. Perhaps he was a showman more than a psychic; how, then, did he perform such stupefying shows? What were the tricks he employed? In the research I did for this book, I came across much scoffing at Home's supposed adventures, but no rational explanations for how he managed his deceits, if indeed his adventures *were* deceitful, as the mind cannot help but insist. Could it be that Home operated so far beyond the seeming bounds of reality that even experts could not discern any duplicity in his methods? Would the Society for Psychic Research ever face a greater challenge?

By the time he reached his early twenties, Home found that his name was known on two continents, and that there was much more ground yet to be covered. "Fairly tall, slim, well-built, in his dress-suit and white tie he looked like a gentleman of the highest social standing." A friend said that he was "very vain of his personal appearance, with a quite innocent and not unpleasing vanity. Always pleasing manners--very affectionate towards all--men, women, and children alike." Yet, in truth, he could not be described quite so simply.

He was, in fact, says Jean Burton, "so unclassifiable a specimen that [people] were hard put to it to know how to approach him at all. He was neither an entertainer nor a holy man; he must be received strictly as an equal; and one must never, never so far forget oneself as to offer him money. Jewels, clothes, fur coats, trips to fashionable watering-places--in some respects his tastes were rather like a cocotte's [a fashionable prostitute]--were acceptable; but money, no. Moreover, he would not even consider invitations unless they came through an intermediary well-known to him, which put an added premium on his eagerly courted friendship."

But he did not look like someone whose courtship would be readily welcomed. Beneath his shock of untamed red hair, through which a comb seemed never to have ventured, was a complexion unusually wan, ashen. He might have dressed elegantly, might have lived stylishly, but never seemed to be in robust health, often feeling weak, enervated. Sometimes he blamed his languor on the strains of his séances, the frequency of which increased as his fame spread; at other times he attributed it to his wearying travel schedule; and occasionally on the need to call up the extraordinary powers necessary to flout reality as he did. All might have been true to an extent, but the deeper truth was that, in his early twenties, he had contracted tuberculosis, a disease for which there was no cure at the time. As he got older, he found himself more and more debilitated, more and more worried about how much time he would be granted on the earth.

Another medium, another malady. A coincidence? Or was it somehow, in some inexplicable way, a requirement for the job?

Before long, Home became the favored medium of European royalty.

In Paris, he conducted séances for the Emperor Napoleon III and his Spanish wife, Eugenie [accent over second "e"] de Montijo. Before the first of them, at the Salon d'Apollon, Home recalled being more nervous than he had ever been before. "The room was packed to the point of suffocation," and that, in turn, caused a problem of suffocating delicacy for the star of the show. As politely as possible, he explained to the Empress that that the maximum number of sitters at a séance should be eight; any more than that, he said, and he might not be able to produce the desired results. Sometimes even eight were too many. He was visibly agitated, fidgety and disconcerted. There would never be a Corinthian Hall for him.

Hearing this, the self-enchanted Eugenie, who had been responsible for assembling a throng consisting of far more than eight people, now had to tell most of her retinue to titter off, clearing the room for Home, the royal couple, and six others. Those excluded, to say the least, were unhappy; their grumbling soon turned to a roar, and Eugenie could not placate them even by assurances that she would insist on Home's adding more séances to his schedule.

The favored six, granted permission to keep their places, arrayed themselves around the wizard and, "in spite of this inauspicious beginning the table soon vibrated and rose from the floor. Prince Murat [the second son of the king of Naples] . . . dropped to his knees to hold the medium's feet." He would later tell friends it was not a hallucination. He would insist that what he saw was real.

Napoleon was an amateur magician, and in his occasional good moods performed tricks for the members of his court; he would easily have spotted the deception if Home had been doing something as amateurish as jiggling the table with his knees. Although not dubious of the medium, like Murat, the Emperor was not completely accepting either, having summoned Home as much out of curiosity as of belief.

Yet he began to believe almost immediately, and not just because of the risen table. Once it descended, he asked questions of Home about people who were strangers to him, both alive and dead. All of the answers, or almost all, were correct. A remarkable result. Yet it was all the more remarkable because the emperor did not really ask the questions--not aloud, that is. Instead, he *thought* them; they never left his mind and made their way down to his vocal chords. It was a silent interrogation by Napoleon and described by those in attendance as an even more amazing performance than they had expected from the wizard. Telepathy, the monarch declared it to be, pure and simple, unerring and unnerving. There is no evidence that he had believed in such a thing before meeting Home.

Afterward, attention turned to the Empress, who was greeted with a different display of paranormal powers than those in which her husband had just partaken. "Almost at once she felt her robe pulled; she started, and uttered a slight cry. Home ... soothingly asked her to place her hand beneath the table, murmuring that if another hand should take hers there, it was one that should cause her no fear. They all waited. 'It is my father's hand,' she breathed in a moment, incredulously. The Emperor hurried over to her and touched it in turn; they recognized the hand, they said, by a characteristic defect, and it seemed to be gloved in silk."

Is it true? Possible? Any of it, all of it? And once again, that constantly nagging question: If the preceding was not true, why did so many people swear to its accuracy? Why, in other venues at other times, had people as diverse as scientists, academics, artists, business leaders and political figures and, going back even further, residents of the Burned-over District, swear that they had seen the un-seeable, learned the unknowable? By now, thousands upon thousands of people had marveled at scores of mediums in a variety of places; was every single one mistaken, or possessed of an ulterior motive? Some people suggested a conspiracy, but for sheer foolishness, the notion ranked with the hot air balloon as an explanation. A conspiracy on an international scale, involving so many people over so much time and distance?

And again ... *why*?

There still exists a letter that Eugenie, "appalled and ecstatic," wrote to her sister, the Duchess of Alba, a day or two after her otherworldly experience. In it, she described the séance precisely as it was described above. As for Home, she told her sister that he was obviously "in very poor health with something strange in his look. He is a Scot, he talks very little, and when asked what we shall be seeing, he answers:--'I don't know anything about it. I am only an instrument.'"

Home also served as an instrument for Queen Sophia of the Netherlands. According to her testimony, "I saw him four times . . . I felt a hand tipping my finger; I saw a heavy golden bell moving alone from one person to another; I saw my handkerchief move alone and return to me with a knot. . . . He himself is a pale, sickly, rather handsome young man. . . . It is wonderful. I am so glad I have seen it."

Such a stir did Home create in Europe that even so prestigious an American magazine as *Harper's* sent a correspondent across the sea to report on his visits with crowned heads. One of his articles told of "the incredible power possessed by this . . . young man, and his exhibitions of turning tables, dancing chairs, and peripatetic chandeliers." *Harper's*, the reader will remember, was the same magazine in which Mark Twain would also defend the existence of unseen forces, and before that was a publication with no history of touting, or even acknowledging, the afterlife or anything else commonly dismissed as in violation of the laws of nature. But a certain acknowledgment came just from association. Just as the geniuses of the SPRs gave cachet to Spiritualism simply by inquiring into its authenticity, so did the very name of *Harper's*. To a degree, it didn't matter what the former concluded or the latter published; the investigators and the magazine had formed a link between themselves and Spiritualism that could not help but suggest the latter's legitimacy. And, in fact, the *Harper's* article was more laudatory, or at least accepting, of the Home phenomenon, than negative.

He went on with his tour of Europe and went on making the inconceivable visible to some of the world's most powerful rulers and went on attracting so much attention that, in time, Pope Pius IX publicly condemned him, charging him with witchcraft. The psychic had become a heretic. It was easier for people to believe the latter than the former.

Shortly after departing from France, he conducted a series of sittings for Czar Alexander II of Russia. At one of them, the medium met and soon afterward proposed to his granddaughter, Alexandrina de Kroll. She accepted. Not that long ago he had so frightened the Cooks that they cast him out into the world. Now he was marrying royalty, and Alexandre Dumas, the famed French novelist, who had written *The Three Musketeers* and *The Count of Monte Cristo*, was serving as the best man at his wedding. Alexis Tolstoy, a second cousin of Leo Tolstoy and also related to another great Russia author, Ivan Turgenev, was a groomsman.

The wedding ceremony attracted hundreds of guests, both inside and outside the church, and proceeded with all "due pomp." But whether a lifetime of bliss would have awaited the couple will never be known. Like her husband, Alexandrina was also tubercular, and died a few years later. Afterward, Home saw less of her than he did when she was alive, but claimed she did not disappear completely. Speaking to Lord Adare, and explaining an apparition that both of them claim to have seen one night when they were in Home's bedroom, he said "she often comes to me." Then she fades away, a cameo in the night.

But before losing his wife, and with Alexandrina proudly at his side, Home kept traveling through countries of which he had never heard as a boy, and kept fascinating those who watched him do what common sense insisted could not be done. Yet he never ceased to insist that his inexplicable skills were not really his own. Rather, repeating the theme of his being but an instrument of inexplicable origin, he would say, "I believe in my heart that this power is being spread more and more every day to draw us nearer to God. You ask if it makes us purer? My only answer is that we are but mortals and as such liable to err; but it does teach that the pure in heart shall see God. It teaches us that He is love and that there is no death."

Home's faith became the basis of faith for many others. As Professor Deborah Blum has written, "He boasted a flamboyant mystic appeal that the staunch mainline Protestant churches of America and Britain--Anglicans, Episcopalians, and Methodists--neither could nor would attempt to match. Perhaps most powerfully of all, he and his counter-parts offered a glimpse of possibilities through open doors that their critics--churchmen, skeptics, and scientists alike--would slam without a glance."

Blum does not mention Catholicism. Perhaps because, at least at this stage of his career, it was the only mainstream religion to show official interest in Home. For reasons unclear, the Church had changed its sacred mind and no longer found the medium guilty of witchcraft. In fact, he was summoned to Rome on one occasion for an audience with the pope. Pius IX "questioned him intently as to his past life and his psychic experiences," wondering about, if not admitting the certainty of, any possible connections between Home's practices and those of the Church. It would be fascinating to read a transcript of the dialogue between the two men. Unfortunately, not even a summary of the conversation exists.

Of course, to a majority of men and women in all nations, Home continued to be a fraud, the world's most skilled practitioner of hokum. This they believed regardless of their faith, regardless of Pius IX's tacit endorsement--and this, when his travels took him back toward the west, "England's foremost poetess" would eventually come to believe. But not at first, not in 1855. At that time, she would be regaled by Home's particular brand of magic.

Elizabeth Barrett Browning, "dark eyes glowing in her small ivory-pale face," first experienced a Home séance at the residence of a respected British solicitor named John S. Rymer. No sooner had she taken her seat at his table than she felt a tingling in the air, as if distant presences were straining to drift closer to her. At a later point in the séance, she claimed that she had seen "spectral hands" stroking Home's cheek, and then felt their gentle touch herself. In fact--or in legend--at one point the hands placed a wreath on her head, an arrangement of clematis with so fresh a scent that they seemed to have been picked with an hour or so.

Elizabeth's husband, another of England's foremost poets, stood behind her as the wreath slowly fitted itself to her head. "He expressed no disbelief"; Elizabeth said, "as indeed it was impossible for anyone to have any."

But Robert Browning's pate had not been crowned with a wreath. Nor had he felt any hands upon him, ghostly or otherwise. Despite his wife's brush with the supernatural, which he had apparently seen with his own eyes, the only thing he felt was contempt, and in the years ahead it would grow beyond all bounds of reason.

Robert had accompanied Elizabeth to the séance, but against his will. He had become a non-believer upon simply learning that there *was* such a thing as Spiritualism; once in its actual presence, he thought himself to be on an "intellectual slumming expedition," and not even for his beloved wife would he accompany her again.

Disbelief is one thing. But the vehemence of Browning's reaction is hard to understand, especially since, as the evening wore on, Home continued to astound others at the Rymer house with his mastery of the paranormal. Even, once, with his mastery of the inanimate. After the wreath had been laid on Elizabeth's head, Home instructed the table at which she sat to rise from the floor. It did precisely that, so obedient a piece of furniture that it might have had ears as well as legs. Such a thing could not happen, Browning swore, and he told the medium so. In response, Home invited Browning to conduct an inspection. "I looked under the table," the poet later said, "and can aver that it was lifted from the ground, say a foot high more than once, with no wires or rods to be seen. I don't in the least pretend to explain how the table was uplifted all together."

Nonetheless, after having briefly been turned into a witness for the defense, Browning reverted to his previous prosecutorial mien. "His robust, explosive nature abhorred Home's gentle, effeminate bearing . . . and Browning loathed the childishly caressing behaviour with which Home treated the Rymers." He was angry at the Rymers for having hosted the séance in the first place. And might have been more upset by Home's apparent, yet harmless, flirtation with his wife--if, in fact, Home was actually guilty of such a thing.

The result was Elizabeth's writing to a friend that she, the friend, was not to *"say a word on the subject--because it's a* tabooed *subject in this house--Robert and I taking completely different views, and he being a good deal irritated by any discussion of it."*

As for his inability to discover how Home had levitated the table, Browning was no longer willing to confess ignorance. He had figured it out, he declared, and was not the first person to do so. It was "the scoundrel's naked foot" that was responsible for the trickery, Browning told Nathaniel Hawthorne, or something that had been attached to his foot. That the poet's previous examination had detected nothing of the sort was no longer an impediment to his vitriol. Home was "a cheat and imposture," his so-called vocation nothing but "humbugging." Browning poured fuel on his own fire, his ire getting the better not only of his common sense, but his decency.

And inwardly, he raged all the more at Home's refusal to be fazed by the poet's criticisms.

A few days after the séance, Home visited the Browning home "with his right hand outstretched in amity," the poet declared. "He bore no ill-will--not he!" Browning was flummoxed, and something less than a gracious host. In fact, he would not play host to the medium at all. "If you are not out of that door in half a minute," he told Home, "I'll fling you down the stairs."

Elizabeth interceded. "Oh, dear Mr. Home, do not, do not blame me. I am so sorry, but I am not to blame."

Home nodded at her, then departed. Browning concluded his account of the incident as follows: "What do you suppose he says of me?" he fumed to a friend. "You'll never guess. He says to everybody, 'How Browning hates me!--and how I love him!'"

As for Elizabeth, unwitting observer to her husband's disturbing responses, she wrote again to her friend. *"For my own part, I am confirmed in all my opinions. To me [the séance] was wonderful and conclusive; and I believe that the medium present was no more* responsible *for the things said and done, than I myself was."*

Yet inexplicably, a year after Elizabeth Barrett Browning had expressed these sentiments, she began denouncing Home as bitterly as her husband continued to do. In a letter to another friend, written in the summer of 1856, she stated that, among other things, Home was "weak as a reed and more vulgar." Later in the missive, as paraphrased by psychic researcher Eric J. Dingwall, Elizabeth said that Home "had succeeded in making himself universally disagreeable, *although most people agreed that his phenomena were above Nature.*" (Italics added.)

Perhaps her husband's self-replenishing stores of venom, in addition to the passage of time, which might have made events at the Rymer's seem less real to her, had changed Elizabeth's mind. Then again, it might be that she had simply found it easier to placate him than continue to believe in events that could not help but seem in retrospect like opium dreams. But this is only conjecture. Publicly, she was silent on her reasons for turning against Home.

As for her husband, he was silent about nothing concerning the medium; like a dog with a bone, he chewed on his animus without ceasing. In fact, three years after his wife had died, and fully nine years after the séance he attended, Robert Browning was still so infuriated at Home that he took to verse to continue his campaign against him, publishing a poem called "Mr. Sludge, the Medium." It is, according to Home biographer and supporter Elizabeth Jenkins, "a work of very considerable power. It depicts a ruthless and diabolically clever swindler who pretends to be a medium, growing rich through the public's determination to be hoodwinked, but reserving to himself a faint possibility that there might be something in spiritualism after all."

The poem begins with Mr. Sludge, who has admitted his chicanery, pleading for mercy. Perhaps from Browning himself.

> **Now,** don't, sir! Don't expose me!
> Just this once! This was the first and only time, I'll swear,--
> Look at me,--see, I kneel,--the only time,
> I swear I ever cheated,--yes, by the soul
> Of Her who hears--(your sainted mother, sir!)

Later, Mr. Sludge tries to examine the motives for his duplicity.

> Though, 't was wrong.
> I don't contest the point; your anger's just:
> Whatever put such folly in my head,
> I know 't was wicked of me. There's a thick
> Dusk undeveloped spirit (I've observed)
> Owes me a grudge--a negro's, I should say,
> Or else an Irish emigrant's; yourself

Explained the case so well last Sunday, sir.

And, later still from Sludge, outright defiance, an explanation of his deeds meant not so much to satisfy others as to reveal his own motives.

> Or, finally,
> Why should I set so fine a gloss on things?
> What need I care? I cheat in self-defence,
> And there's my answer to a world of cheats!
> Cheat? To be sure, sir! What's the world worth else?

The poem does have a certain power to it, as Jenkins believes, but it is the power of vituperation more than art. In the main, "Mr. Sludge, the Medium" is a tedious exercise, interminable in its length, pointless and repetitive in its excoriations. One can only wonder at Robert Barrett Browning's enduring hostility.

Less hostile, but not by much, were some other notable authors, although these had had no first-hand experience with Home. "*Mr. Hume, or Home,*" opined Charles Dickens, "*I take the liberty of regarding as an imposter. . . . But be assured that if he were demonstrated a humbug in every microscopic cell of his skin and globule of his blood, the disciples would still believe and worship.*" [Italics in original.]

And from George Eliot: "I could not choose to enter a room where he held a séance. He is an object of moral disgust to me."

Eventually, even after a second marriage, Home became an object of moral disgust not just to George Eliot, but to numerous others. Rumors began to circulate that he engaged in homosexual dalliances. Lord Adare claimed to have slept with him, a statement that, if true, calls into question the nobleman's reliability as a witness to "The Great Elongation." Perhaps it also explains why Adare and Home managed to see the same apparition of Home's first wife while the two men were in Home's bedroom.

According to rumors of a different sort, Home had previously been expelled from Paris "for a variety of grave misdemeanors," although their nature was not revealed overseas. A New York newspaper, though, charged that he had been banished from the entire French nation for stealing [pound sign] 30,000. Other than the single report of this paper, though, there is no evidence that Home ever stole anything from anyone, nor does the paper provide so much as a single detail.

Still, Home was feeling besieged. He sought peace from the accusations against him by settling in Italy for a time. There, he said, "although some persons . . . did all they could to injure me by false statements, I was only the more cherished by those who best knew me." But few knew him well enough to protect him from a public thrashing. In Florence, "he was set upon and injured by a group of fearful peasants who tried to murder him for practicing sorcery." He might have considered sanctuary in the Vatican, but it seems that the Pope had changed his mind again, now deciding that Home was not a friend of the church after all, and making it known that he was no longer welcome within its walls.

So the medium fled back to Paris, apparently not having been banished from the French capital for more than a brief period. There he met with neither violence nor threats of it. Still, the tide of public opinion, so long having flowed in Home's direction, had clearly reversed its course.

Yet all was not as bleak as it seemed for the incredible flying medium. William Makepeace Thackeray, the author of *Vanity Fair*, among other novels, had at one time agreed with Browning that Home was guilty of "dire humbug," and, further, that he appealed to the "dreary and foolish superstition" of unworthy minds. It was said of Thackeray that he was not a man to be easily fooled, and certainly not gullible enough to be taken in by so obvious a scoundrel as Home.

Yet there were some of Thackeray's friends who believed in the wizard, and pleaded with him to attend a séance. He refused, would not lower himself. They refused to stop pleading. If nothing else, they said, it would be such a lark, and even more important, would give added substance to his indictments, perhaps even leading to a public statement, or a demonstration of his own, that would bury the notion of Spiritualism once and for all. The latter point seemed to register with him, and so he eventually agreed.

Sitting at Home's table, Thackeray found himself subjected to a spectacular series of assaults on his senses. One of the other guests at the séance declared that no sooner had the lights dimmed than "every article of furniture took to moving about to its own accord." A smaller object also moved, a bracelet falling from the wrist of a woman. It "lay on the table surrounded by a luminous appearance."

And that was just the beginning of the momentous evening. Moments later a piano began to play, apparently without benefit of hands; another hand melted when someone attempted to squeeze it; a voice sang in the distance; a piece of paper suddenly appeared on the table with the words "Love her always" written upon it--and then the *piece de resistance*: Once again having decided to ignore the restrictions of gravity, Home rose from his chair and began to float above it. The sitter who wrote of the performance said that he had tried to pull the medium down by grabbing his feet, but could do no more than hold on; Home had rigidly affixed himself to the air. Whether biographer Elizabeth Jenkins saw this or was informed by others, she swears it is true. When Home finally called a halt to the proceedings, "[his] hands were burning hot and his eyes full of tears."

Thackeray saw it all and reacted rationally to the irrationality surrounding him. He had no choice, he said, but to accept the evidence of his eyes. The same was true of Robert Bell, a journalist who had accompanied Thackeray, and spent the séance taking notes, as well as looking for wires or other objects that would explain Home's miraculous acts. He discovered none. The two men returned to their separate apartments afterward in a state of total disequilibrium.

Before long, this particular séance became the subject of an article in a new but already popular literary magazine called *Cornhill*. It was Bell who wrote the piece, not Thackeray, but the latter was the editor of the journal, and thus provided de facto endorsement of all that was in it.

> It is not to be expected [Bell concluded] that any person who is a stranger to these phenomena, should read such a story as this with complacency. Yet here is a fact which undoubtedly took place, and which cannot be referred to any known physical or mechanical forces. It is not a satisfactory answer to those who have seen such things, to say that they are impossible: *since, in such cases, it is evidence that the impossibility of a thing does not prevent it happening.* (Italics in original.)

With a wobbling pencil, and perhaps an equally wobbling sense of reality, Thackeray appended a note to the end of Bell's manuscript. The reporter was a man of "good faith and honorable character," Thackeray declared, the pair of them having been friends for twenty-five years. And since he sat by Bell's side throughout the séance, he could attest to the fact that his friend had written the truth as seen by all who surrounded them.

His endnote finished, Thackeray signed off and sent the article to the printer.

Its title was "Stranger Than Fiction."

Thackeray was not only an acclaimed figure in literary circles, but numbered among his friends several equally acclaimed men of various degrees of stature in a number of professions. As he expected, most were upset by the story. He did not, however, realize *how* upset they would be. Allowing himself to be hoodwinked was the least of it, they charged; but capitulating as he did, he served as an accomplice to deeds virtually criminal in their chicanery. And he had changed his position so suddenly, so unexpectedly; no one could give a reason for such puzzling behavior.

Angered though he was by the responses to the *Cornhill* account, Thackeray responded calmly. "It is all very well for you," he said, "who have probably never seen any spiritual manifestations to talk as you do; but had you seen what I have witnessed, you would hold a different opinion."

Although he was separated from the furor by an ocean, and although Browning had earlier complained to him of Home, Nathaniel Hawthorne "recorded many instances of Home's powers; he did so with complete conviction." But despite the occasional haunting quality of his novels and, more especially, his short stories, Hawthorne, as had previously been the case, zigged and zagged on the subject of Spiritualism.¨¨¨¨¨¨ When he heard of the wreath's alighting on Elizabeth Barrett Browning's head, he accepted her husband's claim that trickery was involved. But summing up his views on the paranormal, Hawthorne would write one of the strongest endorsements yet produced for an alternate view of the universe: "These soberly attested incredibilities," he said, "are so numerous that I forget nine tenths of them . . . they are absolutely proved to be sober facts, by evidence that would satisfy us of any other alleged realities."

Also of mixed mind was Frank Podmore, who was now officially allied with the SPR and who looked into the Home phenomenon, even

---

¨¨¨¨¨¨ When I first came across the word "Spiritualism" in my research, it was capitalized. Since then, I have encountered it with both a small "s" and a capital. I have chosen to use the latter in this volume because (a) it is how I first saw it spelled, and (b) because Spiritualism, no matter how vilified, came to be considered a religion, and all other religions begin with capital letters. Thus my use of the capital "S" is not an endorsement of the belief; it is, rather, a decision based on what I believe to be proper usage, only that.

though he had "a strong prejudice" against the medium. Of course, he had previously admitted a prejudice against all claims of paranormal activity, only to end up attesting to the validity of Eusapia Palladino. As far as William James and others were concerned, this was evidence of Podmore's objectivity, to follow the evidence wherever it led. But doing so was not easy; as far as Podmore was concerned, the evidence followed a road with many twists and turns, forks and cutoffs.

Initially he believed Home to be a fraud. Then he called him a trickster, a conjurer, although conceding that he was quite a skilled one. But these were superficial judgments, off the top of his head. Careful research brought Podmore to more nuanced conclusions, and writing in the *Journal of the American Society for Psychical* he tilted toward acceptance of Home's most famous feat.

> the evidence for his levitation phenomena rests, not on any one case, taken by itself, but on the mass of cumulated testimony offered by scores of witnesses. However completely one case might be explained away, the other cases still remain to us--each case standing on its own merit--and many of them excellently observed, if not so well recorded.

Frederic Myers also joined Podmore in examining Home's career, and "was inclined to consider [him] a rare talent, a medium with unusual gifts for tapping into occult forces."

At some point after that, however, the perpetually quixotic Podmore backed up a few steps, now claiming he was unable make up his mind about Home, arriving at a number of verdicts on a number of occasions. He still thought the man might be a magician of sorts, perhaps a hypnotist of sorts, perhaps even an inducer of mass hallucinations. "Probably some of the more marvelous feats described at Home's séances can be analyzed into sensory deceptions of this nature," Podmore thought. Then again, "There is no evidence of any weight that he was ever privately detected in trickery."

And so back and forth he went, twisting and turning, for and against; it was all too reminiscent of the SPR's reaction to Eusapia Palladino. Except that Home ended up with the edge in credibility. If, ultimately, Podmore could not provide an unqualified declaration in Home's favor, he was certain of the medium's importance. "With the marvels wrought through him or by him the main defenses of Spiritualism must stand or fall."

So far, the ism inadvertently brought to its feet by the Fox sisters was still standing.

More curious about Home than anyone else in the SPR was one of its future presidents. Because of a tragic experience in his own life, Sir William Crookes, a towering figure in the world of British science, was able to look at Home from a perspective that would elude that of either Podmore or Myers. Would his findings, too, be different?

When Crookes was thirty-seven, his brother Philip died at sea. Says Home biographer Gordon Stein, "William was quite close to Philip, and the possibility of contacting him 'in the spirit world' was a real motivation to try to apply the rigorous methods of the laboratory to spiritualist manifestations. Although Crookes's fellow scientists warned him that he would be ridiculed for examining spiritualism, Crookes persisted for nearly five years."

As a young man, Crookes had attended London's prestigious Royal College of Chemistry, where "[h]e had brilliant ideas--inspirations they might be called--and he worked them out systematically and pertinaciously." So says the foreword to Stein's biography, the author of which was Sir Oliver Lodge.

Among Crookes's brilliant ideas were "the invention of the eye-catching and puzzling radiometer in 1875, his brilliant experimental work on cathode rays using the eponymous Crookes tube in the 1870s, his dire prediction in 1898 that mankind would starve unless chemists worked out how to 'fix' the abundant supplies of nitrogen in the atmosphere."

And there was his belief in wireless telegraphy, and his pondering of what its waves might be able to carry.

Already a well-established figure in British science when he first met Home, Crookes was "a big man with narrow blue eyes in a narrow, high-cheek-boned face, a dark beard, and a splendidly imperious manner."

Previously, at the SPR's behest, he had looked into the phenomenon known as Kate Fox. "Like other investigators before him, Crookes marveled at Kate's versatility, her capacity, as he testified, to give a message via automatic writing to one person 'whilst a message to another person on another subject was being given alphabetically by means of "raps,"********** and the whole time she was conversing freely with a third person on a subject totally different from either.'"

Although Kate was partially retired when Crookes met her, and her reputation had long been clouded, Crookes became the most distinguished admirer she ever had. He not only saw her; he heard her rapping. Or heard Mr. Splitfoot rapping, if he was still in the Fox sister's employ at the time. "For power and certainty [of the sounds]," Crookes swore, he had "met with no one who at all approached Miss Kate Fox."

It was not a conclusion that enhanced Crookes's reputation among fellow academics.

Neither were his examinations of Home. Nonetheless, the scientist was as scientific as he could be in his methods. He began by refusing to come to Home's residence, insisting instead that Home come to his

---

********** There is some confusion in the various histories and biographies concerning Spiritualism about raps and controls. That is, when did the deceased communicate directly with mediums via raps, and when did they communicate with controls in some sort of verbal form, controls who then communicated with mediums verbally? Did controls ever rely on raps instead of words? Most people who have written about the format of séances do not seem certain, and thus do not make clear precisely how messages are being transmitted from nether realms to mortal habitats. It is a question that, try though I did, I was not been able to answer to my satisfaction, and so I have merely used the language I most often confronted in my readings. So be it. It is, again, the issue of means and ends, and it is the ends that in all cases remain the more important.

laboratory, where he, Crookes, could control the conditions. Further, he insisted that Home could not visit the lab in advance and survey the surroundings. The medium accepted both conditions.

On the appointed day, Home arrived at Crooke's workplace as if he hadn't a concern in the world. For him, it was just another researcher, just another demonstration.

Crookes began by testing his subject's power of telekinesis. One of the trials he devised was to ask Home "to stand by a mahogany board, set horizontally, but not to touch it. . . . To guard against cheating, Crookes asked volunteers to hold the medium's hands and feet.

"'Can you make it move?' Crookes then asked.

Child's play, Home must have thought. Crookes had "attached a measuring instrument to the board, so that each movement would be . . . scratched onto a smoked glass plate. Home stood silent, Crookes reported, just stood there, hands and feet held tightly, while the board rose and fell and the needle scratched a jagged line, peak after valley after peak, across the darkened glass."

Crookes and the volunteers who assisted him looked on in amazement. This was not science as they had ever witnessed it before, was not life on earth as they knew it.

But what they had seen so far were just the preliminaries. Now for levitation--the main event, the big test, what is called in magic "the prestige." Despite what he had just seen with the mahogany board, Crookes could not make himself believe that a human being could turn his back on gravity and drift himself upwards simply by deciding to do so. But what he was about to witness was just that. "On three separate occasions," Crookes later wrote, "have I seen him raised completely from the floor of the room, once sitting in an easy chair, once kneeling on his chair, and once standing up."

Crookes pleaded with Home for an explanation. How was he to describe to others what he had just witnessed without knowledge of how the feat had been accomplished? The medium thought it a reasonable question. He wanted to be helpful. But answering it was a feat *he* could not accomplish. He just *did* decide on raising his body and it *did* drift up. A feeble response, Home must have realized, but as far as he was concerned levitation was just an instinct, and instinct does not lend itself to the precision of words.

Crookes proceeded with his experiments. And he continued to be amazed, to become more and more a believer, something he would never previously have thought possible. Despite knowing full well what the response would be from his fellow academics, he made his conclusions known publicly. He ascribed the powers he had witnessed to a "psychic force" of some sort that Home was able to summon upon demand, despite his not knowing how. Further, Crookes testified, "of all persons endowed with a powerful development of this Psychic Force, Mr. Daniel Dunglas Home is the most remarkable." And further still, Crookes insisted that "no fact in sacred or profane history is supported by a stronger array of proofs."

And so Crookes found himself joining a small but growing group of SPR members who felt that the more they learned of Spiritualism, and the more they accepted what happened before their eyes, the less they knew. One thing he *did* know, however, was that having publicly validated Home, he would have to brace himself for the uproar.

And it could not have come more promptly or vituperatively. To paraphrase Winston Churchill at a later time and in a different context, was an indignity up with which British science would not put. An unsigned article in the establishment journal *Quarterly Review* acknowledged that Crookes had certain basic abilities, but that he was far from being an intellectual. Going on, the article stated, "We speak advisedly when we say that the Fellowship of the Royal Society was conferred upon him with considerable hesitation."

But this was not only irrelevant, a non-reply to Crooke's endorsement of the wizardry he had witnessed, it was untrue. As Deborah Blum points out, "Crookes, after he discovered thallium, had been elected as a fellow of the Royal Society *by unanimous vote* and, it had been noted at the time, *without debate.*" [Italics added.]

Other attacks followed and, like the preceding, they were directed more at the man than his findings. Eventually, Crookes came to believe that both he and his associates, a distinguished group, were being not merely criticized, but slandered. Among those associates was a renowned electrician who would later help to install the first trans-Atlantic cable, and would go on to build some of the instruments that Crookes used to ensure accuracy in his tests of Home.

> Enraged, Crookes stormed down to the [*Quarterly Review's*] offices, demanded a retraction, and demanded that the author be publicly identified. The editor of the journal refused, explaining that it wouldn't be fair to the reputation of the writer, although as Crookes couldn't help but notice, the *Review* seemed unconcerned with his own reputation.

In fact, the *Review* was guilty of what we would today call character assassination, a hatchet job. It was a blade wielded with the ferocity of wrath rather than the accuracy of informed dissent.

"The message seemed clear enough," Blum writes. "Investigating supernatural events was off limits to scientists, unless the findings proved fraud. Those who chose to ignore that rule--unspoken but strictly enforced--would find themselves off limits as well."

It took a long time for Crookes to cross back over those limits and regain his reputation. But so high had that reputation been, and so respected was he as both a scientist and a man, that he did more than merely regain his previous standing, he enhanced it: receiving numerous awards, numerous requests to speak at academic convocations, numerous queries about what he was learning from his various academic fields of pursuit. Banquets were held in his honor, speeches made on his behalf, memberships bestowed in various honorary societies. It was during this period that he received his knighthood and, most notably, almost three decades after swearing to Home's paranormal abilities, he was elected to the presidency of the British Association for the Advancement of Science. He accepted the position gratefully and humbly, yet made it known that, though he still considered himself a scientist of conventional training and methods, his support of telekinesis was unshaken, as was his belief in telepathy and levitation. In fact, he now even accepted "the possibility that the dead might return."

Given the lingering animosity between science and supernaturalism, it is hard to imagine Crookes's being so grandly forgiven. One day's vilification became a later day's deification. Crookes was not merely surprised by the change in his standing; he was overwhelmed. Yet for a reason that he could not understand, he continued to feel the aching that had drawn him to psychic study in the first place, for despite all the time he had devoted to the subject, all the inroads he believed he had made into matters otherworldly, he had never heard from his brother. His brother Philip remained everlastingly silent.

It is not surprising, with all the attention Home was receiving, that "the calls upon him for séances were innumerable." Countless men and women on both sides of the Atlantic remained spellbound by his mystical feats. "Outwardly a lovable character with a magnetic personality and a great fondness for children; suave, captivating to the last degree . . . he made his way easily and found favor with many who would have spurned him under other conditions . . ."

But it was impossible for him to accept all of the invitations he received, even though some came from Far Eastern emperors, Middle Eastern potentates, and wealthy Europeans and Americans who were willing to travel any distance for the privilege of falling under his spell for a night. It is important to note, however, that even at the peak of his renown, Home remained modest about his abilities and, in addition, became as skeptical of most psychics as the majority of scientists were of him. There were far more corrupt mediums than honest ones, Home believed, and those who conducted their séances in darkness, which was most of them, were likely to fall into the former category. "Light should be the demand of every spiritualist," he wrote in 1876. "By no other [tests] are scientific inquirers to be convinced. Where there is darkness there is the possibility of imposture and the certainty of suspicion." Home might have started out in dimly-lit surroundings--it is not certain--but, as he entered his maturity, virtually all of his séances were well-illuminated.

But the older he grew, the fewer he held. Instead, he began to devote more time to his legacy, writing a two-volume biography called *Incidents in my Life*. It was derided by most journalistic outlets, but not all. London's *Morning Herald*, a respectable enough newspaper of the time, said, "The matter has grown too great for laughter." And the *Spectator* provided the following summation: "The facts of this book, whether facts or not, all drive at our conclusion, that the gates between the world of the living and the departed are always open."

Daniel Dunglas Home was, for his time, a rock star sans music. But his time was growing short, and he knew it.

By the time the reviews of his book appeared, Home had been living with the symptoms of tuberculosis for most of his life. He could not do so much longer. He now breathed less easily than he used to, punctuated his conversations with deep, ratcheting coughs, and became so pale as to seem at times a spectre.

In 1884, with but two years left to him, he predicted the course of his demise to his second wife. According to biographer Elizabeth Jenkins, he warned his spouse "that he had been told that his illness was approaching its term and that the end would be long drawn out and painful, though death would come without a pang. The prophecy was only too true. With short intermissions, the rending pain in his lungs made him suffer 'long and cruelly.'"

His suffering ended on June 21, 1886, in Paris. He was thirty-eight years old.

Perhaps *The Dictionary of National Biography*, the most prestigious publication of its kind in Britain, does best at describing this man whose life was too convoluted for a facile obituary, even a lengthy one, which more than likely would have been a tangled web of prose arriving at contradictory conclusions. Home, stated the *Dictionary*, is "a curious and as yet unsolved problem."

The preceding was written a century ago. Daniel Dunglas Home has still not been solved.

Chapter 9

THE CENSUS
OF HALLUCINATIONS

Hallucination.

It is an important word in this book, a few times stated, but implied or suspected numerous other times. Does it explain what so many people believed they saw at Eusapia Palladino's séances, or at the royal residences where Daniel Dunglas Home startled regal presences, so many occasions when the world seemed to tip off its axis? Would a person have to be hallucinating to believe that he had seen a human being levitate, elongate, grow an extra arm, recline on the air as if on a couch, immerse his hand in flames with no sign of discomfort-- and, of course, communicate with the dead?

It might seem so. After all, hallucination has "an alarming sound" to it, as Frank Podmore once said. But is in fact such a general term, such an all-purpose word, that it is capable of being applied to a variety of circumstances, both specific and general, and therefore not particularly helpful. "Its original meaning" wrote Podmore, "is simply wandering in mind, or dreaminess, what would technically be called slight disso-ciation of consciousness."

However, my old copy of *The Random House Dictionary of the English Language* is more precise when it says, in the first of its definitions, that a hallucination is a sensory experience that does not exist except in the mind, and is caused by various physical and mental disorders, or by reaction to toxic substances.

Precise, yes--but again, in the present context, not really relevant. Were the men and women who saw Home's miracles physically dis-ordered? Mentally disordered? Were they overdosing on opium or morphine? Perhaps a few, but not enough to matter.

In its third definition, the *Random House Dictionary* gets even more precise, calling a hallucination a false impression, an illusion, a delusion. These are also general terms, but more plausible to consider now. Still, how does one account for all that has appeared so far in this book? And how is it that so many men and women got the same impression, illusion or delusion, at the same time? They were differ-ent people, from different places, different backgrounds; if they were hallucinating, wouldn't there have been some variety in what they thought they had seen?

So much time has passed; so much remains to be explained; so many attempts to do so have been found wanting . . .

In 1894, six years after Home's death and only partially in response to his life, the Society for Psychical Research finished its most sweeping project ever. To prepare its *Census of Hallucinations*, five years in the making, the SPR placed ads in various London newspapers, seeking people who claimed to have had psychic experiences of one sort or another. Seventeen thousand people responded. The Society's previous magnum opus, *Phantasms of the Living*, which saw the light of day in 1886, was based on a mere seven hundred "cases of apparitions."

Nora Sidgwick, the wife of Henry, who was thought by some to be the brightest of all the lights in the SPR, supervised work on the *Census*. She found that the majority of the 17,000 respondents belonged to "the middle and upper classes. Their social, educational and religious experiences undoubtedly shaped their views on the nature of ghosts, and consequently how and why they were thought to manifest themselves."

It was Oliver Lodge who wrote the foreword to the *Census of Hallucinations* and, as he and others had done before, sounded eminently sensible in pleading for a bridge between science and the supernatural. "It is a most unpardonable blunder," he wrote, "for a scientific man to suppose that everything that can be known is already more or less within his cognizance; and his least justifiable attitude is that which holds that there are certain departments of truth in the universe which it is not lawful to investigate."

Many of the incidents published in the *Census* are similar to incidents already cited in this volume. Think of the adolescent Home, whose friend Edwin appeared at the foot of the boy medium's bed in "a cloud of brightness," visually announcing his death. Think of Henry Clemens, who appeared before his sleeping brother in a casket. About cases like these, the *Census* states that

> the distance between the two persons concerned is often so
> great that if *any* causal connexion can be established between
> a particular experience of one mind and the corresponding
> experience of another--say, between the death of A. in Eng-
> land, and the apparition of A. to B. in Australia--there will
> be no dispute that the causation lies outside the ordinary
> channels of sense.

What the preceding makes clear is that the Society for Psychic
Research is not defining hallucination as did my dictionary, which I
suspect is how most people would define the term if asked. The SPR
proceeded under the assumption that hallucinations are not so much
illusory as "outside the ordinary channels of sense." Which is to say, one
does not have to be hallucinating to have a so-called hallucination, for
the occurrences that are imagined might not be imaginary at all. They
might actually have happened, but for reasons unclear, did not occur on
the ordinary routes along which most of our perceptions travel.

The SPR did not limit its search for information in the *Census* to
England. It also published notices in newspapers in the United States,
Germany, France, Russia and Brazil. The data it gathered suggested a
dissertation on mathematics more than on paranormality.

The American Society for Psychical Research conducted an identical survey of its own and found that people reported seeing apparitions
"at 487 times the rate predicted by chance. The British calculation was
442.6 times chance." How one can predict the frequency of apparitions, the appearance of which no one can predict, is a mystery to me,
but making that determination signaled the beginning of work on the
Census.

Using figures from the British government, Nora Sidgwick went
on to calculate that the odds of a person dying on a particular day were
one in 19,000. Then she determined that "the possibility of a given
single event, such as a recognizable 'hallucination' of a certain person,

occurring on that same day was also one in 19,000. So for every 19,000 deaths, there should be only one such occurrence."

Sidgwick and her co-workers continued moving further and further from the grasp of the layman: Of the 17,000 people who had contacted the SPR, 2,272 declared that they had seen the ghost of a friend or loved one at the approximate time of his death. These 2,272 responses were the only ones that interested the SPR, which is to say that the vast majority of the questionnaires, almost 15,000 of them, were thrown out; the SPR focused only on hallucinations involving interaction between the living and the dead. And most of *these* supposedly appropriate responses would end up being excluded from the final *Census*.

The process was an exhaustive one. The group began by discarding all statements that referred to apparitions appearing in dreams; this was not a substantive enough occurrence for Sidgwick and her colleagues. So, from 2,272, the number of cases that the SPR found worthy of serious consideration was sliced down to about 1,300. Then more slicing, as another exacting standard was imposed; the sightings of apparitions had to have occurred within twelve hours of the death of the person in question. Otherwise, Mrs. Sidgwick believed, the memories of those who claimed to have seen the ghosts might have grown faulty, or perhaps too imaginative.

The next cut eliminated "cases in which there was a chance of prior knowledge of when the death was expected, such as that of an elderly or ailing relative. Then they [the SPR] removed from their list any ghost story that relied on only one person's claim." This last excision might have been the most important of all. The *Census* takers were insisting on verification of the ghost's appearance by more than one person. Whether inadvertently or not, they were applying a fundamental principle of good journalism to good supernatural exploration: never publish a story unless you have two or more sources to confirm it.

The result of this final paring down of the initial 17,000 responses was that thirty-two incidents remained, a mere .0019 percent of the original total. But, as it turns out, that number was not "mere" at all.

At a rate of 1 out of 19,000, they should have seen .0723 instances among the 17,000 surveyed. Instead, they had 32 cases with solid evidence behind them, which was 442.6 times the chance rate of .0723.

Assuming a person can understand the preceding mathematical complexities, it is a surprising conclusion. And the survey conducted in the United States, where the ASPR applied the same methodology to study more than seven thousand respondents, produced virtually identical results. The two censuses suggest, to put it in its simplest terms, is that not all so-called hallucinations can be dismissed as unreal. At the very least, they must be regarded as real enough to justify the rationale behind the two SPRs, that what science cannot understand, science should investigate, not disregard.

The most thorough and bizarrely intrusive investigation ever undertaken by the SPRs had, at this time, just entered its earliest stages. Its subject was as unlike Daniel Dunglas Home as a psychic could be.

Chapter 10

JUST PLAIN MRS. PIPER

It all started one afternoon when she was eight years old, playing in the garden of her home in Nashua, New Hampshire, finding pleasure in the simplest of activities. It was her way. For one thing, she scoured the ground for acorns, and when she found them she dropped them through a hole in the wicker seat of one of the family's patio chairs; she might, in fact, have cut the hole herself, just for that purpose. Then she picked up the acorns from the ground and dropped them through again. And again. That was all. Simple pleasures get no simpler than this; for some reason, the girl took comfort in the motions, the repetitiveness of them, and especially in partaking of them alone. She enjoyed the feel of the sunshine on her face. And she thought whatever random thoughts eight-year-old girls think.

Suddenly, according to several accounts, little Leonora Symonds's world changed forever. She felt a pain on the right side of her head. Something had hit her: a rock, a fist, a piece of lumber--who knew? She cried out in pain, her eyes watering, and looked around. But she didn't see a thing. Her ear and cheekbone had begun to throb, but saw nothing, no object that could have struck her. She rubbed her face lightly, more puzzled and frightened than she had ever been in her young life.

At the same moment, as one of her daughters would pick up the story many years afterward, she heard "a prolonged sibilent [sic] sound. This gradually resolved itself into the letter S, which was then followed by the words, 'Aunt Sara, not dead but with you still.'" The little girl looked around again; just as there was nothing that could have hit her moments ago, there was no person nearby who could have spoken to her now. Still crying, she ran into her house, "holding on to the side of her head," and told her mother what had happened. Mrs. Symonds did not know what to make of it, but obviously her daughter was troubled, and in need of comfort. The woman who had given her birth would provide it as best she could. But both of them were puzzled, and about to be more so.

A few days later, the family received a message. It seemed that in "a distant part of the country . . . at the very hour and on the very day of her little daughter's strange experience, her mother's sister, 'Aunt Sara,' had passed out of the body suddenly and unexpectedly." In other words, she had died, and some kind of mysterious force had notified her niece at the precise moment of her aunt's departure. The child and her parents were startled. It must have been a coincidence, they thought--a bizarre one, but a coincidence nonetheless.

Soon a few of the people who lived nearby learned about the incident and, startled in their own way, could not help but wonder. If little Leonora had really heard what she said she had heard, and if she had an Aunt Sara who died at the same instant, it seemed like more than a coincidence. It seemed more ominous than that. The Symonds's had always fit into the neighborhood so well, seeming to be good people, normal and decent. But now it appeared that there might be something unusual about the little girl, even worrisome. Gossip started and spread quickly.

The child's mother and father were upset. They would not let their daughter be tormented by "the whispering voices or the whispering neighbors. There were children celebrated for psychic gifts; the notorious Fox sisters came to mind."

But the Foxes had been driven out of town. Leonora's parents would not let anything like that happen to them. They were certain that their little girl was not "such a freak. They put the eerie little moment behind them and raised their daughter as an upright member of the Methodist Church."

And so she would always be.

As a student, Leonora excelled in most of her subjects, "which in those days consisted chiefly of the three 'Rs,' spelling, geography, history and grammar." Her specialty was spelling; when classroom competitions were held, it was said that she simply "spelt the others down." When not in the classroom, Leonora was a playfully energetic girl, often the ringleader of a gang of six when they were engaged in their most mischievous activities. Her daughter's biography, however, does not tell us what those activities were, although it is fair to assume that the girls practiced mischief in its mildest forms.

But Leonora had that other side to her as well, a need for quiet moments, for concentration, reflection; when not idly dropping acorns through a chair, she often took to her needlepoint, at which she grew to excel in her teens. She was good at her work, and some of it lasted for more than half a century, eventually being made into baby clothes for her grandchildren.

It was, to all appearances, the most typical of childhoods for the time, with the exception of that single, inexplicable blip in the garden.

Then, when she was sixteen, Leonora was again victimized, and this time there was no mystery about it. It was winter, and she was playing in a deep New Hampshire snowdrift when another child's sled crashed into her leg, injuring her knee. Although she did not know it at first, the accident had also damaged her abdomen, causing her to bleed internally. No surgery was performed, but the impact created a dull ache across Leonora's midsection, one that would be with her, apparently, at least until her first child was born.************ At that point the pain became more pronounced than dull; at times after Alta's birth, her mother's distress left her virtually immobile. A year later, an abdominal tumor was discovered and "continued to make Mrs. Piper's health rather precarious for a long time." Finally, she consented to an operation, a procedure called a laparotomy, which finally eliminated her discomfort.

Except for her knee. There, the sled had done irreparable damage, leaving her with a slight limp for the rest of her days.

The Foxes' headaches, Eusapia's cranial malformation, Home's tuberculosis, and now this.

************ At the age of twenty-two, Leonora Symonds had married a Bostonian shopkeeper of modest means named William Piper. The Pipers had two children, both girls, with Alta preceding Minerva by a year.

Leonora could not understand why the pain in her abdomen had been so much greater after Alta's birth than before. Neither could her husband, nor the battalion of doctors the Pipers consulted before yielding to the laparotomy. Finally, in desperation, shortly before the surgery, Leonora struck out on her own, finding a clairvoyant about whom she had heard. He was a blind man with an almost frighteningly preternatural reputation, and just his touch made the young mother dizzy. There was something about him, something she could not have explained; the moment she met him, Leonora later stated, she lost control of her conscious self. After talking to the blind man for several minutes, she picked up a pencil and scribbled a few words on a sheet of paper. But was it really she who originated the words? The blind man said no. He picked up the paper, stared at it for a few seconds, and said in as calm a voice as he could manage that it was a message from his son. His dead son. History has not preserved its contents, but Leonora told friends that the man called the note "the most remarkable I ever received."

As a result of this and other visits to the clairvoyant, none of which addressed the problem of her aching midsection but all of which produced a show of paranormal aptitude on Leonora's part, "she found that she was becoming the attraction," a junior clairvoyant herself, gradually upstaging the blind man, to whom she also became an object of attraction. Even awe. So much so that he was not for a moment envious of the modest, young white woman. He would be satisfied in the role of mentor. Young Leonora would be his protégé.

At first, she was intrigued by the notion. But her interest quickly faded. She did not want to be a psychic; she wanted to be a housewife and mother, ordinary and respectable and anonymous. Soon she was expecting her second child, all the more reason for her to eschew supernatural tendencies. According to a description of her in 1885, her twenty-sixth year, "she was slightly chubby, neatly dressed, her light brown hair caught carefully up into middle-class respectability. The

Pipers were middle-class respectable. . . . [They] lived with [William's] parents in a tidy house in the Beacon Hill neighborhood" of Boston.*

But Leonora would not be a housewife and mother as often as she wanted to be. And although she would always be respectable, she would not be ordinary and anonymous at all.

Alta wrote the biography to which I referred a few paragraphs earlier and upon which I will continue to rely for certain information in this and following chapters. In the foreword, there appeared the following sentence: "About Mrs. Piper's gifts there is no sort of doubt." It was further stated that her gifts were "unrecognized by orthodox psychology, something which badly needed exploration and elucidation." And it was claimed that "[t]he facts are too strong much longer to be resisted."

It is quite an endorsement. But hardly unexpected. The foreword was written by Sir Oliver Lodge, who seemed to be making an avocation of such encomiums.

Eventually, Mrs. Piper (for that is how she was known to all but her closest friends, seldom by her first name) began to think that her gifts, if Lodge was right and they were truly that, had been given to her service by the Christian God in which she so strongly believed. If that was true, she must not only accept them, but put them to use in the service of her fellow man. Still, it was a difficult decision for her to make. She did not want to be special, to stand out in the crowd that was humanity. But she did. She had been chosen. She had no say in the matter, she decided, other than to accept the responsibilities that accompanied her psychic skill.

One of her first sittings after reaching this conclusion was with a Boston widow named Eliza Gibbens. Like Daniel Dunglas Home, she did not accept money from Mrs. Gibbens, nor did she ever want to accept either money or material goods for her services, "preferring," as Alta wrote, "to devote her time and power to the interests of science rather than to private exploitation." And, of course, to serve her Lord.

Eventually, though, Mrs. Piper found the demand for her services to be so great, and to be taking up so much of her time, that she decided to charge a modest fee. Her husband William was not a wealthy man; the extra money would certainly help his shop remain solvent. But even with the strength of her faith supporting her, she struggled with her decision. She did not want her séances to become commercial enterprises, no matter what the reason. She was not entirely comfortable with them under any circumstances. According to William, she was "bashful" about falling into a trance before others, and did not like the idea of others seeing her in such a condition. It was as if they were spying on her sleeping.

At any rate, Mrs. Gibbens was herself bashful about seeing Mrs. Piper. She did not believe in paranormal experiences, thought the very notion of them antithetical to her religious upbringing. But, at the urging of friends, and especially her husband, she overcame her reluctance, and arranged for a sitting. She was immediately pleased with her decision. From the moment she met the unpretentious woman across the table from her she felt at ease, and after a few minutes of small talk, began to reveal more and more of herself. Mrs. Piper responded when appropriate, and when she did Mrs. Gibbens was amazed. She referred to "the knowledge of which on [Mrs. Piper's] part was incomprehensible without supernormal powers."

For instance, that morning Mrs. Gibbens had spent an hour or two looking for her bankbook. She couldn't find it. She mentioned this to Mrs. Piper. After returning home, Alta swears, Mrs. Gibbens found the bankbook precisely where her mother had said it would be.

So impressed was Mrs. Gibbens that she made an appointment for her daughter, Margaret, to see Mrs. Piper the following day. But so wary was Mrs. Gibbens that she set a trap. She wrote a letter and gave it to Margaret in a sealed envelope, which she slipped into her purse. As the séance began, Margaret gave the envelope to the medium. But she told her not to open it. Nor did Margaret reveal to her anything about the contents of the letter. She was not interested in such details; rather,

Margaret wanted to know something about the person who had written the missive.

> Reading sealed letters was an easy trick for mediums of the day. They could conceal an alcohol-soaked sponge in a hand or sleeve and surreptitiously soak the paper with it, rendering it transparent--and decipherable--until the alcohol evaporated. They had only to briefly distract the visitor until they could return the envelope and reveal its contents.

Mrs. Piper was fortunate that, in this case, her sitter did not want the contents to be revealed. If she had, the medium might have been stumped, for it was written in Italian. The medium knew not so much as a word of the language.

But she divined that the words *were* Italian. She divined that the correspondent was herself Italian, although she now lived in the United States. She also divined, and revealed, something of the woman's habits, of her likes and dislikes, of her friends and the activities in which they mutually engaged. To Margaret Gibbens she told all of this, then returned the letter to her, still sealed, no tampering having occurred.

It was an extraordinary performance, and the one that would, in time, lead her to the world's attention. For Margaret's mother, Mrs. Eliza Gibbens, was also the mother of Alice Gibbens, and Alice was none other than Mrs. William James. As a result, James himself soon paid a call on Mrs. Piper, his first impression being that she was "a simple, genuine, unassuming Yankee girl."

The scholar was immediately drawn to her. But her manner was one thing, a dignity that he was unaccustomed to finding in a medium. But her knowledge of the James family tree was something else entirely, bewildering in its accuracy--even, it seems, to Mrs. Piper herself, who "became increasingly uneasy" as she recited name after name, and fact after fact about James's relatives. For instance, "she mentioned the recent loss of James's waistcoat . . . and she described in detail the death throes of a cat that James had killed with ether." She also knew the nickname by which the family called their second son in the nursery, and only in the nursery.

The session continued. At one point, Mrs. Piper hesitantly said something about a dead child. James's third son, Herman, had passed away two months earlier.

"The medium showed a most startling intimacy with this family's affairs," James said, after the séance ended, "talking of many matters known to no one outside, and which *gossip* could not possibly conveyed to her ears. . . . My own conviction is not evidence, but it seems fitting to record it. I am persuaded of the medium's honesty, and of the genuineness of her trance; and although at first disposed to think that the 'hits' she made were either lucky coincidences, or the results of knowledge on her part of who the sitter was and of his or her family affairs, I now believe her to be in possession of a power as yet unexplained."

To Mrs. Piper's annoyance, which seemed to be growing at the same pace as her reputation, James arranged for other members of the ASPR to attend future sittings; they were just as amazed by what they witnessed as William had been. And, after exposure to others they had probed, the psychic researchers had finally found a subject who seemed, all things considered, normal, a woman whose character was beyond reproach, whose demeanor put those around her at ease. They had found someone, in other words, in whom they felt safe in believing, and for many members of the ASPR this was a turning point.

The problem was that Mrs. Piper treasured her privacy as an antiquarian treasures his first editions; she never sought the fame that James inadvertently helped to bestow on her. In fact, when he told her that he was reporting on her for the *Proceedings of the American Society for Psychical Research*, she asked for at least partial anonymity. He agreed, and referred to her only as Mrs. P. Even that was more than she wanted.

It was solely by continuing to believe that she was doing work that was inspired from above that Mrs. Piper was able to continue as a medium. She held séances both with and without ASPR observation, and her sitters found that her presence "could be a heady experience, leaving one overconfident of opening the doors to immortality." In large part, Mrs. Piper believed, this was due to the control with whom she had recently begun to collaborate. No longer a solo act, she had become such a strong believer in controls that she took them on as avidly as a foster mother opens her heart to waifs. Unfortunately, controversy promptly ensued.

The collaborator with whom she first shared her practice, and the praise it evoked, was a French physician who, so the story goes, had died of leprosy twenty-five years earlier. She pronounced his name "Finney," like the man who had named the "Burned-over District." Another French doctor of approximately the same bygone time had also pronounced his name "Finney," although it was spelled "Finett." But Mrs. Piper insisted that her control's name, its pronunciation not-withstanding, was spelled P-H-I-N-U-I-T, and further claimed that she had reached a point at which she could do nothing without him. Many in both SPRs were surprised, her normality being such that she did not seem to need a spectral assistant. Perhaps she had begun to feel too overwhelmed by her success to carry on alone. Perhaps she wanted someone to distract attention from her. Or perhaps she just felt the need of a companion, like the imaginary friends with whom so many of us have played as children.

Regardless, Mrs. Piper's sitters had no initial reason to doubt Phinuit's existence. Sometimes they declared that they could sense his presence at séances, actually feel his breath on the backs of their necks or his hands on their shoulders. But he was not always that subtle. "[He] was opinionated and vociferous," says James biographer Linda Simon, and "while Mrs. Piper's memory seemed unremarkable, Phinuit could recall minute details of his encounters with sitters. Moreover, besides relaying trivial and mundane messages from the dead to their living relatives, Phinuit gave pointed moral lectures with an arrogance and psychological insight that, James said, Mrs. Piper could never match."

It sounds convincing enough by the standards of the paranormal--if, in fact, there are such things. But Phinuit, it turned out, was a phony--his name, at least, if not his talents--and he would eventually be exposed. The first clue to his mock identity was that he spoke a pidgin variety of French, leading members of the ASPR to wonder why he was not more skilled at his native tongue. Investigators began looking into Phinuit's background, and it did not take long for them to "discover that no such person had lived at the time and in the place that [Mrs. Piper] claimed he had done, [and when confronted with this information] the spirit confessed [through Mrs. Piper] that his name was not Phinuit but 'Scliville,' though he seemed uncertain about that, too. Why he should claim to be someone he was not is difficult to understand, unless he was a fabrication of the medium's mind." And Mrs. Piper hardly seems the type who would engage in fabrication of any sort.

Regardless, the Phinuit or Scliville "scandal" raises an important, previously raised issue in the complicated world of otherworldliness. Was this revelation of a control's falsified identity really an expose [accent over second "e"] of a medium's methods, as some people thought? *Why?* What difference did it make what Mrs. Piper called her invisible assistant? What should have concerned the SPRs and others who now called her into question was neither the name nor background of the control but the precision of his powers. Did he provide his medium with accurate information? (If, in truth, the information *was* provided by the control and not the medium.) I repeat: means and ends, means and ends. Ultimately, quibbling about the name, or even the existence, of a control makes no more sense than scouring British orphanages for the records of Oliver Twist.

After Phinuit's, or Scliville's, outing, teapot tempest though it was in reality, Mrs. Piper announced that she had replaced him with a more mundane-sounding fellow named George Pellew, although nobody could figure out who *he* was, either--and Mrs. Piper provided no clues. She simply allowed the parade to go on: At various other times, she is said to have employed as controls a young Indian girl named Chlorine, followed by a roster of celebrities that included "Martin Luther, Commodore Cornelius Vanderbilt, Henry Longfellow, George Washington, Lincoln, J. Sebastian Bach, English actress Sara Siddons, and Loretta Pachini, a young Italian," allowing none of these once famous people to continue resting in peace. Surely a woman as benign, even shy, in her manner as Mrs. Piper could not have been so tyrannical a boss as to fire her controls at a whim. Regardless, this muddle about the names of her controls makes one believe that there was a glitch in the lady's respectability after all.⁕⁕⁕⁕⁕⁕⁕⁕

Eventually the name Rector would be added to the list of her associates, and after that would come the most unlikely fellow of all.

But most of Phinuit's successors did not always serve their mistress in the same manner that he had. Often they whispered to Mrs. Piper, and she took dictation from them in the form of automatic writing. She placed a sheet of paper before herself. Then the control handed her a pencil, "placing it between the fore and middle fingers; it was at once grasped, and writing began." Her sitters did not see her receive the pencil, nor did they see or hear the control whispering as he or she told her what to transcribe. When she completed the message, she passed it to the appropriate sitter, and the sitter and Mrs. Piper talked briefly about its contents.

It was, in its way, a fitting process, reminiscent of her first day as an official medium, when she wrote the note for the blind man, ostensibly recited to her by his son.

Mrs. Piper was one of the few clairvoyants to describe what it was like to sink into a trance. To the researchers in New York and London, it was fascinating information.

⁕⁕⁕⁕⁕⁕⁕⁕ It is not certain, but Phinuit seems to have been the control who stayed longest with Mrs. Piper, not departing from her service until she traveled to London. Most of the others came and went quickly.

I feel as if something were passing over my brain, making it numb; a sensation similar to that I experienced when I was etherized, only the unpleasant odour is absent. I feel a little cold, too . . . and people and objects become smaller until they finally disappear; then I know nothing more until I wake up, when the first thing I am conscious of is a bright, very very bright light, and then darkness, such darkness. My hands and arms begin to tingle.

But then, said Alta Piper about her mother, "she always resumes the conversation at that point where it was broken off before the sitting began."

What Mrs. Piper did not mention about her trance states was that she seldom returned from them empty-handed. Usually--and, one assumes, courtesy of her controls--she would bring her sitters an aphorism or two from the other side. It was always in a Biblical tongue, always providing a fine Christian moral. Among them:

"Be more passive, living in the faith that nothing of wrong can come to thee . . ."

"Know and understand thyself in all things and become stout-hearted, brave and noble . . ."

"We would have thee read good books; go out for open fresh air; bathe in the sunlight of thine earthly world which God hath given thee to enjoy."

"Always think before thou dost give expression to thy thoughts . . ."

"Throw thy pride to the winds and have Charity."

"Live simply, humbly, peacefully with God . . ."

A sermon and a séance, each a communication from a different sector of the afterlife. Two for the price of one.

William James investigated Mrs. Piper for eighteen months. He was both confused and disappointed by the controversy about her controls' names, wondering how she had allowed herself to sink into such a pointless mire. But he never lost faith in her honesty. If she were going to lie, he reasoned, surely she would have chosen a more important matter than the name of her go-between. He simply dismissed the subject from his eventual evaluation of her, declaring himself "as absolutely certain as I am of any personal fact in the world that she knows things in her trances which she cannot possible have heard in her waking state, and that the definite philosophy of her trances is yet to be found." Usually a cautious man, James knew it was not a cautious statement. He knew a thunderstorm of criticism would rain down on him. So he took cover before he could be drenched.

After the eighteen months had passed, he recused himself from further involvement with Mrs. Piper. In fact, he recommended that no members of the ASPR should involve themselves with her any longer, proposing instead that its sister group invite her to London for more study, starting from scratch. The SPR eagerly agreed, and it was Richard Hodgson who sent a formal invitation. When Mrs. Piper received it, she

> was not only amazed but greatly perturbed as well. What *could* these investigators be thinking about? Did they really . . . expect her to leave her husband and two little children and travel three thousand miles across the Atlantic Ocean merely for further probing, and testing, and experiments? Surely this was more than could legitimately be expected of her! And, yet, what if she refused? What construction would be put upon such a decision were she to make it?

Of course, she had already put a construction on her tasks. She was a humble disciple doing her Master's work--demanding work, to be sure, and work she would not continue to do forever. *Could* not do forever. But now was not the time to cease, and not just because she still thought of herself as a missionary whose mission was unfinished. There were practical considerations as well. Mrs. Piper had never been abroad. Perhaps she would never have the opportunity again. The SPR was offering to assume all expenses for the trip, including food and lodging, and not only for herself, but also for her two daughters. William would stay home and tend to matters at the shop.

The Piper ladies departed late in the autumn of 1899--Leonora, Alta and Minerva sailing to England, both excited and apprehensive about a series of sittings and experiments that had been arranged by the SPR at Cambridge.

By the time they arrived, Mrs. Piper had grown into a proper middle age, where she always seemed to have belonged. The photograph Alta included as her biography's frontispiece shows her mother's expression to be more stern than her manner. Her hair has been cut short and is neatly combed; her nose sharply bisects her face; and her gaze is both alert and somehow dissatisfied.

She has clothed herself dowdily, in appropriate Victorian style, but allows the accessory of a necklace, although it seems more plain than showy. A shawl is draped over her shoulders. Which is all to say that her photograph reveals a woman who neither looks nor acts as if she possesses supernatural abilities. In a field of prima donnas, she stood out no more than a member of the chorus. As far as her appearance was concerned, that is. Her abilities, however, put her at center stage.

Frederic Myers met her and her daughters in Liverpool, and "the sober little American medium stirred in him a sensation like the rising warmth of a hot-air balloon. He defined the feeling as hope." The reference to a hot-air balloon seems to be purely coincidental.

Off to Cambridge the foursome went, where they met Hodgson, who had arranged the séances. He was surely congenial with Mrs. Piper, but it is hard to believe, even at the start, that he did not look at her through dubious eyes. Despite his previous conversion to the ranks of Eusapia and Daniel Dunglas Home supporters, he retained his reputation as the SPR's leading "fraud-buster," and without even meeting Mrs. Piper he "refused to accept that it was spirits of the dead who were communicating through her." Even Sir Arthur Conan Doyle feared that Hodgson would somehow sunder Mrs. Piper's reputation, believing him to be "the greatest detective who ever put his mind to this subject."

It is questionable, then, how much ease Mrs. Piper could have felt in Hodgson's company, especially since he was "a big, burly, vigorous man with a fresh, ruddy face and a shock of sandy brown hair. . . . He hoped, eventually to hear and learn from nature as [his favorite poet] Wordsworth did. In fact, he scheduled time for it in his daily plans. Hodgson was . . . ever disciplined in his habits, always determined in approaching his goals."

For now, though, his goal did not involve learning from nature, but from what was ostensibly the *super*natural.

Sir Oliver Lodge, on the other hand, was of quite a different opinion from Hodgson. Shortly after Mrs. Piper's arrival, he persuaded a friend of his, a physician, to attend one of her Cambridge sessions. He agreed, but grudgingly. He told Lodge that he "would do nothing helpful, not say one word to this so-called medium. He would give the same response to anything she said--correct or incorrect. He planned to do nothing but grunt."

Phinuit was still employed as Mrs. Piper's aide-de-camp at the time, at least he seems to have been, and although neither he nor his boss had the slightest idea who Lodge's doctor friend was, or that he would even be attending on this particular night, Phinuit knew the man had four children. One was a thirteen-year girl to whom the control referred to as a "little daisy." But to the family's sorrow, the girl had a mark over one eye and was to a degree crippled, having difficulty walking.

Changing the subject to the doctor himself, Phinuit sympathized with him for occasionally being plagued by indigestion. He commended him for medicating himself with glasses of hot water.

Shortly afterward, the physician departed from the séance in a huff. Lodge followed, and later elicited from him an angry confession that everything Phinuit had told him was true. Well, not every detail--but close enough. For instance, although Little Daisy did have a scar over her left eye from an accident as an infant, she was not crippled.

Still, the physician, perturbed that his previous dubiety had been so effectively challenged, decided to visit Mrs. Piper a second time. It was then that he became a true, if unwilling, convert. No sooner had the gentleman seated himself and the medium descended into her trance than Phinuit's voice filled the room. He had made some mistakes at the prior session, he said, and was glad to have the chance to rectify them. It was not Daisy who struggled to walk; it was one of her friends. But Daisy had problems of her own, having lost her hearing after a severe fever a few years earlier.

Phinuit still hadn't gotten it all right. But he was willing to correct himself about Daisy, and had been man enough to offer an apology in the first place--and this was all the doctor needed to hear. He virtually leapt out of his chair and bounded away from the sitting, fearful that there might be an even more piercing accuracy to what the control said next. As for Lodge, he said, "I have satisfied myself that much of the information she possesses in the trance state is not acquired by ordinary commonplace methods, but that she has some unusual means of acquiring information."

But what *was* that means? To Myers, Lodge rejected the suggestion that she had some unusual means of acquiring information, something perhaps like a telegraph line to the spirit world. Rather, Lodge believed, Mrs. Piper was more likely a gifted telepath, somehow attuned to faint stirrings in the air, little puffs of arcane knowledge, invisible waves passing through the air between medium and sitter. It was a foreshadowing of what Thomas Edison would later say to Guglielmo Marconi, a statement that would have unforeseen repercussions for both of them.

At any rate, Myers notwithstanding, Mrs. Piper was off to an impressive start among the British.

The SPR began its lengthy series of tests on her--Mrs. Piper found them interminable--by examining her psychometric abilities. Lodge had an uncle named Robert, who lived in London, and Robert had a twin brother who had died twenty years earlier. At Oliver's request, Robert provided "a curious old gold watch" from his late brother that he had kept all this time. Lodge gave it to Mrs. Piper and she began to examine it without looking, as if, sightless, she were reading an inscription in Braille. Then the room was filled with the "rumbling Phinuit voice, declaring that . . .

- The watch's owner was an uncle of Lodge.
- His name was Jerry.
- Jerry had been close to his twin.
- His twin was named Robert.
- But Robert had never killed a cat for a childhood lark, whereas Jerry once did so.
- Two of Jerry's most cherished boyhood possessions were a small rifle and a snakeskin.
- The brothers swam in a creek together and one afternoon almost drowned.

All correct, every last bit of it, down to the swimming incident, which the boys had kept a secret in their early years, because they feared that if word of their misadventures got back to their parents, they would be punished.

It was almost too much, even for Lodge. So, although apparently with a certain half-heartedness, he decided to play the unaccustomed role of devil's advocate. At his own expense, he dispatched a detective to meet with the now-elderly Robert and various family friends to find out whether Mrs. Piper had somehow found out about Lodge's plan and sent an agent of her own to London in search of information. The agent contacted Robert, who told him that no one had contacted him about his late brother. Friends of Jerry reported the same. The detective made a thorough canvass of Robert and Jerry's old neighborhood and found that not a single question had been asked by anyone about either of the brothers. He checked back issues of local newspapers for information about the twins. Again, nothing. "Mrs. Piper has certainly beaten me," the agent reported back to Lodge, deflated. Lodge, on the other hand, although not surprised at the news, must have beamed at hearing it.

"Thus the mystery," wrote Frenchman M. Sage in a book about Mrs. Piper's experiences with the SPR, "grows deeper and deeper." Lodge agreed, giving the book his ultimate imprimatur. He wrote the foreword.

Upon hearing the reports of these initial séances, Hodgson tried to remain neutral. Not so, however, with several of his colleagues in the SPR. In addition to Lodge, there was Henry Sidgwick, one of the founders of the group, who believed Mrs. Piper to be "a medium who in a trance state seemed to have a power of getting information telepathically from the minds of those who sat with her, and sometimes something beyond this."

And from Frank Podmore: "The result of these early séances was to leave all those who had carefully studied the matter profoundly convinced that Mrs. Piper was gifted, at the lowest, with some supernatural faculty of acquiring information."

Even more carefully observed sessions followed, more impressive results followed, more ennui descended on Mrs. Piper.

Hodgson was not troubled by the medium's fading enthusiasm. There was a larger issue at stake here, he believed, and this being the case, he could see no choice other than to insist that she conduct a few more séances than she was expecting, solely under his aegis. Wearily, unenthusiastically, she agreed. But these tests, she made it known, would be the last to which she would submit--larger issue or not. The SPR agreed, determining that their final trials of Mrs. Piper would be the most exhaustive and securely monitored they had ever conducted, of her or anyone else.

Of course, the SPR had always been meticulous in its methods. The mediums they studied were only those deemed the most reliable, and still they were forced to endure a series of preliminary measures to ensure that reliability. Sometimes these measures were, to put it mildly, extreme.

> In one brutal series of tests devised by physiologists from the University of Naples [for Eusapia Palladino], the experimenters bound Eusapia's hands and arms with cords. They tied the cords onto iron rings on the floor and dripped lead seals onto the knots. As [future SPR president Charles] Richet reported, even after being bound for hours, she was able to summon those odd ectoplasmic hands--"some frail and diaphanous, some thick and strong"--all of which dissolved like mist when touched.

In Robert Stemman's volume *Spirit Communication*, there is a photograph of the British medium Leslie Flint with his hands being immobilized and several strips of what appear to be adhesive tape across his mouth. On his face is an expression that combines pain with surprise. He had agreed to participate in an experiment; he must have felt instead as if he were being held hostage.

Later, Mrs. Piper would be subject to worse treatment. At the first few of her séances for Hodgson, he determined to find out whether Mrs. Piper's trance state was the real thing or a clever piece of stagecraft. "He'd put ammonia-soaked cloth under her nose, dumped spoonfuls of salt, perfume, and laundry detergent into her mouth, pinched her until she bruised, all without provoking a flinch." All right, he concluded, the trance was genuine. That was one item off his checklist. On to the next.

But extraordinary steps had been taken even before the sittings began. When Mrs. Piper and her girls arrived in London, they settled in with the Lodges, and more to placate Hodgson than to satisfy his own desire for security, Lodge turned his abode into a kind of fortress. "He insisted on replacing the entire staff of their home, hiring new servants before the Piper family arrived. He locked away the family Bibles and photograph albums. Upon their arrival, he searched the Pipers' luggage. He insisted on reading all their mail before they saw it. He monitored the most casual conversation at meals, driving Mary [Lodge's wife] crazy with his insistence that she talk about nothing but general current events." Nothing, in other words, that might possibly come up at a séance. Or so Hodgson reasoned.

But none of it mattered. Mrs. Piper continued to be one of the most accurate mediums the SPRs had ever encountered. Hodgson's blood vessels swelled with exasperation.

But he would not give up. When Mrs. Piper announced she was leaving London and returning with her daughters to Massachusetts, Hodgson begged her to let him accompany her. She refused. He persisted. And persisted and persisted until finally, she surprised not only herself but much of the SPR by allowing Hodgson to accompany them. But only Hodgson, no other members of the SPR. And only for a short, unobtrusive stay. He agreed. Perhaps the prospect of returning home brightened her spirits at the same time that it diluted her better judgment.

It was not a good idea. Back in the United States, Hodgson decided that even more extreme security measures were in order. "It appears," wrote Alta Piper, "that one very wet morning as Dr. Hodgson and a sitter entered the house in Arlington Heights, the lady deposited her dripping umbrella in the stand provided for that purpose near the front door. Whereupon Dr. Hodgson, who was already halfway up the stairs, noticing her action immediately rushed down again, and seizing her by the arm admonished her brusquely thus--'You idiot! Haven't you any more sense than to do a thing like that? Don't you know that you might be accused of being in collusion with Mrs. Piper if you leave your umbrella there? It might be thought that by this means you were conveying a note, or other information to Mrs. Piper, through one of her daughters, for instance.'"

Hodgson also ordered Mrs. Piper and members of her household not to undertake any "suspicious journeys," under which category came visits to nearby cemeteries. He did not want anyone copying dates and inscriptions from tombstones. Hodgson was just as suspicious of more conventional sources of information. "He prevented Piper from reading a newspaper prior to each sitting."

As should be apparent by now, and will soon become even more apparent, Mrs. Piper was not just Hodgson's current assignment for the SPR; she had become, as was accurately noted, his "personal obsession." An American psychologist who knew Hodgson said that, by the time he passed away, his fixation on the medium had gone so far that it "wrecked" his mind. Perhaps having been vilified for approving of Eusapia and Home, he was determined never again to give his approval so easily. If at all.

It was with this resolve that Hodgson, like Lodge, employed a detective. Actually, several of them. Their orders were to follow Mrs. Piper on her daily rounds outside the home, no matter where she went, no matter how long she stayed. Even more pointlessly, he began a one-man stakeout of the Piper residence from across the street. The heights of absurdity kept rising.

> He hovered over the house like a bird on a nest, ignoring even the worst weather in order to maintain his watch. The winter of 1888 was one of the worst in history; the blizzards that swept the East Coast in March would kill more than 400 people. Hodgson remained undeterred. When conditions were so abysmal that the Pipers' hilly street was just a glare of ice, he borrowed a sled and coasted back down toward the train station, three-fourths of a mile through the blurring cold.

According to the Frenchman Sage, who exaggerates the time frame, but not the state of mind, "during some fifteen years, [Hodgson] hardly lost sight of her for a moment."

Mrs. Piper did not anger easily. Hodgson accomplished the feat with a minimum of effort. She began to believe that he was something in addition to an investigator; he was a stalker (although the word was not in use at the time), and she wrote to James, expressing her concern. She threatened to stop holding séances altogether; at the very least, she was "sorely tempted" to cease doing so under Hodgson's supervision.

James was, to say the least, disturbed to hear this. "At every moment," he said at about this time, "Mrs. Piper gives the sitters details which they maintain that they never could have known. Consequently, she must read them instantaneously in the minds of persons, sometimes very far distant, who do know them." She was, in other words, too valuable to the cause of paranormal studies to be allowed her escape. It was crucial that he do something to placate her.

He thought of trying to reason with Hodgson. But that seemed impossible at this point, as Hodgson was behaving like a man who had escaped from the grasp of reason. Instead, James replied to Mrs. Piper's letter with a missive he wrote as carefully as he composed his essays on psychology. "[I]t took all James's diplomatic skills to smooth her down," according to Deborah Blum. "He repeated his own respect for her, and teased her to see the silly side of detectives fruitlessly trailing such a sober couple, as William went to his department store job and Leonora ran errands to the baker and the greengrocer." Mrs. Piper, however, did not see a silly side, not of any SPR behavior toward her. Nonetheless, James kept trying to lighten her mood. "I hope neither you nor your husband will take the thing seriously," he wrote to her from America. "It has its very comic side and you are the ones who can best afford to laugh at it."

But he was wrong about that. The Pipers were the ones who could *least* afford to laugh at it. There is nothing funny about feeling like prey, even if the predator is a scientist who only seeks the truth, intending no harm, despite his ever more bizarre actions.

Finally, finally, it was over. Unable to think of any other trials to which to subject Mrs. Piper, he gave up. Contrary to his intention, he had proven to the best of his considerable ability that Mrs. Piper was a medium who did not deceive, did not cheat, did not in any way exploit those who believed in her. She had no hidden assistants flashing her information, no threads to make objects move "invisibly," no prop arms, no kneecaps pushing tables off the ground; she was a medium who had established herself to Hodgson as being genuinely endowed with the rarest of powers. Mrs. Piper had joined Daniel Dunglas Home in providing the SPRs with the strongest evidence yet that avenues to the afterlife existed. More than that, they were in fact open to traffic. Not open to all, not open in any comprehensible or consistent manner, not open according to eternally-held scientific principles, but open nonetheless.

Had it been anyone other than Hodgson who so successfully vetted Mrs. Piper, he would have been triumphant. He had made an invaluable contribution to the SPR while adhering to the most rigorous standards he could apply. But Hodgson never felt triumphant about his work; the best he could do, with the passage of time, was feel a certain pride in it. But to read between the lines of the following is to see that he did so as if holding a grudge against his own accomplishments.

> I cannot profess to have any doubt but that the "chief communicators" . . . are veritably the personalities that they claim to be; that they have survived the change we call death, and that they have directly communicated with us whom we call living through Mrs. Piper's entranced organism. Having tried the hypothesis of telepathy from the living for several years, and the "spirit" hypothesis also for several years, I

have no hesitation in affirming with the most absolute assurance that the "spirit" hypothesis is justified by its fruits and the other hypothesis is not.

Richard Hodgson, once the SPR's "atheist" par excellence, was that no longer. In fact, he eventually wanted to take his hypothesis a step further than he had ever previously contemplated, to prove the greatest impossibility of all, that a constant dialogue could be opened between the living and the dead, one that did not rely on mediums and séances but on direct channels, accessible to all, that had not yet been discovered. It is this to which he seems to be referring when he said to an associate, looking back on his findings with Mrs. Piper, "Indeed, I might add much thereto."

But he ran out of time before he could.

December 20, 1905: Despite having gone to bed early, she could not fall asleep until about one. She awoke again at four, feeling a strange quality to the darkness, although she couldn't have said what it was. It felt as if a fog had settled over her, thick and black and smoky. She remembered her dream of only moments ago, and, despite its ghoulish nature, revisited it as calmly as she could.

She had been walking toward a tunnel, planning to enter it, when she suddenly saw a man approaching her, blocking her way. She stopped, looking at him, certain she knew who it was but, for the moment, unable to place him. He had a beard, but the light was dim and he was standing at an angle so that she could make out no other feature of his face.

She began to approach the tunnel entrance again, but the man held up his hand. He did not want her to step any closer. "As his fingers reached toward her, she startled awake."

Later, she told her daughter Alta about the dream. She said that, just before she snapped to wakefulness, she realized that the man who blocked her way was Richard Hodgson.

December 20, 1905: After stopping for a few drinks at the Tavern Club, one of his favorite haunts, Richard Hodgson went to another place where he spent some of his spare time, the Union Boat Club. He was not a sailor, but a handball player, and the club had a number of courts. He had just begun to play against a frequent foe when he suddenly fell, swinging at the ball and missing and dropping onto the floor with a thump. There was nothing over which he could have tripped; he had simply collapsed, tumbling onto his back and, after a few seconds, beginning to gasp, to choke. He writhed from side to side, struggled to breathe, then stopped, turning perfectly still. Hodgson had suffered a massive heart attack. He was fifty years old.

William James was devastated by the news, lamenting his friend's demise by calling him "the manliest, unworldliest, kindliest of human beings. May he still be energizing somewhere."

It was, according to some, a prescient wish. Before long, several of his friends and associates came to believe that Hodgson was not only still energizing, but in the most unlikely of somewheres imaginable.

Chapter 11

THE HODGSON LEGACY

Richard Hodgson was buried three days after he died. He had no wife, children or extended family to mourn him, and James expected but a modest turnout at the funeral. He could not have been more surprised. "Everyone was there," he stated, "from simple personal affection for the man in the coffin. I stood at the foot of the stairs and saw everyone come down. *All* the women, and many of the men, were crying." It is doubtful that Mrs. Piper was among those who shed tears, and not known whether she was even in attendance.

A few days later, the world of British Spiritualism turned upside down. Mrs. Piper conducted a séance. Her control, a fellow named Rector, was whispering in her ear, and Mrs. Piper was jotting down what he told her. All was proceeding as it usually did when suddenly Mrs. Piper started clutching her pencil more tightly than before, white-knuckling it, and her hand began to shake. The sitters were alarmed. One asked her whether she was all right. The sitter received no answer, concluding that the medium was too deep in the valley of her trance to hear him.

Suddenly, pressing so hard on her pencil that she broke the point, smearing whatever it was that she was attempting to write, she grabbed another piece of paper and managed to scrawl a large letter "H" atop it with what was left of the lead. She continued writing scratchily, in smaller letters: o-d-g-s-o-n. Hodgson. Rector had given her the name of Mrs. Piper's recently deceased tormenter. It was, in a manner of speaking, a job referral, for Rector had decided he would no longer serve as Mrs. Piper's control. Henceforth, for reasons known only in the after-life, and perhaps a bit fuzzy even there, the position now belonged to the least expected of candidates, the medium's very recently departed prince of tormentors, Richard Hodgson.

For some Spiritualists it had always been difficult to believe in the notion of controls in the first place. But to believe in Hodgson's playing that role for Mrs. Piper was to make the implausible into the incredulous. One asks: Whose idea was this anyhow? Did Hodgson want to continue his association with Mrs. Piper or vice versa? If the latter, why would she have come to such a seemingly self-flagellating decision? Hodgson hardly seemed qualified to make the transition from real enemy to imaginary friend. Maybe he had gone undercover, in a manner of speaking. Determined not to let death get in his way, he would keep investigating his subject, but in the guise of an ally rather than a skeptic. Which brings us back to the question of why Mrs. Piper would go along with the scheme in the first place. Which cannot, of course, be answered.

Hodgson would remain Mrs. Piper's posthumous colleague for about seventy séances.

William James attended one of the odd couple's first joint sessions and told friends he had broken out in a cold sweat. Nothing about this new pairing made any sense to him, including the fact that Hodgson failed to recognize him, and that James could not recognize the comportment Hodgson had assumed as an employee of the world beyond mortality. As the sitters took their places, preparing to hear Mrs. Piper's opening remarks to them, "[t]he Hodgson control tended to announce himself with the unfamiliar heartiness of a politician on the campaign trail, exclaiming, 'Well, well, well! I am Hodgson, delighted to see you. How is everything? First rate?'

"Hodgson, as all who knew him were aware, had never talked that way in his life.

"Yet the glad-handing usually gave way to a familiar friendliness, as if the ghost--if it was such--had to pull free from Mrs. Piper before emerging as himself.

"The spirit Hodgson teased his old close friends, turned quiet and serious with those he knew less well. One woman had told James that she and R.H. 'were such good friends that he was saucy toward her, and teased her most of the time.'"

James did not know what to make of this, any of it. He was especially bewildered by the information that Mrs. Piper was now revealing, through Hodgson, of the SPR and its members, their accomplishments and biases and quirks. She had never hinted at possessing such knowledge before, and some of what she said was not even known to James. Who could be providing it if not her new control. She also revealed other knowledge that was new to her, speaking about arcane points of law and psychology, subjects that Hodgson had studied many years ago; and speaking about poetry, especially the work of Hodgson's favorite, Wordsworth. In fact, it has been said by some that she recited long stretches of Wordsworth's verse. She did all of this in Hodgson's voice, with that new, bluff presentation of his.

Still, and try though he might, James could not allow himself to be certain about Hodgson's spirit being in the service of the supernatural. According to Christine Wicker, who wrote the history of Lily Dale, "[he] was never convinced. The spirit's mannerisms were sometimes forced and seemed overdone."

Most other members of the ASPR, a group incapable of being easily swayed, seem to have accepted the notion of Hodgson's being Mrs. Piper's control all along--and not just her control, but a trustworthy one at that. After poring over numerous statements Hodgson had made while working with his former *bete noire* [circumflex over the first "a" in "bete"], the researchers approved the following statement for their journal: "The total amount of truthful information communicated by the R.H. control to the various sitters is copious."

The ASPR did not publish comments like this without an exhaustive examination of every available detail.

Yet there remained those, perhaps a majority of ASPR members, who could not accept the transformation of Hodgson from "terrible enemy of fraud" to glad-handing psychic sidekick. It was true that, as a dead man, their old colleague seemed to retain much, of what he knew when alive, but there were oddities in addition to the overly-enthusiastic heartiness in which he spoke. He also showed lapses in knowledge where none could be expected--for instance, when it came to some details of his childhood. According to Joseph McCabe, the author of a highly critical book about Spiritualism, "When Hodgson died in 1905 and left a large amount of manuscript in cipher, [Mrs. Piper] could not get the least clue of it. When friends put test questions to the spirit of Hodgson about his early life in Australia, the answers were all wrong." Among the questions was the name of a schoolmaster he had as a child; the Hodgson spirit reportedly could not remember it. Of course, it is possible that the mortal version of the man might have forgotten it as well. It is also possible that something had been lost in transit from one realm of being to the other.

But apart from the charges made against Hodgson for inaccuracy, more serious charges were now being made against Mrs. Piper. For the first time, her reputation was being seriously challenged. Said Martin Gardner, an author of mathematics and science texts, long known and well-respected as a debunker of what he refers to as "pseudo-science," the medium had been deceitful well before Hodgson became her control. "She once told James a ring had been stolen," Gardner wrote, "but it was found in James's home. Three times Phinuit tried vainly to guess the contents of a sealed envelope in James's possession, even though [Phinuit] supposedly contacted the dead woman who wrote the letter."

He also charged Mrs. Piper with failing to recognize a "sting operation" that was the work of James's sister, Alice. From the beginning of the relationship between the Jameses and the medium, Alice had been the most dubious member of the family toward the notion of an afterlife. So when brother William asked for a lock of her hair to give to Mrs. Piper--supposedly, "'vibrations' from personal items helped her make contact with appropriate spirits,"--Alice pulled a switch. She gave him some strands of hair from a friend of hers, recently deceased. Mrs. Piper, apparently, could not tell the difference. So much for her skills at psychometry, according to Gardner.

But how much can be made of this? That Mrs. Piper failed in some instances did not mean she failed in all. And Gardner has been accused of being self-servingly selective in the examples of error--or fraud--about which he wrote. Did he choose Example A specifically because he could see a possibility for deceit? Did he then neglect Example B because no such possibility made itself apparent?

Neither Gardner nor anyone else whose work I consulted during my research for this book has been able to present detailed criticisms of the whole of Spiritualism. Of many individual incidents? Yes. Of the entire faith? No. In fact, to this very day the most effective condemnations of Spiritualism are variations on the same theme, the ones that come most readily to virtually anyone's mind:

It doesn't make sense.

It's illogical.

It's impossible.

It defies all the laws of science.

If there really *is* such a thing as Spiritualism, why have so few examples of it been recorded in daily life, and from there made their way into newspapers and magazines, social media, and television?

These are not specific arguments, rebuttals of specific incidents. They address nothing fundamental, nothing nuanced. But in some ways they could not be more compelling. They travel through our minds along well-worn pathways, without obstruction. They seem unassailable, making perfect sense. Making perfect "common sense."

But Spiritualism *doesn't* make sense. It *is* illogical. It *is* impossible. . . . It is, thus, impervious to criticism for the same reasons that it elicits so much of it.

Except that when one digs deeper into the subject, beneath the surface of sense that we call common, one finds it more and more possible to assail. Or at least to question, to wonder, to doubt. Some individuals who have done this state their position as follows: there are countless claims of Spiritualistic practice that are either true or, if fraudulent, have not been detected as such by the greatest minds in the world studying the claims with the greatest diligence and strictest standards. There are those who insist that this is simply two different ways of saying the same thing. Maybe, maybe not.

More so than Gardner, it was physiologist Ivor Lloyd Tuckett who offered what might have been the most sweeping of all denunciations of Mrs. Piper. Claiming that he had thoroughly researched her methods and results, although probably without attending a séance, he wrote that her gifts were not gifts at all. Rather, she was guilty of "*[muscle]-reading, fishing, guessing, hints obtained in the sitting, knowledge surreptitiously obtained, knowledge acquired in the interval between sittings and lastly, facts already within Mrs. Piper's knowledge.*"

It is impossible to know, at this distant point in time, whether McCabe and Gardner were correct in their charges, or the events that led to them. But their reputations, especially Gardner's, were such that one must treat their findings thoughtfully. Like James and his fellow members of the SPRs, the two men did not issue edicts irresponsibly.

Tuckett, however, is a different matter. His is a dismissal of Mrs. Piper that fails utterly to dismiss, laughable in its foaming spew. In fact, Tuckett could have concocted his accusations without examining Mrs. Piper at all, so random and therefore meaningless are they, so lacking in substance as well as specificity.

Although I never would have suspected it when I started working on this book, the supporters of Spiritualism, especially those affiliated with the SPRs, are a more distinguished, informed, and reasonable assembly than the naysayers.

Chapter 12

THE WHITE CROW

More than any other person, it was probably Mrs. Piper who inspired the statement. And when William James uttered it, he made what is arguably the most memorable defense ever spoken in defense of psychic research. Or, to be more precise, he made a statement so remarkable for its simplicity, succinctness and perception that it became a rallying cry for those who believe that psychic research is a worthwhile pursuit. It did not become a rallying cry that changed anyone's mind, and not just because it was wrapped in a metaphor and therefore mildly indirect. It did not change anyone's mind--or at least did not change a significant number of minds--because most minds are inflexible when it comes to the subject of paranormality.

The metaphor was, rather, a kind of valedictory, James's final and most enduring word on Mrs. Piper and her fellow explorers of the afterlife. It was an unreserved sanction of her authenticity, his ultimate judgment on what the two SPRs had learned and contributed to a scientific world that remained largely indifferent to, and certainly unaccepting of, virtually anything to which the groups were devoted.

It had been a long road for James. Pragmatism, after all, insists "that only principles that can be demonstrated not only theoretically, by deduction, but practically, by use, deserve intelligent consideration." To carry such demanding principles into the study of the supernatural had been a great burden. No one of James's character had ever toted so heavy a load into such forbidding territory. He bore up as well as could be expected under the load, deriving what satisfaction he could from his belief that the SPRs proved the validity of treating the afterlife as a worthy subject of study, and, further, proving the existence of the afterlife, at least to a few people.

Early in his studies of Mrs. Piper, James had "invited eight colleagues from Harvard to observe [her], telling them of recent extremely positive developments. Five refused, one informing James that even if something happened, he wouldn't believe it. 'So runs the world away!' James wrote. 'I should not indulge in the personality and triviality of such anecdotes were it not that they paint the temper of our time.'"

He might have been able to understand his mates in the academe being confounded if they had witnessed Mrs. Piper. After all, even he did not always comprehend what he was seeing. "If I may be allowed a personal expression of opinion at the end of this notice," James summarized at one point, "I would say that the Piper phenomena are the most absolutely baffling thing I know."

But the Harvard faculty members he had contacted did not witness Mrs. Piper, nor did the majority of them even look cursorily at reports of her séances. They simply refused to expose themselves to the SPRs' experiments and conclusions, reminiscent of children who believe that if they ignore something it will go away; if they close their eyes they cannot be seen. And their refusal to visit Mrs. Piper after receiving a personal invitation from a figure like William James was but an added source of annoyance to him, a personal affront. He did not believe that self-imposed barriers were worthy of those whose who had dedicated their lives to the search for truth and knowledge. And he wondered whether his colleagues, masters of certitude, were afraid that they, too, might end up sharing James's conclusions about Mrs. Piper, calling the basis of their entire careers into question.

In her biography of James, Linda Simon, whose professorial career includes positions at Harvard and Skidmore, could not help but address the issue of Mrs. Piper's seemingly inexplicable talents. Granted, she did so through James's eyes, but also with an eminent historian's objectivity.

> Besides transmitting messages aloud, she engaged in automatic writing, using her right hand both to write down spirit communications and, cupped, to serve as a mouthpiece into which sitters sent their own messages to the control. No matter how rarely she saw a sitter, Piper was able to recall minute details of their relationships, their problems, and their lives. She was voluble and forthcoming, very different from other mediums, who conveyed only terse and hesitant

messages. Piper may have been a talented actress with a pro-
digious memory; James thought not. Acknowledging the
"dramatic improbability" of finding a true psychic, still, he
believed.

In fact, he believed so strongly in a form of life after death that he
offered what seems a strangely cold consolation to his sister Alice. Long
an emotionally troubled woman, Alice wrote to James from London in
1901 to tell him she was now under assault physically as well; a tumor
had been discovered in her breast. Doctors informed her she did not
have long to live.

When James replied, he told Alice that, in his opinion, she had
never taken much pleasure in being alive, and thus should be able to
depart from mortality with relative ease. The sentiment is not as callous
as it seems. Mrs. Piper had by this time helped to convince James that
life existed after death, at least in some form. As a result, he could write
to his sister, "When that which is *you* passes out of the body, I am sure
there will be an explosion of liberated force and life until then eclipsed
and kept down." She would still be his sister, James pronounced; she
would simply be taking a different form.

In the same year that James retired as president of the American
Society for Psychical Research, the British physicist William Barrett
published a thumping endorsement of both SPRs, in some of whose
work he had participated. "Barrett's book, *On the Threshold of a New
World of Thought*, rang like a victory cry when it appeared in 1909,
declaring that he and his colleagues had proved their case, from the
newest results with Eusapia Palladino to more than twenty years of
consistent evidence provided by Leonora Piper."

James's own valedictory, as might be expected, was much more
restrained. It was thoughtful, sensible, making little mention of his critics. It is remembered, however, for but a single sentence, the one at the
end, one that has been repeated vocally and in print countless times
by psychic researchers in the century since. James said: "If you wish to

upset the law that all crows are black, you must not seek to show that no crows are; it is enough if you prove one single crow to be white."

It was, of course, Leonora Piper of whom he spoke. She was, for James and many others, the white crow.

But there is another possibility. There is the possibility that people who are not white crows have had, and perhaps intermittingly continue to have, white crow moments. Sam Clemens was not a psychic, but apparently he had one. James Fenimore Cooper was not a psychic, but he also seems to have had one. A theatrical agent with whom I have worked told me of his white crow moment. And I know of many other men and women, both through personal testimony and literary references, who have had isolated experiences that defy the normal restrictions imposed by time and space.

Of course, such moments do not account for Daniel Dunglas Home or Leonora Piper and others who, by all accounts, were full-time white crows, psychics virtually from their youngest days. But to many people, including those who dismiss the Homes and Pipers of history, the notion of white crow moments in otherwise black crow lives is acceptable, if for no other reason than that isolated incidents of the paranormal are easier to dismiss than lifetimes full of them. A solitary white crow moment, after all, can be a coincidence, a serendipitous occurrence, an accident. And such isolated moments are easier not to dismiss at all, to accept as simply bizarre, unrepeatable occurrences. Perhaps, as William James came to believe, the laws of science come in a greater variety than has henceforth been acknowledged.

As Sir Oliver Lodge wrote in the foreword to Alta Piper's biography of her mother, "Her life work has been devoted to providing material for a nascent science, including a kind or variety of interaction between mind and matter, which, though puzzling and unusual, has already had instructive and beneficent and comforting results."

It serves as a farewell salute of sorts for Mrs. Piper, too.

In 1901, as Alice James prepared to die and her brother tried to assure her that another form of existence awaited, Leonora Piper announced that she was retiring. It was time, at long last time, and she was sure her Lord would understand. She would conduct no more séances. She was fatigued to the marrow by them and, despite decades of sharing her gift, of being observed and analyzed, poked, prodded, probed, and pestered, she was still unable to explain the exact nature of her gift. She remained doubtful that her trance states were "spiritistic," she said. In addition: "I am inclined to accept the telepathic explanation of all the so-called psychic phenomena, but beyond this I remain a student with the rest of the world."

Mrs. Piper had first proclaimed her intention to retire several years earlier, when Hodgson--the psychic investigator, not the control--was tormenting her with his vigilance. She told a reporter from the *New York Herald* that she "would never hold another sitting with Mr. Hodgson, and that [she] would die first." (Ironically, of course, *he* would die first, and she would continue to hold sittings with the deceased version of Mr. Hodgson.)

Her goal at the time of her first announcement was a simple one. "I . . . desire to become a free agent, and devote myself and my time to other and more congenial pursuits."

It was not that easy. She was too renowned a figure by then to disappear into the placid waters of the quotidian. Against her will, she continued to serve the Almighty by conducting séances. But she presided over fewer of them than before, slowing the pace even further when Hodgson signed on as her second in command. Her séances gradually became shorter than they used to be, and just as often involved fewer sitters. When, in 1901, she declared her retirement for the second time, she was true to her word. She phased herself out of sojourns into the afterlife and settled down comfortably into more congenial pursuits, which included gardening, hosting friends, tending her children and grandchildren, and spending more time with her husband. She was able to maintain such a life for almost half a century.

Gradually reporters lost interest in her and the public began to forget her. The SPRs might still have been trying to make sense of her feats, for all she knew--but she *didn't* know, and was delighted with her ignorance. Eventually, other than a few relatives, neighbors and long-time friends, it seemed that only the rare individual remembered either her name or the furor whose cynosure she had so inadvertently been, and upon which she never tried to capitalize. The once-famous psychic had sunk happily into anonymity.

Leonora Evelina Symonds Piper passed away on July 3, 1950 of bronchopneumonia, in Arlington, Massachusetts, where she was also buried. She was ninety-three years old.

By then, the membership of the SPRs had been handed on to a new generation, one that might not even have realized how much Mrs. Piper meant to those who had come before. But to those who did know, she is and ever has been, the white crow. And to those who believe she had left a legacy to the future, it was that death--although it was certainly end of life as we know it--did not have to be the end of communication.

So William James had long believed. "[W]hen," he asked rhetorically, "was not the science of the future stirred to its conquering activities by the little rebellious exceptions to the science of the present?" But he had posed the question forty years before Mrs. Piper's passing, giving up his own hold on mortality in 1910, a victim of heart disease at the age of sixty-eight. If he had realized that more than a century would pass without science having been stirred to any more of the conquering activities that mattered so much to him, he would have been sorely troubled. His beliefs, however would not have been altered. Too firmly, he was certain, were they rooted in the experiential.

Which is to say, the pragmatic.

Chapter 13

MACHINE DREAMS

Even as a young man, Sir Oliver Lodge "believe[d] . . . that both spiritualist messages and wireless waves could travel through the 'ether.'" He continued to collect evidence for the rest of his life, studying the results of SPR experiments, attending séances, taking part in laboratory-controlled tests, interviewing those for whose books he wrote forewords. But he was always a spectator, never a participant in conversation with a citizen of the great beyond. Until, that is, the day when he chatted briefly with his Aunt Anne.

He was sitting at a séance in London conducted by Mrs. Piper, expecting to do nothing more than observe, as usual, when out of the void he heard his aunt's "well-remembered voice." And he recognized her well-remembered advice, so often provided, if not always heeded. Their dialogues had been brought to a halt by her death several years earlier, but suddenly there she was again, talking with her nephew as if they were in the midst of a discussion that had been suddenly interrupted. Lodge swore it was true, and provided details. Somehow, some way, his mother's sister had "crossed over," meaning that she had become a wraith who could return to life vocally, and perhaps, in time to come, even in some more tangible manner.

In her years as a human being, Aunt Anne had been "a beloved woman of lively intellect who had abetted [Lodge's] drive to become a scientist against the wishes of his father." Yet she was also proud that her nephew was becoming a scientist of the afterlife, joining William James and so many others of strong intellectual bent in proving that such a person, such a job title, could actually exist. "She had once told Lodge that after her death she would come back to visit if she could, and now . . . . she reminded him of that promise."

It is one thing to believe in Spiritualism as an abstract principle, another to know that many friends and associates have communicated with former mortals now residing elsewhere. But is still another to find oneself engaged in dialogue with a dead relative. Lodge did not actually see her, but hearing from her was more than enough to leave him both shaken and elated. Despite which, his reaction to his initial post-mortem encounter with Aunt Anne seems oddly dispassionate. "This," he stated, "was an unusual thing to happen." That is all he said. Nothing more. Perhaps he was *so* shaken and elated that he hadn't the energy to express the depth of his emotions.

Later, however, he expanded on the effect of his visit with Aunt Anne. It had left him "thoroughly convinced not only of human survival," Lodge said, "but of the power to communicate, under certain conditions, with those left behind on the earth."

Several years afterward, he would be addressed by another departed member of the family, and it would be the most thrilling, emotionally piercing, and lingering experience of his life.

By then, an unbearably long time had passed without his having heard once more from Aunt Anne. He wondered where she had gone, and why, and what her life was like now that life as she had previously known it was gone. He went to séance after séance, but without hearing from her again. Surely she wasn't ignoring him. Was he doing something wrong? Were there restrictions on communicating from the other side, difficulties that he couldn't possibly imagine? Whatever the reason, those certain conditions to which he had referred had not occurred again.

Then, in 1915, he received the news, a telegram from the British government, a thunderbolt. His son, his beloved Raymond, twenty-six years old, had taken a fatal bullet in the Great War. For Lodge, the telegram was something of a fatal bullet to his own being. It was not, however, a total surprise, and not just because lethal violence was Europe's pervasive curse at the time, the storm that had risen from hell. Lodge "believed that he had been warned of Raymond's death by his old friend, the late Frederic Myers, in a 'cross correspondence' message." Even so, he could not bring himself to accept the reality of an abyss so wide and deep having opened in his life. Learning that it had, that he had fallen to the despised *Boche*, he found that his desire to talk to his son was as profound as his grief.

Most of the séances he attended at this time, hoping to reach Raymond, were conducted by Great Britain's most respected medium, Mrs. Gladys Osborne Leonard. She reminded Lodge of Mrs. Piper, as "she was a little bit terrified of her own work. No, 'terrified' is not the right word; she held the work in a certain degree of awe that sometimes interfered with communication." Perhaps, knowing how important the transmission was to so distinguished a sitter, Mrs. Leonard was too nervous to operate at peak efficiency. Time after time, with Lodge sitting at her table, his heart pounding with runaway tension, she failed in her mission to reach his son. Until one night, one glorious night that vindicated every minute of his life Lodge had devoted to psychic research, she did not fail. Her call, so to speak, went through. Raymond got in touch. As Lodge later told friends about the moment, he

> heard his son say, "I love you. I love you intensely. Father, please speak to me." The conversation continued, and a few minutes later Lodge heard, "Father, tell mother she has her son with her all day on Christmas Day. There will be thousands and thousands of us back in the home on that day, but the horrid part is that so many of the fellows don't get welcome. Please keep a place for me. I must go now."

In his lifetime, Sir Oliver Lodge would write more than forty books. Prior to the death of his son, his titles included such well-respected and scarcely-read volumes as *Modern Views of Electricity*, *Electric Theory of Matter*, and *Electrons, or the Nature and Properties of Negativity*. In 1916, the year that England joined forces with the French for the disastrous Battle of the Somme, he produced a volume of an entirely different sort. *Raymond Or Life And Death* was published by the Andesite Press and bore a seal on the front of the dust jacket that read "Scholar Select," meaning that the volume had been read by a panel of respected academics and judged to be of significant cultural content.

"I recommend people in general," Lodge said, in explaining his departure from previous subjects, "to learn and realize that their loved ones are still active and useful and interested and happy--more alive than ever in one sense--and to make up their minds to live a useful life till they rejoin them."

The book was a popular one, going through thirteen printings. A best-seller, it was especially meaningful to families like Lodge's, all too many of them, who had lost a child on the battleground.

Yet the book is not easy reading. Lodge's prose is often dense, as if designed for his fellow academics rather than the average reader. "Death," he writes in a chapter designed to minimize the event's finality, "is not extinction. Neither the soul or the body is extinguished or put out of existence. The body weighs just as much as before, the only properties it loses at the moment of death are potential properties. So also all we can assert concerning the vital principles is that it no longer animates that material organism."

In Britain's scientific community, the book was *not* a best-seller. Most of its members received the volume with respect for the author's feelings, but not for the veracity of his ideas, and few went so far as to actually read the entire thing. British academics had long known of Lodge's beliefs in the afterlife, most disagreeing with them but willing to make a distinction between Sir Oliver the physicist and Sir Oliver the Spiritualist.

In 1922, with his son still very much alive to him, Lodge published *Raymond Revisited*. The title, however, is misleading, for after the 1915 séance, Lodge never heard from his son again, was never revisited.

But neither did he lose hope. In fact . . .

After a few years went by, Sir Oliver received an unexpected grant from a British shipbuilder, his name not having survived the years. But as a result of the grant, Lodge was able to turn his attention to a wireless device unlike any that he, Marconi, Crookes, or anyone else had ever contemplated before. His enthusiasm for the project far out-stripped his common sense.

This particular wireless, like the telegraph he had worked on inter-mittently for so many years, would also rely on the beaming of invisible rays, thereby making possible a connection by means never employed before. But at this point the two kinds of devices differ markedly. Lodge's assignment, according to the grant provision, was "to design a machine specifically to test for the spiritual ether." Or, as Lodge viewed his assignment, to penetrate the barrier that death had imposed on father and son, to enable him to listen to a treasured voice that could no longer be heard through conventional means. The shipbuilder, a devout Spiritualist, had nominated Sir Oliver to be the Alexander Gra-ham Bell of the paranormal.

No one knows how he began to design his contraption. No one knows how he even began *thinking* about designing it. How does one conceive such a project, one that makes the scientific mind reel? What tools would be required for such a device? What parts? How would they work together to capture the attention of people who were no longer people as we understand the term? Where *were* those people? And by what route would a message sent by a human being reach the former human being for whom it was intended? What was to prevent a message intended for Raymond Lodge from instead reaching the proprietor of an eighteenth century roadhouse? And, of course, most fundamentally, how could Lodge be sure that the message would even exist after he sent it, or believed that he had sent it?

No attempt at such an instrument had ever been made before, as far as Lodge knew, and after his own work was completed he left behind no blueprints, no notes, to inspire those who might want to attempt the task in the future.

But that he labored assiduously on his device cannot be doubted, inspired by having already heard from two deceased members of his family. But *they* had contacted *him*, at their whim. Now he wanted to reverse the process; *he* wanted to be the one initiating the contact. If the former were possible, there must be a way to achieve the latter as well. Or so Sir Oliver reasoned as he set to work.

The respected scientist, according to some of his mates in the academe, had finally been tipped over the edge. His long service to the SPR *was* the edge; now the shipbuilder's grant had made him take a few more steps forward. Lodge became the world's first subsidized fantasist, causing his colleagues to look upon his efforts with a condescension that was sometimes bemused, at other times barbed, although at all times sympathetic.

Lodge paid them no mind. In such secrecy did he work that no one is certain how long it took him to proceed from inspiration to finished product. It is believed, however, that once his labors were complete, the main components of his ether-reacher were two dynamos, which, when up to speed, would

> spin metal disks into a blur, whirling them 4,000 revolutions per minute, producing a sizzling electrical charge. Its purpose was to test a favorite theory of the spirit believers, that the ether had a natural affinity for charged atoms, that its ability to carry electrical energy might be thus responsible for psychic powers. The machine contained instruments to measure any "etheric" effect on the sparking, electrically charged disks.

Finally, it was time for a trial. Lodge turned on his machine. And the disks, as intended, blurred. The dynamos urging them on whirred. A sizzling electrical charge crackled through the air. To Lodge, it looked and sounded as if the machine were doing precisely what it was supposed to do. The ether, however, did not respond. Not a single one of the gauges on his machine that was designed to register a response from otherworldly provinces made a sound, a movement, the slightest blip. Except for the blurring and whirring and crackling, there was nothing. Lodge made adjustments, refinements, reconfigurations. The results, or lack of them, were the same.

The British shipbuilder, although disappointed, paid Sir Oliver for his time, thanked him for his trouble, and perhaps sought another inventor to carry on with his quest.

As for Lodge, he still did not give up hope. Five years after his failed attempt to reach the afterlife with a mechanism inspired by the telegraph, he tried again on the radio. At the behest of the Society for Psychical Research, Lodge asked the Director-General of the British Broadcasting Corporation for permission to use the airwaves for an experiment in telepathy.

Writes Lodge biographer W.P. Jolly, "A group of people in the office of the SPR were shown certain objects of which they had no prior knowledge. The objects, which were successively displayed to them at intervals of five minutes, were two separate playing cards, a Japanese print, a bunch of white lilac, and a man wearing a grotesque mask. Listeners were asked to record any impressions they might have of the nature of the objects and post them without delay to the SPR."

More than twenty-five thousand people responded, some from the United States, some from as far away as Australia. "But when analysed these results gave no evidence of primary significance that telepathy had occurred." Not even the kind of minimal results that the SPR's *Census of Hallucinations* believed it had established as fact.

Sir Oliver had been optimistic when the radio experiment was first proposed. When it, too, proved a failure, he once again bore up as best he could, trying to persuade the BBC to make another attempt to reach beyond the end of mortality. But it was not interested.

Lodge took that news well, too. He was a rock. Nothing could make him change his mind, or even waver. His resolve was, depending on one's point of view, the ultimate in either folly or faith. But at this point he seems to have been fresh out of ideas. He could think of nothing else to do but hope that Raymond would call him again. He did not.

In 1970, more than four decades after the BBC's trial run in mass telepathy, the *Sunday Times* of London conducted another. It received six thousand responses. Not a single one gave verifiable evidence of ethereal communication, or prompted the *Times* to carry on further with its attempt to find such evidence. The topic, in fact the very subject of Spiritualism, seemed to be of less interest to the populace than it had previously been.

By this time, Lodge had been dead for thirty years. He was eighty-nine when he breathed his last, and during the three decades in which his mortal self had been interred, Lodge himself had only once initiated communication with a living person. It could not have been a stranger choice. The Scottish inventor John Logie Baird, who is credited with giving the world's first public demonstration of television on January 26, 1926, does not seem to have been a believer in intercourse with the afterlife. Nor is there any reason to believe that he knew or had even heard of Sir Oliver. Nonetheless, Baird told one and all, Lodge had indeed gotten in touch with him, although for some reason he chose not to reveal either the method or the contents of the transmission. He said only that he had not been surprised to have heard from the afterlife, not even by a stranger.

The first time that Guglielmo Marconi met Thomas Edison was probably in 1901, within a few months of the former's having astonished the scientific world by achieving the greatest triumph of his life. It was a world to which he did not belong; he was, after all, an autodidact with no academic credentials. Nonetheless, it was he, not the academically trained scientists, who had first sent a wireless signal from Europe to North America. As someone said, it was the greatest crossing of the Atlantic by an Italian since Columbus had made the passage four centuries earlier. Edison, also an autodidact without formal scholarship, was eager to make Marconi's acquaintance. The feeling was mutual.

The elder by thirty-seven years, Edison did most of the talking. Which was fine with the younger man, who was happy to learn.

Sometimes, though, Edison sounded more like a daydreamer than the world's greatest transformer of ideas into products. At one point he said, "You know Marconi there are sounds going all around us right at this moment in this room. . . . If we only had the means to detect these tiny vibrations we would be able to select out of all of these the ones we desired to hear."

Marconi nodded, although it was not agreement so much as the acolyte's paying tribute to his superior. But he was not really clear about what Edison was trying to say. One day, though, he would understand perfectly, this after a lifetime of denying that anything even remotely resembling Spiritualism could exist. For Spiritualism is exactly what Edison was hinting at, and what Marconi himself would consider in his last days.

In 1937, with death on the near horizon for him, Marconi became a different man. He began to believe, or to try to believe. He wanted to be a man of faith, a man who did not die, not as he had understood the term all his life. He remembered now, if not before, what Edison had said to him: "Sounds going all around us right at this moment in this room." He had referred to "Tiny little vibrations." Life in so many various forms surrounded us day and night, Edison was saying, life from the past no less than the present.

Marconi lay in bed, half-delirious in his terminal state, trying his hardest to form thoughts: If a microphone were sensitive enough, far more sensitive than any even imagined so far, one that was capable of receiving those tiny vibrations, would it be able to pluck them out of the air and listen to anything that had ever been said? Would it be able to pluck out, say, the Sermon on the Mount? Not a recording of it, not some clergyman's rendering--the real thing, as spoken by Jesus himself, two millennia ago. If Marconi could actually hear Jesus, hear him speaking some of the most inspiring words He ever uttered, wasn't He still alive, even more alive than even his most committed worshippers dared to hope?

Perhaps if Marconi had been younger and more energetic, less feverish, he would have tried to create a microphone like the one he envisioned. But he could not do it now, not ever, and he passed away with the idea stored somewhere in the back of his mind.

Edison, however, had already tried something similar.

In some of the earliest movies he ever made, ghosts play starring roles. In 1900, for example, Edison produced *Uncle Josh in a Spooky Hotel*, a comedy with a running time of slightly more than a minute. This short, short subject "consists of a shrouded ghost that appears behind Josh and slaps him as he talks to his landlord. Josh retaliates, thinking the landlord has hit him. The ghost then reappears to slap the landlord, who hits back at Josh. The film ends with both of them seeing the ghost and running out of the room."

Certainly more slapstick in this case than thrills. But, as far as the filmmaker was concerned, fiction with a basis in fact.

Edison believed that ghosts were real, members of a celestial cast of characters that actually existed--in some form, through some means. Although he did not think of them precisely as others did, his interest in spectral presences was genuine, perhaps a by-product of the vast imaginative powers that had enabled him to become the world's foremost creator of the new. But it was not enough for him to bring to the screen celluloid ghosts who entertained; he wanted to interact with genuine ghosts who communicated personally, who could tell the living what to expect in the future and learn what was happening in the world they had left behind. And so he "conceived the theoretical foundations for his device to contact the dead." After which he went to work.

Edison had determined that human bodies "are composed of myriads and myriads of infinitesimally small individuals, each in itself a unit of life, and that these units work in squads." He referred to these squads as swarms, and he believed they lived eternally. What he did not know, however, was where to find the members of a specific swarm, much less the entities that comprised them, after the corporeal self had died. Nor did he understand how to converse with them. But that would not stop him from trying.

According to Roy Stemman, a journalist and self-described "skeptical believer," Edison spent the last seven years of his life no less dedicated than Lodge, "developing a 'Spirit Finder' device which he hoped would locate a frequency between long and short waves to be used as a telepathic channel between the living and the dead."

Edison had decided that surviving units of life had already found their telepathic channel, that they were already "broadcasting" from beyond death's curtain. But because their frequency had not yet been located, the waves they emitted were either silent, too faint, or too circuitous in their pathways, to be heard by existing instruments. Edison wanted to change that. "What [he] had in mind was an apparatus which operated like a valve," says biographer Ronald W. Clark. "In a modern powerhouse, a man with his one-eighth of a horsepower could turn a valve which started a 50,000 horsepower steam turbine. In [Edison's Spirit Finder] apparatus, the slightest effort which it intercepted would be magnified so many times that it would produce a usable record."

Edison continued his theorizing in an article for the *Scientific American*.

> If our personality survives, then it is strictly logical or scientific to assume that it retains memory, intellect, other faculties, and knowledge that we acquire on this Earth. Therefore . . . if we can evolve an instrument so delicate as to be affected by our personality as it survives in the next life, such an instrument, when made available, ought to record something.

(Another Edison biographer explains as succinctly as possible why his subject believed that "our personality survives." Writes Neil Baldwin, "If the great sequoia tree could go on for centuries, why not some essence of human personality?")

But the fact that Thomas Edison was attempting to communicate with the dead would not stay confined to the pages of a small-circulation, if high-prestige, magazine; it escaped from *Scientific American* and has remained unconfined ever since. At one point, Edison himself admitted his efforts. "I have been at work for some time building an apparatus to see if it is possible for personalities which have left this earth to communicate with us."

Even a century later, the topic was being discussed, this time in a play that the *New York Times* found to be "a colorful footnote to American history." In 1995, Mark St. Germain's *Camping With Henry and Tom* was first presented on a New York stage, with the former character being Ford and the latter Edison. The third major role in the cast is that of Warren G. Harding, the president of the United States, and the play is based on an actual excursion into the woods by the three men, a small vacation--an escape from fame, responsibility and, in the case of Ford and Edison, from the re-ordering of the American way of life.

One night, seeking more privacy than they had known since childhood, the three of them hid themselves even deeper in the woods than they had originally intended, sneaking away from Secret Service agents assigned to protect them. Ford climbs behind the wheel of his Model T and, having no idea where he is going, motors his mates through the rugged terrain of backwater Maryland, surrounded by huge Doric columns of tree trunks. Suddenly, a deer dashes in front of the car, but not fast enough. Ford hits it, and although the animal manages to remain breathing and escapes, the vehicle is disabled. The men are not injured; they are, however, stranded, with no means of contacting the outside world, or any sense of exactly where they are. For a few days, the characters are not so much vacationing as dwelling in exile.

One night, as they are sitting around a campfire awaiting rescue, Edison leans against a tree stump trying to read a book. But it is not easy; the light is dim and flickering, and he is frequently interrupted by his contentious mates. Finally, the inventor gives up and sets the book on the ground. Ford, wondering what it is, picks it up.

EDISON: Put it down, Henry.

FORD: *(Looking at title)* Sir Arthur Conan Doyle.

HARDING: A mystery! I love them.

FORD: "The World of the Supernatural."

EDISON: It's a mystery why he wrote it. Sherlock Holmes couldn't find one clear thought in it.

HARDING: Then why are you reading it?

EDISON: It's the only kind of human folly I still enjoy. The kind I can toss across the room whenever I'm sick of it.

FORD: *(Excited)* You're building it, aren't you?

EDISON: I didn't say that, Henry.

FORD: You're thinking about it, then. Admit it!

HARDING: Building what?

FORD: I've been after Mr. Edison for years to invent a machine to contact the dead.

HARDING: *(Taken aback)* Well. Good luck to you.

EDISON: We can't build a fire, and the man thinks I can find a [sic] afterlife.

FORD: If anybody can do it, you can.

HARDING: I don't know which would be more terrifying. Finding it, or not finding it.

One of Edison's longest-serving and most trusted assistants, Dr. Miller Hutchinson, worked with him on the Spirit Finder, and was as adamant as his employer that one could be constructed. His certainty was matched by his lack of knowledge on how to proceed. But: "Edison and I are convinced," Hutchinson wrote, "that in the fields of psychic

research will yet be discovered facts that will prove of greater significance to the thinking of the human race than all the inventions we have
ever made in the field of electricity."

When Edison died in 1931, neither he nor Hutchinson had made
any progress on the Spirit Finder, and despite Roy Stemman's assertion that the men were "developing" such a device, that they had been
working on it for "some time," neither a prototype nor drawings exist
today. But, like Lodge, who also left nothing behind, Edison never lost
faith in the idea behind what was perhaps the sole invention he could
never master.

Unlike Lodge, though, who supposedly made post-mortem contact with Baird, Edison has remained silent ever since his interment. In
fact, as of 2022, the once budding religion of Spiritualism has become
virtually silent as well. The worship of technology is the new American
creed, one that engages more people than any other faith ever did, so
it is perhaps inevitable that one day someone will attempt to cross the
final frontier of communication by coming full circle, in a manner of
speaking, recalling the Fox sisters by employing an Apple. Not the kind
that taps on the floor; the kind that require tapping on a keyboard.

If it happens, that someone will be someone who believes the world
behind the black curtain is just a few extra terabytes away.

EPILOGUE

In conclusion, I find it worth repeating a point made earlier: Broadly speaking, the supposition behind Spiritualism is the supposition behind most organized religions. When people die, they do not really cease to exist; they merely take up residence in another realm of being, one that the living have not yet discovered and perhaps are never destined to locate. Spiritualism teaches that the deceased and the living are somehow able to communicate, while Christianity teaches that the same is possible between the living and the Almighty. Christians hope that God will answer their prayers, Spiritualists that the departed will renew, if only for a short time, their previous relationships. The former is more common than the latter; in neither case, though, is the communication of the conventional variety.

Thus Spiritualism cannot be dismissed *in principle* without inflicting wounds on Roman Catholicism, Protestantism, and other forms of worship. I admit the comparison is not an airtight one. I admit that many Christians will find it specious, insulting, even offensive to the religious beliefs they hold. I ask those who are offended not to mistake me; I am not, repeat *not*, equating the Christian God with someone's long deceased Uncle Fred, which, if it were a joke, would be a tasteless one. I am, rather, calling attention to the fact that neither can be reached by normal methods of communication. But the fact that this is so must be acknowledged in any serious study of Spiritualism, and any serious attempt to understand the reasons for its grip on the American past.

At present, it is irrelevant. Spiritualism is history more than current events. Yet in its time--the Industrial Age in the United States, the Victorian Era in England--it provided consolation, or at least flickers of hope, to millions of men and women who needed just such a balm. More so than today, the world of yesterday was often nasty, brutish, short, and poisoned by both poverty and industrial pollution. The robber barons dined on pheasant while the starving men and women in their employ fired rickety old rifles at pigeons or sparrows, hoping to bring down a rare treat for the evening meal. These men and women, and too often their children, sometimes toiled seven days a week, often from sunup until sundown, in factories and shops that were dangerous to their health and even more of a threat to their odds of a lengthy life span. Their only salvation came in the religions in which most of them had been raised, religions that promised a better life when they reached the hereafter, rather than during the here-and-endlessly dismal now. For some of them, always a relative few, this was not enough. They were receptive, even eager, to direct their spiritual longing elsewhere.

And then Spiritualism came along, providing an alternative. One of its basic beliefs, although not necessarily stated in the words I am about to use, has been that "reality" is misused as a singular noun, that the proper usage is "realities," plural. Yet it is a belief to which little heed seems ever to be paid--this even though more than a century ago, Albert Einstein established a kind of alternate reality with his theory of relativity. And if there is one alternative reality, surely the possibility for others also exists. It is precisely this possibility, a surrogate reality, that lies at the core of Spiritualism. It does not promise a heaven, but something almost as heartening, the opportunity to talk to those no longer slogging their way through way through life on earth. These people thereby enjoy a form of continued existence, just as if they were Methodists or Episcopalians. And those they had left behind will find their sorrows less sorrowful. So it is believed, so it is hoped.

It surprises me, at such a late stage of my life, that I am just now learning about Spiritualism. But I understand why; information is hard to come by.·········· I have dozens of books in my home library that are devoted, at least in part, to the history of the latter half of the nineteenth century. I looked through the indices of them all. I found one reference, only one, to Spiritualism. I checked the indices of more volumes in nearby libraries, large and small, again wanting to find the appropriate pages for Spiritualism. For the most part, I failed. I turned up a few, but only a few. And most of the references I discovered were no longer than a paragraph or two, and in a few instances were nothing more than a single sentence. None of them even hints at the relative importance of Spiritualism in its time.

When I searched the indices of a different set of books, those on the current state of religious activity, I fare even worse. Today, the number of people who identify themselves as Spiritualists, at least in the United States, is so small that it literally doesn't register. According to the most recent study by the non-partisan Pew Research Center in Washington, D.C., six percent of Americans are Jewish, .9 percent Buddhist, .7 percent Hindu, and .3 percent of those surveyed identified themselves as members of something called the United Church. Next to the word Spiritualism, there is nothing, a blank, a black hole. So few people expressed a belief in it that they do not rate a percentage, not even a percentage preceded by a decimal point.

I take issue, thus, with an article published on May 24, 2021 in the online version of *The New Yorker*. The article refers to a resurgence of interest in Spiritualism in the twenty-first century. It reports out that one out of every three Americans say they have conversed with the dead.

·········· I do not, however, know *why* it is hard to come by, and that is a lacuna immensely frustrating to me. Of course the information exists; something as momentous as Spiritualism's virtual disappearance from the public record cannot occur without a reason. But that reason, or those reasons, have remained hidden from view despite my diligent attempts to find them. I can speculate, but cannot state with anything approaching certainty.

It further reports that there are 100 Spiritualist churches in the United States, and 300 in the United Kingdom. Let me address these points:

One out of three is a remarkable statistic, but it tells us more about people claiming to have conversed with the deceased than it does about people identifying themselves as Spiritualists. It is possible, perhaps commonplace, for men and women to believe in post-mortem communication without even knowing that the belief is the fundamental tenet of a religion. And many of those who *do* know that they are officially Spiritualists do not identify themselves as such because they also worship more traditionally, more "respectably," attending services at Roman Catholic churches, Protestant churches, and synagogues. As the *New Yorker* article points out, "plenty of people hold spiritualist beliefs within other faith traditions or stand entirely outside organized religion."

As for the number of Spiritualist churches, most of them are storefronts more than cathedrals. And, even so, the number is not impressive. In the United States, there is one Spiritualist worship site for every 3,200,000 people. In the United Kingdom, there is one for every 224,333 men and women.

There might be a resurgence in belief in dialogue with the departed. There is, however, no resurgence in Spiritualism.

The buildings in London and New York that house the SPRs, they are still standing, but serve more as museums now more than institutions that try to extend the frontiers of research and knowledge. They are memorials more than active enterprises. Surely there was a Daniel Dunglas Home of the twentieth century, even if he didn't levitate or elongate or put on other such circus-like displays of paranormality; surely there is a Leonora Piper of the twenty-first, even if she is not quite as accurate or unassuming. But no one has found them, or has seriously inquired into their existence, and as far as I know, no one with the cachet of William James even seems to be looking.

I have found it impossible to learn how many members are enrolled in the ASPR at present, just as I have found it impossible to learn the specifics of how either of the SPRs is funded, and how today's amounts compare to yesterday's. I do know this: I visited the ASPR library twice; it is a large room, impressive in its belle epoque style and superbly stocked, a trove for an author with my interests. But on both of my visits I was alone, the only person seated among the books.*¨¨¨¨¨ I saw dust motes bustling thickly in the air. I heard a phone ring only once. And I heard the soft footsteps of the librarian as she occasionally glided through the room to replace or remove a volume from the shelves. On my first visit, I asked her about the people who worked at the ASPR. She said that the woman in charge of the organization was away on business that day and another was at home, sick.

But that was it. That was everyone, three people, the entire staff, which works out to one employee for each floor of the once-elegant Manhattan brownstone, a building on Central Park West that has long since taken on the patina of the shabby-genteel.

Nonetheless, the ASPR and SPR achieved the goals of their heyday, meticulously examining claims of the paranormal and publishing their results, despite all the booing and hissing from the scientific sidelines. In recent years, although without specifically referring to matters

---

¨¨¨¨¨¨¨ Interestingly, one of my predecessors in using the facility was Peter Aykroyd's son, the comedian and actor Dan, a scholar of the paranormal like his father. There are a few places in *Ghostbusters* when Dan's character, Ray Stantz, breaks into what sounds like inspired riffing on the supernatural; the ghost that he and his partners have just busted in a hotel ballroom, for example, is described as "a focused, non-terminal repeating phantasm or a Class-5, full roaming vapor."

To moviegoers, it was gibberish. To Aykroyd it was not. He took notes for the *Ghostbusters* script at the ASPR, determined on making the script as accurate as possible--accurate, that is, as he understood the term. Dan knew his findings would play as humor on screen; in fact, he was counting on it. But he didn't care. He would get laughs from the audience while at the same time being true to himself and his beliefs. Two birds with one stone.

Decades later, when I took a seat in the library, I was fortunate. No full-roaming vapors of *any* class interrupted my studies.

supernatural, a scholarly fellow named Aaron Lassig, who identifies himself as half-philosopher, half-mechanical engineer, estimates that the percentage of discoverable knowledge of which science is presently aware is 0.00000000002368. Then he adds, I trust with a grin, "But this is only approximate."

Another approximation I encountered, this one on the question-and-answer website Quora, is exponentially higher, soaring all the way to almost one percent, leaving a mere ninety-nine percent of the world's knowledge unknown to those who occupy the world.

If either of those numbers is accurate, or close to accurate, or even within a light year or two of accurate, there is room aplenty to accommodate many more realities.

In the preceding pages I have written much that the reader is certain to reject. And that the author himself cannot help but question, having arrived at destinations I never imagined even existed when I began writing this book. I have, in other words, however inadvertently, cannot help but fear that I have reported here and there about events that did not happen. But not many, I like to think, and I urge the reader to understand that some falsehoods are as important a part of history as many truths, especially if they represent widespread views of their era, views that tell us much about the tenor of times past, the cultural values, and the need that people possess to believe what they believe.

But to me, nothing strains credulity more than the notion that every claim of authenticity made by members of the two SPRs about a psychic's accuracy is either prevarication or error. If the former, why? To accept the notion that the smartest minds in the world, thousands of them, engaged in a conspiracy to delude lesser minds is a more preposterous assumption than accepting the veracity of the feats of Home and Piper and many others.

I am not at ease sounding so adamant. But I write with a passion for logic and a respect for the archival record, and I believe I have been faithful to both.

In conclusion to my conclusion, I quote from Sir William Crookes, after he finished conducting several days of experiments with Daniel Dunglas Home. Precisely what Home demonstrated on those particular days is not known. What *is* known is that, afterward, Crookes met with some acquaintances and related in detail not only what he had just seen, but what precautions he and his associates had taken to make sure Home had not been deceitful.

His listeners were silent throughout Crookes's presentation, the air thick with the scent of incredulity. Surely you don't believe that kind of thing is possible, one of his colleagues finally responded.

"I never said it was possible," Crookes replied, in the most measured terms he could manage. "I only said it was true."

ACKNOWLEDGMENTS

This is rather a brief section of my book, but not because I received so little help in assembling the material. Rather, I received a great deal of assistance--which is always necessary when one writes history--but from a relatively small number of people.

Carolyn Zygmont of the Westport Public Library is always the first to receive my gratitude when I complete a book. But this one was different--in part because my knowledge of a secular afterlife was so limited before I decided to write about it; in part because of the topics complexities. As a result, Carolyn was even more indispensable than usual; both the number of questions I asked and the range of information I requested were greater than ever for *When the Dead Talked . . . and the Smartest People in the World Listened*. But Carolyn's ability to provide the information I needed, or to guide me in my own searches, was also greater than ever. Caryn Friedman and Margie Freilich-Den, who staff the reference desk at the library in the adjoining town of Norwalk, also provided much needed guidance and support.

Some of the books and documents upon which I relied were not available in Westport, Norwalk, or in other public libraries anywhere; they were, instead, tucked away in private collections or in the collections of universities in at least six states. I heartily thank Susan Madeo and Christine Lorusso for obtaining these obscure volumes for me. Obscure, yes, but containing crucial information. And the details were often difficult to assemble. I hope I have done so logically, credibly, and fairly.

There were also two easier-to-procure books that proved invaluable to me. I referred to one of the authors several times in the text; the other I cite for the first time here. For those who found it edifying to read *When the Dead Talked . . .* and would like to read more on the topic, I recommend Professor Deborah Blum's *Ghost Hunters: William James and the Search for Scientific Proof of Life After Death.* Very little has been written for general a general audience on this subject; Professor Blum's volume was easily the most valuable, comprehensive, and academically sound of them all.

The other author is Erik Larson, who does not even know about the journey upon which he set me. On page 13 of *Thunderstruck,* a book he published after his extraordinary *The Devil in the White City,* he briefly refers to William James encountering a medium named Leonora Piper and being "enthralled" by her. I remember reading the sentence, reading it again, and then dropping the book onto my lap, startled. Could it possibly be? The father of pragmatism was enthralled by a woman who supposedly communed with the dead? The towering American intellect of his time believed in the unbelievable? If it was good enough for William James, it was certainly good enough for me. It seemed a pairing that was almost oxymoronic, and, more than anything else that appears in the previous pages, it was this pairing, and the ramifications thereof, that drew me to write those pages.

Larson's adjective led to my research on James's research into the afterlife, which in turn led me to the work of the SPRs, which in turn led to this volume, and one startling fact after another, one startling occurrence after another, an education in an important part of the American and British past with which I was totally unfamiliar.

For her kindness in clearing up a few matters about the Fox sisters' anatomical prowess, my gratitude goes to Melissa Grafe at the Cushing/ Whitney Medical Library at Yale University.

Without Junelle James, the librarian of the American Society for Psychical Research, the young lady with the soft footsteps, *When the Dead Talked . . .* would not have been possible. The Society's great repository of information and high ethical standards made it invaluable to me. One day I asked Junelle if the SPR had any books or articles about a controversial medium who was once well known. I received scowl in response. Then she asked whether I *had* to include her?" I will not admit whether I did or not; the point of the anecdote is to call attention to the rigors of the ASPR in presenting only information that it finds valid. Junelle was suspicious about this particular person, and convinced that the ASPR had proven her suspicions well-founded.

From Lily Dale, I found out more about Spiritualism than just Lily Dale's contribution to it. I spoke to, and learned greatly from, Susan Glasier, the Village Manager, and Ron Nagy, the Museum Curator. They sent me off on tangents that led to tangents of their own, which I quickly learned were not tangents at all.

I thank Alan Neigher for various reasons--not to mention his stimulating congeniality--and, as well, express my gratitude to Lorraine Battipaglia for providing a valuable suggestion about the order in which some of the information in this book should be presented.

And I express my gratitude to Nicky Bradley, who proved himself to be a fussy, pedantic, and nit-picking proofreader. In other words, the perfect colleague for a fussy, pedantic, and nit-picking author. I am very appreciative.

Finally, since I wrote much of *When the Dead Talked . . . and the Smartest Minds in the World Listened* despite the inconveniences of a blood clot, an occasionally aching back, some painful symptoms of celiac disease, a mysterious bout with fatigue, and an arthritic knee, a memento of so many years on the basketball court. I express my gratitude to the American medical profession. Well, to certain members thereof.

BIBLIOGRAPHY

Private Papers, Periodicals, Selected Internet Sources

AH Stuart, Nancy Rubin, "The Fox Sisters: Spiritualism's Unlikely Founders," *American History Magazine*, August, 2005. (Online version)

BioScience Peter Moller and Bernd Kramer. "Review: Electric Fish," *Bioscience* (American Institute of Biological Sciences), December 1991.

Brooklyn Eagle, January 21, 1901.

BW Lisa Baker Whelan, "Between Worlds: Class Identity and Suburban Ghost Stories, 1850-1880" *Mosaic: 35.1*, (March, 2002), pp. 133-148.

DP Declaration of Principles, National Spiritualist Association of Churches.

FD "Piper, Leonora E." encyclopedia2.thefreedictionary, various sources.

JAH "Journal of American History," Robert W. Delp. London: Oxford University Press on behalf of Organization of American Historians.

JASPR "Journal of the American Society for Psychical Research."

JSPR "Journal of the Society for Psychical Research."

NY New Yorker, Casey Cep. "Why did So Many Victorians Try to Speak With the Dead?" May 24, 2021, unpaginated. (Online version)

NYT New York Herald, January 22, 1901.

NYT New York Times, March 17, 1905.

NYW New York World, October 22, 1988.

PASPR Proceeding of the American Society for Psychical Research.

PGA Doyle, Sir Arthur Conan, M.D., LL.d. *The History of Spiritualism, Volume II*, Chapter One, Project Gutenberg Australia. Date first posted: July, 2003. (Online version)

PSPR "Proceedings of the Society for Psychical Research."

PSY Bradley, Megan E. "William James," *PSYography*. Frostburg, Maryland: Frostburg State University, retrieved by Wikipedia, September 21, 2013.

RA Banks, Joe. "Rorschach Audio: Ghost Voices and Perceptual Creativity." *Leonardo Music Journal Volume 11*, 2001.

Rap Abbott, Karen. "The Fox Sisters and the Rap on Spiritualism," *The Smithsonian* magazine, October 30, 2012.

SPR Journal of the Society for Psychical Research, Volume VI, November, 1894, online version.

SWC The Haunted Museum (authors). "Story of the White Crow," www.prairieghosts.com/piper.html, 2003-2008.

WHE World History Encyclopedia. Mark, Joshua J. "Ghosts in the Ancient World," October 30, 2014, accessed on October 6, 2021, www.worldhistory.org/ghost/.

Books

Aykroyd, Peter with Angela Narth. *A History of Ghosts: The True Story of séances, Mediums, Ghosts, and Ghostbusters.* New York: Rodale, 2009.

Baldwin, Neil. *Edison: Inventing the Century.* New York: Hyperion, 1995.

Barrett, Sir William. *Death-Bed Visions.* London: Metheun & Co., 1926.

Blum, Deborah. *Ghost Hunters: William James and the Search for Scientific Proof of Life After Death*. New York: Penguin, 2006.

Branch, Edgar Marquess and Robert H. Hirsh, eds. *The Works of Mark Twain: Early Tales and Sketches*, Volume I. Berkeley, California: University of California Press.

Brandon, Ruth. *The Spiritualists: The Passion for the Occult in the Nineteenth and Twentieth Centuries*. London: Weidenfeld and Nicolson, 1983.

Braude, Stephen E. *Immortal Remains: The Evidence for Life After Death*. Lanham, Maryland: Rowman and Littlefield, 2003.

Brock, William H. *William Crookes (1832-1919) and the Commercialization of Science*. Aldershot, Hampshire, England: Ashgate Publishing, 2008.

Buckland, Raymond. *The Spirit Book: The Encyclopedia of Clairvoyance, Channeling, and Spirit Communication*. Canton, Michigan: Visible Ink Press, 2005.

Burns, Eric. *All the News Unfit to Print: How Things Were . . . and How They Were Reported*. Hoboken, New Jersey: John Wiley & Sons, 2005

Burton, Jean: *Heyday of a Wizard: Daniel Home, the Medium*. New York: Knopf, 1944.

Chernow, Ron. *Titan: The Life of John D. Rockefeller, Sr.* New York: Random House, 1998.

Christiansen, Rupert. *The Victorian Visitors: Culture Shock in Nineteenth-Century Britain*. New York: Atlantic Monthly Press, 2000.

Christopher, Milbourne. *Houdini: The Untold Story: The dramatic life of the world's most famous magician, escape artist, and investigator of psychic phenomena*. New York: Thomas Y. Crowell, 1969.

Clark, Ronald W. *Edison: The Man Who Made the Future*. New York: Putnam, 1977.

Conot, Robert. *A Streak of Luck: The Life & Legend of Thomas Alva Edison*. New York: Seaview Books, 1979.

Cross, Whitney R. *The Burned-over District: The Social and Intellectual History of Enthusiastic Religion in Western New York, 1800-1850*. Ithaca, New York: Cornell University Press, 1950.

Crowe, Catherine. *The Night Side of Nature Or Ghosts and Ghost Seers*. London: Wordsworth Editions, 2000.

D' Albe, E.E. Fournier. *The Life of Sir William Crookes*. New York: D. Appleton and Company, 1924.

Darrow, Kathy D., ed. *Nineteenth-Century Literature Criticism*, Volume 220. Detroit: Gale, 2010. [electronic version]

Davies, Owen. *The Haunted: A Social History of Ghosts*. Houndmills, Basingstoke, Hampshire, U.K.: Palgrave Macmillan, 2007.

Dingwall, Eric John. *Some Human Oddities: Studies in the Queer, the Uncanny, and the Fanatical*. New Hyde Park, New York: University Books, 1962.

Douglas, Alfred. *Extra-Sensory Powers: A Century of Psychical Research*. London: Victor Gollancz Ltd., 1976.

Doyle, Arthur Conan. *The History of Spiritualism, Vol. 1, 2*. New York: Arno Press, 1975.

Fisher, Paul. *House of Wits: An Intimate Portrait of the James Family*. New York: Henry Holt, 2008.

Fitzsimmons, Raymond. *Death & the Magician: The Mystery of Houdini*. New York: Atheneum, 1980.

Fuller, Randall. *The Book That Changed America: How Darwin's Theory of Evolution Ignited a Nation*. New York: Viking, 2017

Gallagher, Winifred. *How the Post Office Created America: A History*. New York: Penguin Press, 2016.

Gardner, Martin. *Are Universes Thicker Than Blackberries?: How Mrs. Piper Bamboozled William James.* New York: Norton, 2003.

Goodwin, Doris Kearns. *Team of Rivals: The Political Genius of Abraham Lincoln.* New York: Simon & Schuster, 2005.

Habegger, Alfred. *The Father: A Life of Henry James, Sr.* New York: Farrar, Straus and Giroux, 1994.

Hall, Trevor H. *The Enigma of Daniel Home: Medium or Fraud.* Buffalo, New York: Prometheus Books, 1984.

Hansel, C.E.M. *The Search for Psychic Power: ESP and Parapsychology Revisited.* Buffalo, New York: Prometheus Books, 1989.

Hart, Professor Hornell. *The Enigma of Survival: The Case For and Against the After Life.* Springfield, Illinois: Charles C. Thomas, 1959.

Hawthorne, Nathaniel. *The French and Italian Notebooks,* edited by Thomas Woodson. Columbus, Ohio: Ohio State University Press, 1980.

Home, D.D. *Incidents in My Life.* New York: A.J. Davis & Co., 1864

Houdini, Harry. *Houdini: A Magician Among the Spirits.* New York: Arno Press, 1972.

Howe, Daniel Walker. *What Hath God Wrought: The Transformation of America, 1815-1848.* New York: Oxford University Press, 2007.

James, William. *Essays in Psychical Research.* Cambridge, Massachusetts: Harvard University Press, 1986.

Jenkins, Elizabeth. *The Shadow and the Light: A Defence of Daniel Dunglas Home, the Medium.* London: Hamish Hamilton, 1982.

Johnson, Paul. *Modern Times (Revised Edition): From the Twenties to the Nineties.* New York: HarperCollins, 1991.

Jolly, W.P. *Sir Oliver Lodge.* Rutherford, New Jersey: Fairleigh Dickinson University Press, 1975.

Kalush, William, and Larry Sloman. *The Secret Life of Houdini: The Making of America's First Superhero.* New York: Atria Books, 2006.

Kaplan, Fred. *The Singular Mark Twain.* New York: Doubleday, 2003.

Kelly, Edward F., Adam Crabtree and Paul Marshall, ed. *Beyond Physicalism: Toward Reconciliation of Science and Spirituality.* Lanham, Maryland: Rowman and Littlefield, 2015.

Kerr, Howard and Charles L. Crow, eds. *The Occult in America: New Historical Perspectives.* Urbana, Illinois: University of Illinois Press, 1983.

Kurtz, Paul, ed. *A Skeptic's Handbook of Parapsychology.* Buffalo, New York: Prometheus Books, 1985.

Kuzmeskas, Elaine M. *Connecticut in the Golden Age of Spiritualism.* Charleston, South Carolina: History Press, 2016.

Lamont, Peter. *Extraordinary Beliefs: A Historical Approach to a Psychological Problem.* Cambridge, England: Cambridge University Press, 2013.

-------. *The First Psychic: The Peculiar Mystery of a Notorious Victorian Wizard.* London: Little, Brown, 2005.

Larson, Erik. *Thunderstruck.* New York: Crown, 2006.

Leichtman, Robert R. *Sir Oliver Lodge Returns: From Heaven to Earth.* Columbus, Ohio: Ariel Press, 1979.

Leonard, Todd Jay. *Talking to the Other Side: A History of Modern Spiritualism and Mediumship: A Study of the Religion, Science, Philosophy and Medium that Encompass this American-Made Religion.* New York: iUniverse, 2005.

Lewis, R.W.B. *The Jameses: A Family Narrative.* New York: Farrar, Straus and Giroux, 1991.

Lodge, Sir Oliver. *Raymond, or Life and Death*. Project Gutenberg: Ebook, 2016.

Markel, Howard. *The Kelloggs: The Battling Brothers of Battle Creek*. New York: Pantheon, 2017.

Masini, Giancarlo. *Marconi*. New York: Marsilio Publishers, 1976.

McArthur, Tom and Peter Waddell. *The Secret Life of John Logie Baird*. London: Hutchinson, 1986.

McCabe, Joseph. *Is Spiritualism Based on Fraud? The Evidence Given By Sir A.C. Doyle and Others Drastically Examined*. London: Watts, 1920.

Menand, Louis. *The Metaphysical Club: A Story of Ideas in America*. New York: Farrar, Straus and Giroux, 2001.

Mercier, Charles A. *Spiritualism and Sir Oliver Lodge*. London: Watts & Co., 1919.

Neville-Sington, Pamela. *Fanny Trollope: The Life and Adventures of a Clever Woman*. New York: Viking Penguin, 1998.

Owen, Alex. *The Other World: Spiritualism and psychical Research in Victorian Britain, 1850-1914*.London: Virago, 1989.

Piper, Alta. *The Life and Work of Mrs. Piper*. London: Kegan Paul, Trench, Trubner & Co., 1929.

Podmore, Frank. *The Newer Spiritualism*. London: T. Fisher Unwin, 1910.

Raboy, Marc. *Marconi: The Man Who Networked the World*. New York: Oxford University Press, 2016.

Robbins, Anne Manning. *Past and Present with Mrs. Piper*. New York: Henry Holt, 1921.

Sage, M. *Mrs. Piper & the Society for Psychical Research*. New York: Scott-Thaw, 1904.

Sconce, Jeffrey. *Haunted Media: Electronic Presence from Telegraphy to Television (Console-ing Passions)*. Durham, North Carolina: Duke University Press, 2000.

Salter, W.H. *Trance Mediumship: An Introductory Study of Mrs. Piper and Mrs. Leonard*. London: Society for Psychical Research, 1950.

Sankovitch, Nina. *The Lowells of Massachusetts: An American Family*. New York: St. Martin's, 2017.

Seldes, Gilbert. *The Stammering Century*. Gloucester, Massachusetts: Peter Smith, 1972.

Sidgwick, Arthur and Eleanor Mildred Sidgwick. *Henry Sidgwick: A Memoir by A.S. and E.M.S.* London: Macmillan, 1906.

Simon, Linda. *Genuine Reality: A Life of William James*. New York: Harcourt, Brace, 1998.

Stein, Gordon. *The Sorcerer of Kings*. Buffalo, New York: Prometheus Books, 1993.

Stemman, Roy. *Spirit Communication: A comprehensive guide to the extraordinary world of mediums, psychics and the afterlife*. London: Piatkus, 2005.

Stephen, Sir Leslie and Sir Sidney Lee, eds. *The Dictionary of National Biography*. London: Oxford University Press, 1921.

St. Germain, Mark. *Camping with Henry and Tom: A Play in Two Acts*. New York: Samuel French, 1995.

Tuckett, Ivor Lloyd. *The Evidence for the Supernatural: A Critical Study Made with "Uncommon Sense."* London: K. Paul, Trench, Trubner [two dots over the "u" in "Trubner"], 1911.

Turner, Frank Miller. *Between Science and Religion: The Reaction to Scientific Naturalism in Late Victorian England*. New Haven: Yale University Press, 1974.

Weinberg, Barbara. *Talking to the Dead: Kate and Maggie Fox and the Rise of Spiritualism*. San Francisco: HarperSanFrancisco, 2004.

Wellman, Judith. *Grass Roots Reform in the Burned-Over District of Upstate New York: Religions, Abolitionism and Democracy*. New York: Garland Publishing, 2000.

Wells, H.G. *The War of the World*. New York: New York Review Books, 1960.

Wicker, Christine. *Lily Dale: The True Story of the Town That Talks to the Dead*. San Francisco: HarperSanFrancisco, 2003.

Wolfe, Tom. *The Kingdom of Speech*. New York: Little, Brown, 2016.

NOTES

Glossary

- "a medium with special powers," Aykroyd, p. 15.
- "let us define it," quoted in ibid, p. 229.
- "The phenomenon is," Podmore, p. 59.

Before He Was Mark Twain . . .

- "in 1858 the Clemens brothers," Blum, p. 73-4.
- "with his throat cut," quoted in Burns, p. 64.
- "her right hand almost severed," quoted in ibid, p. 64.

1. Apples in the Night

- "adept mimics," Weisberg, p. 15.
- "infected district," quoted in Cross, p. 3.
- "the '"Burned-over District,'" Menand, p. 90.
- "the prevailing western analogy," Cross, p. 3.
- "spook house," quoted in Blum, p. 16.
- "a gruesome portrait," ibid, p. 17.
- "[s]light but sturdy," and, "ebullient fourteen-year-old," Weisberg, p. 12.

- "The first way in which," Seldes, p. 331.
- "sometimes it seemed," quoted in ibid, p. 331.
- "two mischievous children," Christopher, p. 28.
- "I then asked," Weisberg, p. 19.
- "Now count five," *Rap*, p. 2.
- "that it was murdered," quoted in Weisberg, p. 20.
- "William Duesler summed up the position," Kerr and Crow, eds., p. 83.
- "Margaret Fox's sister," Weisberg, p. 32.
- "[o]ne of the greatest religious movements," *AH*, p. 2.
- "God's chosen people," quoted in Markel, p. 24.
- "[s]enators, judges, and professors," Christopher, p. 28.
- "Rochester rappings," Seldes, p. 332.
- "regarded them with awe," *AH*, p.3.
- "Rochester was a hotbed," *Rap*, p. 2.
- "WONDERFUL PHENOMENA," *NY*, unpaginated.
- "remained perplexed," ibid, p. 6.
- "Blinding cascades of light," ibid, p. 6.
- "Margaret and Catherine Fox," Seldes, p. 332-3.
- "that the human personality," Aykroyd, p. 5-6.

2. The Loudest Joints

- "[h]is purported ability," *JAH*, Vol. 54, No. 1 (June, 1967) p.44.
- "'Poughkeepsie Seer,'" quoted in Weisberg, p. 26.
- "'John the Baptist,'" quoted in *Rap*, p. 3.
- "the feeble-bodied, untutored son," Aykroyd, p. 9.
- "The circumference of his head," quoted in ibid, p. 10-11.
- "Maggie, Kate, and Leah Fox," *Rap*, p. 3.

- "In addition to the rappings," Fitzsimmons, p. 9
- "All this sounds sufficiently ridiculous," quoted in Kerr and Crow, eds., pp. 90-1.
- "The sisters went to bed," Weisberg, p. 109.
- "The sisters explained," Kerr and Crow, eds., p. 90.
- "So popular were the séances," Weisberg, p. 109.
- "at the home," ibid, p. 110.
- "Had she died of illness?" Blum, p. 19.
- "witnessed a [Fox] session," *Rap*, p. 4.
- "their most influential backer," Habegger, p. 321.
- "Greeley had heard the raps," Weisberg, pp. 108-9.
- "emerged from the hotel," ibid, p. 109.
- "arousing national interest," Fitsimmons, p. 9.
- "All over America," ibid, p. 10.
- "To believers," ibid, p. 10.
- "giving their trances," Blum, p. 62.
- "By the 1840s," *AH*, p. 4.
- "Well-educated, would-be sophisticated people," Wolfe, p. 49.
- "Manifestations," quoted in Seldes, p. 335.
- "I answered," quoted in ibid, p. 335-6.
- "they left behind dozens of circles," Kerr and Crow, eds., p. 92
- "Reasoning by way of exclusion," Weisberg, p. 124.
- "the raps did not occur," Hansel, p. 233.
- "made by the sisters," Fitzsimmons, p. 10.
- "so adept that they performed," *AH*, p.7.
- "explaining that it helped," Kerr and Crow, eds., p. 95.
- "Spiritualism is a humbug," quoted in Christopher, p. 182.
- "I do this," quoted in Houdini, p. 5.

- "On October 21, 1888," *Rap*, pp. 4-5.
- "this horrible deception began," quoted in ibid, p. 5.
- "a black-robed, sharp-faced widow," quoted in ibid, p. 5.
- "The entire house," and, "agreed that the sounds," *NYW*.
- "Like most perplexing things," and, "A child at twelve," ibid.
- "death-blow," quoted in Weisberg, p. 253.
- "MODERN SPIRITUALISM," quoted in ibid, p. 255.
- "demonstrated clearly where," Fitzsimmons, p. 11.
- "end-stage alcoholism," *AH*, p. 8.
- "The desire to establish," Weisberg, p. 102.
- "[o]ne of the first individuals," ibid, p. 102.
- "God's telegraph," quoted in ibid, p. 102.

3. The Boom, Part One

- "popular fascination," Blum, p. 13.
- "Would to God," quoted in Weisberg, p. 256.
- "remained one of the world's," quoted in Weisberg, p. 231.
- "Darwinian theory," Fuller, p. 42.
- "The greatest event," quoted in Johnson, p. 48.
- "my boy is gone," quoted in Goodwin, p. 419.
- "was drawn to the spiritualist world," ibid, p. 422.
- "MARS INHABITED," *NYT*, August 30, 1907.
- "was also criticized," Sankovitch, p. 254
- "Spiritualism often attracted," Turner, p
- "Do as I do," quoted in Wicker, p. 100.
- "According to the *New Haven* (Conn.) *Journal*," Hall, p. 29.
- "along with railroad man," Wicker, p. 7.
- "[t]he 1880 census," Kuzmeskas, p. 107.

- "a warmly satisfying," Cross, 347.
- "a Russian bureaucrat," Weisberg, p. 231.
- "on a mission," ibid, p. 231-2.
- "She couldn't bear to be parted," ibid, p. 232.
- "end-stage alcoholism," *AH*, p. 8.
- "body, reeking of old dirt," Blum, p. 24
- "One day," quoted in ibid, p. 241.

4. The Boom, Part Two

- "[t]he religious and quasi-religious fervor," Aykroyd, p. 17.
- "Spooksville," and "Silly Dale," quoted in Wicker, p. 13.
- "It was so popular," ibid, p. 65.
- "Spiritualist religious practice," ibid, p. 22.
- "[n]onresident mediums," and, "visit from around the world," Weisberg, 260.
- "Spiritualism is the most comforting," www.smithsonianmag.com/history/in-good-spirits-43969706/?no-ist.
- "To hang a shingle," Wicker, p. 37.
- "In 1916," Weisberg, pp. 266-7.
- "*We affirm that communication,*" *DP.*
- "Public sanitations codes," *BW,* p. 136.
- "frustrated, disappointed," ibid, p. 136.
- "the supernatural was used," Darrow, unpaginated [electronic [electronic version]
- "would not be easily deluded," ibid, p. 20.
- "Well, he wants you to know," quoted in Wicker, p. 28.
- "a significant portion," ibid, p. 138

- "the supernatural was used," Darrow, unpaginated [electronic version]
- "Some years ago," Crowe, p. 154-6.
- "Professor De Morgan was willing to concede," Burton, p. 163.
- "the most influential single book," quoted in Blum, p. 330, n15.
- "a pioneering attempt," www.amazon.com/Phantasms-living-v-1-Edmund-Gurney/dp/B0065GCLSW.
- "criticized by a number," Douglas, p. 76
- "Fraud had already created," Aykroyd, p.

5. High Societies

- "the great head," Larson, p. 10.
- "In 1883," Aykroyd, p. 51-52.
- "[t]wo young female shop-assistants," Douglas, p. 241.
- "I knew it would be unpopular," quoted in Blum, p. 259.
- "hailed as a major work," Blum, p. 40
- "However, he did accept," Turner, p. 59.
- "earned a reputation," Aykroyd, p. 48.
- "Myers was, like Sidgwick," Blum, p. 42.
- "He expected psychical research," Turner, p. 117.
- "And then a scream," quoted in Blum, p. 93.
- "Of my fright and horror," quoted in ibid, p. 93.
- "a terrible death," quoted in ibid, p. 94.
- "Our plan," quoted in ibid, p. 41.
- "Fraud had already created," Aykroyd, p. 47.
- "some kind of fourth dimension," Wolfe, p. 64.
- "a physiologist from France," Simon, p. 191.
- "including sixty academics," Weightman, p. 93.

- "to examine without prejudice," quoted in Larson, p. 12.
- "His ardent yet rational approach," Aykroyd, p. 48-9.
- "Truth is stranger than fiction," quoted in Raboy, p. 44.
- "Further, Twain said," Blum, pp. 172-3.
- "[t]he society's official aim," Brandon, p. 68.
- "With the discovery," Raboy, pp. 84-5.
- "Rays of light," quoted in Weightman, p. 96.
- "before Marconi, Crookes was sneered at," quoted in ibid, p. 51.
- "excited into being," Blum, p. 86.
- "The evidence published," quoted in ibid, p. 86.
- "When Crookes raised the idea," Raboy, 86.
- "the head of the astronomy department," Simon, p. 191.
- "that only principles that can be demonstrated," *SWC*, p. 1.
- "Father of American psychology," *psy*, unpaginated.
- "He'd developed an innovative approach," ibid, p. 5.
- "considered one of the most influential thinkers," Aykroyd, p. 123.
- "camp meeting," and, "extremely depressing," quoted in Simon, p. 190.
- "We spent the evening," quoted in ibid, p. 190.
- "James had never been," Blum, p. 7.
- "There remains, of course," Hawthorne, p. 400-401.

6. The James Boys

- "had yet to accomplish," Blum, 227.
- "Spiritualism in the mid-and late," Fisher, p. 478.
- "William plunged on into," ibid, p. 477.
- "Psychical research was clearly costing," Blum, p. 221.

- "wild facts," quoted in Simon, p. 188.
- "what is possible," D' Albe, p. viii.
- "To scientific men such as James," Simon, p. 141.
- "It is not a scientific way," quoted in Turner, p. 54.
- "Hardly, as yet, has the surface," quoted in Blum, p. 6.
- "Are the much despised," quoted in Simon, p. 190.
- "he worried that [if] scientists," ibid, p. 26.
- "every book of human history," and, "No matter where you open," ibid, p. 80.
- "central to every major civilization," *WHE*, unpaginated.
- "rare and precious kinship," quoted in ibid, p. 80.
- "this perpetual association," quoted in ibid, p. 92.
- "Not all churches," ibid, p. 81.
- "if chemistry and physics," ibid, pp. 109-110.
- "the laity and some ministers," Kerr and Crow, eds., p. 72
- "Are the much despised 'spiritualism,'" quoted in Simon, p. 190.
- "a table, encircled by a brass rail," ibid, p. 366.
- "She is poorly," quoted in Blum, p. 153.
- "'Spirits' said [Alfred Lord] Wallace," quoted in ibid, p. 261.
- "the Widow's Mite was front-page news," ibid, p. 261-2.
- "is certain that," and, "I caught him," James, Henry, p. 280.
- "an entire oeuvre," Habegger, p. 312.

7. The Peasant Vamp

- "As a little girl," www.survivalafterdeath.info/mediums.palladino.htm, p. 1.
- "upper bourgeoisie," ibid, p. 1.
- "the chairs began to dance," *PGA*, p. 3.

- "sobbing violently," ibid, p. 8.
- "Eusapia had a peculiar depression," ibid, p. 10.
- "short, heavy . . . with charm," Aykroyd," p. 52.
- "but they could not explain," https://en.wikipedia.org/wiki/Eusapia_Palladino.
- "Palladino was no simple case," Lamont, *Extraordinary Beliefs*, p. 189.
- "Afterward the participants," Christopher, p. 31.
- "avowed skeptic," Aykroyd, p. 53.
- "an invalid woman," www.survivalafterdeath.info/mediums.Palladino.htm, p. 2.
- "She seems to lie," ibid, p. 3.
- "to urine tests," Aykroyd, p. 54.
- "[t]he most notorious medium," and, "had no qualms," Kalush and Sloman, p. 419.
- "truly feminine languor," and, "strange and feeling passion," quoted in Simon, p. 367.
- "I am filled with confusion," quoted in Doyle, Vol. 2, p. 13.
- "becoming instrumental for Palladino's reaching," https://en.wikipedia.org/wiki/Eusapia_Palladino, p. 5.
- "an esteemed bacteriologist," Aykroyd, p. 49.
- "a big powerful man," quoted in Larson, p. 41.
- "It was as if," quoted in ibid, p. 42.
- "and the feeling," quoted in ibid, p. 42.
- "tilted back against the wall," quoted in ibid, p. 42.
- "mechanical connexion," quoted in ibid, p. 42.
- "dark and hot and very still," ibid, p. 41.
- "Professor Galeotti," and, "One [the left arm] is on the little table," *PGA*, p. 6.

- "[m]uch similar testimony," ibid, p. 6.
- "History is silent," ibid, p. 42.
- "that everything rested," Brandon, p. 258-9.
- "Her methods are too detestable," quoted in Simon, p. 368.
- "that associating with the slippery Palladino," ibid, p. 368.
- "jugglery and imposture," https://en.wikipedia.org/wiki/Eusapia_Palladino, p. 3.
- "The mystery of," www.unexplainedstuff.com/Mediums-and-Mystics/Mediums-and-Channelers-Eusapia-palladino-1854-1918.html.
- "a piece of cheesecloth," Blum, p. 312.
- "I have always said," quoted in ibid, p. 312.
- "his usual prejudice," Barrett, p. 75.
- "Here, for the first time," www.survivalafterdeath.info/mediums/palladino.htm, p. 11.
- "However the facts," *JSPR*, Volume VI, November, 1894, p. 360.
- "thoroughly convinced not only," quoted in Larson, p. 13.

8. The Incredible Flying Medium

- "of high social standing," Hall, p. 103.
- "expressed his wonder," quoted in Burton, p. 228.
- "I very much doubt," quoted in ibid, p. 228.
- "Either the facts must be admitted," quoted in Hall, p. 104.
- "that the observers," ibid, p. 126.
- "placed against a wall," Burton, p. 218.
- "Among these visitors," Lamont, *First Psychic*, p. 30-31.
- "was investigated by physicians," ibid, p. 31.
- "a tremulous phosphorescent, ibid, p. 31.

- "one of the most famous men," ibid, p.xiii.
- "I was very delicate," Home, p. 27.
- "Scotchy," quoted in ibid, p. 2.
- "In his lighter moods," Burton, p. 19.
- "would visit the other," Lamont, *First Psychic*, p. 14.
- "About a month," Home, pp. 18-19.
- "grew more dense," ibid, p. 19.
- "Before the apparition vanished," Burton, pp. 19-20.
- "laid siege to the [Cook] house," ibid, p. 23.
- "Daniel, fear not my child," Jenkins, p. 13.
- "I see no way out," quoted in ibid, p. 16.
- "When an invisible hand," Burton, p. 153.
- "the staunch Presbyterians," Aykroyd, p. 41.
- "gentlemen of education and means," quoted in Burton, p. 26.
- "Hannah Brittan is here," quoted in ibid, p. 32.
- "[T]he spirit has informed me," quoted in ibid, p. 32.
- "Spirits were seen distinctly," quoted in ibid, p. 48.
- "featured raps, strains of ghostly music," Weisberg, p 221.
- "strong men blanched," ibid, p. 221.
- "As Home took it," Jenkins, p. 155.
- "Fairly tall, slim," quoted in Burton, p. 5.
- "very vain of his personal appearance," quoted in Podmore, p. 33.
- "so unclassifiable a specimen," Burton, p. 4.
- "The room was packed," ibid, p. 94.
- "in spite of," ibid, p. 95.
- "Almost at once," ibid, p. 95.
- "appalled and ecstatic," Jenkins, p. 77.

- "in very poor health," ibid, p. 77.
- "I saw him four times," Swedish court documents quoted in en.wikipedia.org/wiki/Daniel_Dunglas_Home.
- "so successful," Blum, p. 30.
- "due pomp," ibid, p. 30.
- "she often comes to me," quoted in Jenkins, p. 239.
- "I believe in my heart," quoted in Blum, p. 23.
- "He boasted a flamboyant," ibid, pp. 30-31.
- "questioned him intently," Jenkins, p. 74.
- "England's foremost poetess," Burton, p. 65.
- "dark eyes glowing," ibid, p. 65.
- "spectral hands," Blum, p. 22.
- "He expressed no disbelief," quoted in Burton, p. 67.
- "intellectual slumming expedition," ibid, p. 65.
- "I looked under the table," quoted in Blum, p. 22.
- "His robust, explosive nature," Jenkins, p. 39.
- "*say a word on the subject*," quoted in Burton, p. 66.
- "the scoundrel's naked foot," quoted in ibid, p. 69.
- "a cheat and imposture," quoted in Podmore, p. 45.
- "humbugging," quoted in ibid, p. 68.
- "with his right hand outstretched," and, "If you are not out," ibid, p. 70.
- "Oh, dear Mr. Home," quoted in Christiansen, p. 141.
- "What do you suppose," quoted in Podmore, p. 70.
- "*For my own part*," quoted in ibid, p. 71.
- "weak as a reed," quoted in Dingwall, p. 105
- "had succeeded in making himself," ibid, p. 105.

- "a work of very considerable power," Jenkins, p. 147.
- "**Now**, don't, sir!" www.telelib.com/authors/B/BrowningRobert/verse/dramatispersonae/mrsludge.html.
- "*Mr. Hume, or Home,*" quoted in Burton, p. 149.
- "I could not choose," quoted in Jenkins, p. 253.
- "for a variety," quoted in ibid, p. 82.
- "although some persons," Home, p. 126.
- "he was set upon," Aykroyd, p. 43.
- "dire humbug," and, "dreary and foolish superstition," quoted in Lamont, p. 37.
- "every article of furniture," quoted in Jenkins, p. 115.
- "lay on the table," quoted in ibid, p. 115.
- "Love her always," quoted in ibid, p. 115.
- "[his] hands were burning," quoted in ibid, p. 115.
- "It is not to be expected," quoted in Home, p. 215.
- "good faith and honorable character," quoted in Blum, p. 30.
- "Stranger Than Fiction," quoted in Jenkins, p. 115.
- "recorded many instances," ibid, p. 59.
- "These soberly attested incredibilities," quoted in ibid, p. 59.
- "a strong prejudice," ibid, p. 107.
- "the unreliability of evidence," ibid, p. 122.
- "the evidence for his levitation," *JASPR*, Volume III, 1909, p. 718.
- "was inclined to consider [him]," Blum, p. 107.
- "Probably some of the more," quoted in ibid, p. 108.
- "There is no evidence," quoted in Jenkins, p. 91.
- "With the marvels wrought," quoted in Blum, p. 108.
- "William was quote close to Philip," Stein, p. 52.

- "[h]e had brilliant ideas," quoted in D' Albe, p. v.
- "the invention of the eye-catching," Brock, p. xiii.
- "a neurotoxin so potent," Blum, p. 45.
- "Rays of light," quoted in Weightman, p. 96.
- "a big man," Blum, p. 45.
- "Like other investigators before him," Weisberg, p. 224.
- "For power and certainty," ibid, p. 225.
- "to stand by a mahogany board," Blum, p. 47.
- "the prestige," from the motion picture of the same name, released in 2006.
- "On three separate occasions," quoted in Weisberg, p. 224-5.
- "psychic force," and, "of all persons endowed," quoted in ibid, p. 48.
- "no fact in sacred or profane history," quoted in Kurtz, p. 190.
- "the leaders of British science," Blum, p. 48.
- "We speak advisedly," quoted in ibid, p. 48.
- "Crookes, after he discovered thallium," ibid, p. 48.
- "Enraged, Crookes stormed down," ibid, p. 48.
- "The message seemed clear enough," ibid, p. 49.
- "the possibility that the dead," ibid, p. 230.
- "I never said it was possible," quoted in Aykroyd, p. 47.
- "the calls upon him," Jenkins, p. 155.
- "Outwardly a lovable character," ebooks.Cambridge.org/chapter. Jsf?bid=CBO9780511910586&cid=CB.
- "Light should be the demand," quoted in Blum, p. 61.
- "The matter has grown," and, "The facts of this book," quoted in ibid, p. 141.
- "that he had been told," Jenkins, p. 259.
- "a curious and as yet unsolved," Stephen and Lee, eds., p. 1121.

9. Census of Hallucinations

- "an alarming sound," Podmore, p. 6.
- "Its original meaning," ibid, p. 81.
- "cases of apparitions," Davies, p. 8.
- "the middle and upper classes," ibid, p. 9.
- "It is a most unpardonable blunder," *PSPR*, Volume X (Containing Part XXVI), 1894, p. 24.
- "the distance between the two persons," ibid, p. 28.
- "at 487 times," Blum, p. 183.
- "The possibility of a given single event," ibid, p. 183.
- "cases in which," ibid, p. 183.
- "At a rate of 1 out of 19,000," ibid, p. 183.

10. Just Plain Mrs. Piper

- "a prolonged sibilent [sic] sound," Piper, p. 12.
- "holding on to the side," ibid, p. 12.
- "a distant part of the country," ibid, pp. 12-13.
- "the whispering voices," Blum, p. 97.
- "such a freak," ibid, p. 97.
- "which in those days," Piper, p. 14.
- "spelt the others down," quoted in Piper, p. 14.
- "continued to make," Sage, p. 5.
- "the most remarkable," quoted in Blum, p. 98
- "she found that she was becoming," ibid, p. 98.
- "she was slightly chubby," ibid, p. 97.
- "About Mrs. Piper's gifts," and, "unrecognized by orthodox psychology," Piper, p. ix.

- "[t]he facts are too strong," Piper, xi.
- "preferring to devote her time," Piper, p. 39.
- "bashful," quoted in Simon, p. 201.
- "the knowledge of which," quoted in Blum, p. 98.
- "Reading sealed letters," Blum, pp. 98-99.
- "a simple, genuine," quoted in Fisher, p. 478.
- "became increasingly uneasy," Blum, p. 100.
- "she mentioned the recent loss," Simon, p. 200.
- "The medium showed," quoted in Douglas, p. 108.
- "could be a heady experience," Blum, p. 245.
- "Finney," "Finett," etc., Gardner, p. 254.
- "[He] was opinionated and vociferous, Simon, pp. 201-202.
- "discover that no such person," Stemman, p. 202.
- "Martin Luther, Commodore Cornelius Vanderbilt," Gardner, p. 254.
- "placing it between fore and middle fingers," *PSPR*, Volume XXIII (Containing Parts LVIII-LIX), 1909, p. 132.
- "I feel as if something," quoted in Piper, p. 67.
- "she always resumes the conversation," ibid, p. 67.
- "Be more passive," and, "Know and understand," quoted in ibid, p. 109.
- "We would have thee read good books," quoted in ibid, pp.109-10.
- "Always think before," quoted in ibid, p. 111.
- "Throw thy pride to the winds," quoted in ibid, p. 112.
- "Live simply, humbly," quoted in ibid, p. 112.
- "as absolutely certain as I am," quoted in Hart, p. 55.
- "was not only amazed," Piper, p. 47.
- "the sober little American," Blum, p. 161.

- "fraud-buster," and, "refused to accept," Stemman, p. 30.
- "the greatest detective," quoted in Sage, 101.
- "was a big, burly, vigorous man," Blum, pp. 83-4.
- "would do nothing helpful," p. 164.
- "little daisy," quoted in ibid, p. 164.
- "I have satisfied myself," quoted in Stemman, pp. 29-30.
- "a curious old gold watch," Blum 165.
- "rumbling Phinuit voice," ibid, p. 165.
- "Mrs. Piper has certainly beaten me," quoted in Piper, p. 56.
- "Thus the mystery," Sage, p. 35.
- "a medium who in a trance state," Sidgwick, p. 502.
- "The result of these early séances," Podmore, p. 171.
- "In one brutal series of tests," Blum, p. 226.
- "He'd put ammonia-soaked cloth," ibid, p. 181.
- "He insisted on replacing the entire staff," ibid, p. 163.
- "It appears that one very wet morning," Piper, pp. 62-3.
- "suspicious journeys," ibid, p. 44.
- "He prevented Piper," Aykroyd, p. 203.
- "personal obsession," Blum, p. 142.
- "wrecked," quoted in Oppenheim, p. 376.
- "He hovered over the house," Blum, p. 142.
- "during some fifteen years," Sage, p. 7.
- "sorely tempted," quoted in ibid, p. 142.
- "At every moment," Sage, p. 36.
- "[I]t took all James's diplomatic skills," Blum, p. 142
- "I cannot profess," quoted in Stemman, p. 30.
- "I might add much thereto," quoted in Blum, p. 230.
- "As his fingers reached," ibid, p. 272.

11. The Hodgson Legacy

- "Everyone was there," Blum, p. 273.

- "[t]he Hodgson control tended to announce," quoted in Blum, p. 286.

- "[he] was never convinced," quoted in Wicker, p. 213.

- "were such good friends," and, "*absolutely characteristic*," quoted in Blum, p. 286.

- "The total amount," *PASPR*, Vol. III, July, 1909, Part I, p. 473.

- "terrible enemy of fraud," Sage, p. 7.

- "When Hodgson died in 1905," McCabe, p. 104.

- "She once told James a ring had been stolen," Gardner, p. 256.

- "'vibrations' from personal items," ibid, p. 257.

- "*[m]uscle-reading, fishing, guessing*," Tuckett, p. 329.

12. The White Crow

- "that only principles," www.prairieghosts.com/piper.html, p. 1.

- "invited eight colleagues from Harvard," Blum, p. 190.

- "If I may be allowed," quoted in ibid, p. 223.

- "Besides transmitting messages aloud," Simon, pp. 288-9.

- "When that which is *you*," quoted in Blum, p. 172.

- "Barrett's book," ibid, p. 292-3.

- "spiritistic," quoted in Simon, p. 307.

- "I am inclined to accept," quoted in Blum, p. 254.

- "would never hold another sitting," quoted in ibid, p. 254.

- "I . . . desire to become a free agent," quoted in Simon, pp. 306-7.

- "[W]hen was not the science," quoted in ibid, p. 369.

13. Machine Dreams

- "believe[d] . . . that both," Weightman, p. 287.
- "well remembered voice," quoted in Sungook, p. 96.
- "a beloved woman," Larson, p. 13.
- "She had once told Lodge," ibid, p. 13.
- "This was an unusual thing," and, "thoroughly convinced," quoted in ibid, p. 13.
- "believed that he had been warned," Weightman, p. 286-7.
- "she was a little bit terrified," Leichtman, p. 55.
- "On one occasion," ibid, p. 287.
- "I recommend people in general," quoted in Jolly, p. 287.
- "Death is not extinction," Lodge, p. 296.
- "to design a machine," Blum, p. 197.
- "Spin metal disks," ibid, p. 197.
- "A group of people," Jolly, p. 228.
- "But when analysed," ibid, p. 228.
- "attempted to 'transmit,'" Weightman, p. 287.
- "consists of a shrouded ghost," Davies, p. 212.
- "conceived the theoretical foundations," Sconce, p. 81.
- "are composed of myriads," quoted in ibid, p. 82.
- "skepticalbeliever,"www.coasttocoastam.com/guest/stemman-roy/57953.
- "developing a 'Spirit Finder' device," Stemman, p 108.
- "What [he] had in mind," Clark, p. 235.
- "If our personality survives," quoted in Stemman, p. 108.
- "If the great sequoia tree," Baldwin, 377.
- "I have been at work," www.thoughtco.com/edison-and-the-ghost-machine-2594017.

- "a colorful footnote," www.nytimes.com/1995/02-21/theater/theater-review-american-luminaries-venture-into-the-woods-with-agendas-in-tow.html.
- "EDISON: Put it down, Henry," St. Germain, p. 23.
- "Edison and I are convinced," quoted in Stemman, p. 108.
- "it is difficult to imagine," Sconce, p. 82.
- "I might mention," www.nobelprize.org/nobel-prizes/physics/laureates/1909/marconi-lecture/pdf.
- "Marconi's impatience with what he saw," ibid, p. 456.
- "one of the first followers," quoted in ibid, p. 655.
- "there are sounds going all around us," quoted in Raboy, pp. 155-6.
- "[n]ear the end," and, "Marconi worked to create," Sconce, p. 61.
- "believed that radio technology," *RA*, p. 77.
- "simply vibrate," http://www.deathreference.com/Ce-Da/Communication-with-the-Dead.html#ixzz4AfbjSFkh.

13. Epilogue

- "a medium who was gaining notoriety," Larson, p. 13.
- "Intending to expose her," ibid, p. 13.
- "Theodore Roosevelt," Simon, *Dark Light*, p. 190.
- "a focused, non-terminal," transcribed by author from VCR of *Ghostbusters* on March 19, 2017.
- "plenty of people," *NY*, unpaginated.
- "But this is only approximate," quoted in quora.com/What-percentage-of-discoverable-knowledge-has-been-discovered-already-by-science.
- "I never said it was possible," quoted in Aykroyd, p. 47.

ABOUT THE AUTHOR

Eric Burns is a two-time winner of the American Library Association's "Best of the Best Award"—in 2004 for *The Spirits of America: A Social History of Alcohol*, and in 2007 for *The Smoke of the Gods: A Social History of Tobacco*. A later book, *1920: The Year That Made the Decade Roar*, was named one of the best non-fiction works of 2015. And, in a starred review, *Publishers Weekly* said of Burns's *The Golden Lad: The Haunting Story of Theodore and Quentin Roosevelt*, "this is how biographies should be written." It was the first biography he had produced. In his previous career, Burns was chosen as one of the best writers in the history of television journalism, and twice won an Emmy for his scripts.

TO MY READERS

Thank you for reading *When the Dead Talks...And the Smartest Minds in the World Listened*. Book reviews are often overlooked, but they are critical to helping authors gain visibility. Your feedback is important to me. Please take a moment to write an honest review on the e-retailer of your choice. Every review makes a difference. Have a great day.

—Eric Burns

INDEX

Made in the USA
Coppell, TX
01 February 2024

28459198R10173